Survival Guides

Timothy L. Hudson

Cover design by Adam Parsons.

Back cover photo of Mr. Hudson by Adam Parsons.

ISBN Number 0-9764052-7-X

First printing, April 2006

ThomasMax Publishing
P.O. Box 250054
Atlanta, GA 30325
404-794-6588
www.thomasmax.com

This book is dedicated
to my wife Sheila, whose patience and understanding
long ago passed my understanding.

From The Author

You hold in your hand the end result of a 10 year old experiment. That was when I decided to start a daily email devotional. My goal was small: to send an encouraging devotional each morning to about 100 students at UGA. Little did I know that nothing stays contained on the internet! Today the Survival Guide has over 7500 subscribers in 26 different countries. Those more tech savvy than I tell me that the number of readers is probably between 12,000 and 15,000. This fantastic "experiment" is now available to you in this collection of 365 of these daily email "Survival Guides."

Thank you for purchasing this book! It has been a tremendous blessing to assemble these devotionals inspired by God's Word into a collection of daily readings. Each devotional is given in an easy to read format to help you survive and thrive in your daily walk with Jesus. My prayer is that this book becomes part of your daily spiritual discipline.

But there is another reason to thank you for your purchase. All proceeds from the sale of this book go to Christian Campus Fellowship at The University of Georgia. Talk about a win-win scenario! You get a good book and we get financial support to continue ministering to students at UGA. CCF is a non-denominational ministry that is fully funded by donations from churches and individuals like you. CCF has been a lighthouse beaming forth the love of God at UGA since 1976. My wife, Sheila, and I have been blessed to lead this dynamic mission since 1982. The 2006-07 academic year will be our 25th year here.

You can order additional copies of this book directly from CCF (with more of the purchase price going to CCF instead of to the bookseller) by emailing CCF at Survival_Guide@ugaccf.com, by calling 706-548-9625 or by writing to Survival Guide, P.O. Box 609, Athens, GA 30605.

The Survival Guide continues in its email form. To subscribe simply email SGsubscription@ugaccf.com

"THIS IS THE ONLY RACE WORTH RUNNING. I'VE RUN HARD RIGHT TO THE FINISH, BELIEVED ALL THE WAY."
2 TIMOTHY 4:7

One of the greatest gifts God can give us is determination. Determination is a characteristic of God's that He shares with us through His Spirit. When we get it we're no longer quitters or the type of people who are easily defeated.

A good definition of determination is "being resolute or firm in purpose." Godly determination, then, is being resolute or firm in purpose to a righteous course of action, then staying with it. We must be determined to overcome the past, to go forward and not stagnate. We must not be afraid of difficulty, for things worth having never come easy.

When we find ourselves being double-minded about something we know is the righteous thing to do, we need to remind ourselves that God wants us to approach righteous living with determination—then stick with it—rather than going in some other direction because of worry or discouragement or the opinions of others.

God provides everything it takes to succeed in whatever He calls us to do. If we have truly made Jesus the Lord of our life, then we determine to "run hard right to the finish" because Jesus lives in us.

Ask God for the determination to fight the good fight of faith until the battle is won and Jesus returns to give us the final victory!

Survival Guide for **January 2**

"LOOK AT MY HANDS; LOOK AT MY FEET—IT'S REALLY ME. TOUCH ME. LOOK ME OVER FROM HEAD TO TOE. A GHOST DOESN'T HAVE MUSCLE AND BONE LIKE THIS." LUKE 24:39

Jesus could say to doubting Thomas, "Touch me. Look me over from head to toe." Can you say that? Do you dare let people get close enough to see your strengths and your weaknesses?

All of us who are the Church, we must let people look us over "from head to toe" and see if we are real. That means taking off the masks, getting rid of the religious façade that hides our struggles, and saying to the world, "Look me over from head to toe. I'm real. I struggle with my kids. I battle with my temper. I worry about my bills. I don't always read the Bible and pray as I should. But God has made a difference in my life, and what He has done for me, He can do for you."

Ghandi once said, "If more Christians were like Christ, I would be one too!" Unfortunately, the ones he met preached love, but practiced discrimination. They taught the new birth, but perpetuated the same old system of poverty and despair that benefited the few and enslaved the multitudes.

Jesus said, "I am the Good Shepherd." (Jn 10:11). The word translated "good" in the original Greek means "winsome or attractive." Do we make Christ attractive to others? What a shame that so often we do not!

The world cares little for the "spiritual experiences" we have "in church." How is your influence at home? Or at school? Or at work? Can you look at those around you today and say, "Look me over from head to toe?"

Ultimately, that's the only test that matters.

Survival Guide for **January 3**

". . . JESUS CAME UP AND WALKED ALONG WITH THEM."
LUKE 24:15

A story is told about a farmer whose land flooded. As the waters rose around him, he prayed for God to save him. Just about that time a man on a raft floated by and offered him a hand, but he stayed put and prayed even harder. As the waters kept rising, he climbed up to the roof top where he saw a police officer waving to him from a motor boat. But again he refused to leave, confident that God would deliver him. Finally, an army helicopter lowered a rope ladder down to him, but he refused to grasp it. So he drowned and went to heaven and complained to God, "I prayed so hard, why didn't You save me?" Whereupon God replied, "I sent you a raft, a motor boat and a helicopter—what else did you want Me to do?"

Even though we often look in the wrong place for God, the truth is we will never find ourselves in any situation where He is absent. The problem is never God's presence; it is our perception.

After the Crucifixion, two discouraged disciples were walking home to Emmaus; their hopes lay buried in a tomb. As they walked along, a "stranger" began walking beside them, warming their hearts with His presence and comforting them in their loss. At the journey's end, they shared a meal together and suddenly the stranger revealed Himself to them, then He disappeared. It was Jesus! He had been with them all the time.

God's presence probably isn't accompanied by lightning bolts or drum rolls, but if we look for Him—we will find Him. Jesus doesn't have to be felt for His presence to be real.

Focusing the lens of faith is all that is needed to reveal God's presence.

Survival Guide for **January 4**

". . . LONG BEFORE HE LAID DOWN EARTH'S FOUNDATIONS, HE HAD US IN MIND." EPHESIANS 1:4

Have you ever seen a designer at work? First he starts with an idea. He sees it, then he creates it. You were in God's mind before you were in your mother's womb. Regardless of whose child, sibling or spouse you are, you were God's idea. Never forget that!

You weren't born because of what your parents did or didn't do. No, you were born because of something God did. He's the One Who mixed the genes that gave you your identity, your personality, and your purpose. He made you and He doesn't make mistakes. (Ps 139:16).

God didn't allow you to be aborted or miscarried, stillborn or die of SIDS. He didn't allow that childhood accident or illness to take you out. He never took His hand off your life for one moment. Even if you were neglected and abused, deprived and denied, God is the One Who brought you through and kept you from losing your mind.

He is also the One Who brought you to an understanding of Jesus as your Lord and Savior and raised you up so that you could fulfill His purposes in spite of every effort to destroy you, admonish you, defame you or discourage you.

The fact is . . . if you hadn't gone through everything you have gone through, you wouldn't be the person you are today. God knows that! He's been in the process of creating you, fashioning you, molding you, designing you, refining you and perfecting you since the moment He thought of you.

When God thought of you, He had a good idea!

Survival Guide for **January 5**

"... WE'VE BEEN THROWN DOWN, BUT WE HAVEN'T BROKEN." 2 CORINTHIANS 4:9

Do you ever feel like a failure?

When I feel like a failure I look at an area of your life where I keep failing and do five things. Try these whenever you find yourself in a period of negative thinking:

1. Check your expectations. Write them down. Then ask yourself, "Are they realistic? Do I expect to do everything perfectly on the first try? How many mistakes will I allow myself before I succeed?" Then adjust your expectations to reality.

2. Try something different. Brainstorm at least 20 or 30 new methods then try at least half of them. Go ahead—if the first 15 don't work, just tell yourself, "OK, now I know that it's at least a 16 or 17-step process"—and keep going.

3. Utilize your gifts. You will be intuitive and effective only in the area of your strengths; so use your strengths and avoid your weaknesses. There are people all around you whose dreams will come true by helping to make yours come true. Bring them into your life.

4. Learn to bounce back. No matter how many times you fall down, get back up and start again. Most of the time those who fail are not actually defeated; they simply quit. Follow Paul's example: "... We get knocked down, but we get up again and keep going." (2Cor 4:9 TLB).

5. Factor God in. Solomon says, "Listen for God's voice in everything you do, everywhere you go; He's the One Who will keep you on track." (Prov 3:5).

One of God's ideas, just one, can turn everything around for you, so talk to Him today.

Survival Guide for **January 6**

"SATAN HAS TRIED HIS BEST TO SEPARATE ALL OF YOU FROM ME, LIKE CHAFF FROM WHEAT." LUKE 22:31

Jesus told Peter that Satan wanted to sift him "like chaff from wheat." Just as wheat is separated from chaff, so Satan wants to separate us from God. One way he accomplishes this is through temptation, so here are some tips for overcoming temptation:

(1) When you fall, refuse to stay down. Don't accept the lie that says, "If you were really a Christian you wouldn't fall." Birth and growth are separate processes. When Jesus saves us, our spirit is immediately changed, but until our emotions, appetites and desires come under His Lordship, we are vulnerable. This has nothing to do with our salvation and everything to do with becoming mature. Salvation can't be earned through work; becoming mature is, however, the work of a lifetime.

(2) Be quick to confess your sins. David said, "The Lord is near to the brokenhearted, and saves the crushed in spirit." (Psalm 34:18 NRSV). God always responds to a penitent heart. He meets us at our lowest point and walks with us through the valley where even our closest friends won't go.

(3) Once you are free, stay free. When a plant is uprooted, it may look good for a while, but unless it is replanted in healthy soil and properly tended, it will die. When God delivers us from something harmful, he delivers us to something healthy. He takes us out of bad situations in order to place us in good ones.

So, look out for "The Separator." You will win over temptation only if you take him seriously.

Survival Guide for **January 7**

"OPEN MY EYES THAT I MAY SEE WONDERFUL THINGS IN YOUR LAW." PSALM 119:18(NIV)

Here are four ways to come to the Word with open eyes:

1. Come humbly.
   "Like new born babies, crave pure spiritual milk, so that by it you may grow up . . ." (1Pet. 2:2 NIV). What's more helpless than a baby? Or more needy? Or more dependent? That's how we should approach the Bible. . . like babies going after a bottle.

2. Come hungry.
   "He satisfies the thirsty and fills the hungry with good things"(Ps 107:9 NIV). What we hunger for determines what satisfies our hunger. Accept no substitutes! Refuse to be satisfied with the junk food of television, movies, or music when you can sit at God's table with Him and have a gourmet meal.

3. Come persistently.
   Ask more from each verse. Paul speaks of "the manifold wisdom of God" (Eph 3:10 NIV). The word manifold means that each verse is like a diamond—every angle brings another beam of light. Martin Luther said, "Study your Bible like you pick apples. First, shake the tree, then shake the limbs, then shake the branches, then shake the twigs, then look under every leaf."

4. Come openly.
   Don't read the Bible to find out what is wrong with your neighbor—let it convict you not them. Personalize what you read. Pray, "Lord, talk to me. What are You saying to me in this?"

Come with open eyes and experience God's Living Word!

Survival Guide for **January 8**

"IF YOU DON'T KNOW WHAT YOU'RE DOING PRAY TO THE FATHER. HE LOVES TO HELP. YOU'LL GET HIS HELP, AND WON'T BE CONDESCENDED TO WHEN YOU ASK FOR IT." JAMES 1:5

Anytime you don't know what you are doing is a good time to ask God for help. But there are three particular occasions when hearing from Him makes all the difference in the world.

> 1. Ask God before you consider the needs of others. Why? Because their needs are driving them; only the plan of God should be leading you. You are not their answer—God is! How can your words strengthen them or solve their problems, if you haven't first asked God for wisdom? Paul said, "I received from the Lord what I also passed on to you." (1Cor. 11:23 NIV). Before you can give it, you have to receive it.

> 2. Ask God before you entertain the ideas of others. Why? Because ideas are not commands. Be careful—it is easier to get into things than it is to get out of them. Don't make the wrong commitments and end up bound by promises you can't (or shouldn't) keep. Love others, but be led only by God's spirit. "In his heart a man plans his course, but the Lord determines his steps." (Pr 16:9 NIV).

> 3. Ask God before you listen to the complaints of others. Why? Because you are not responsible for their happiness. Stop being co-dependent, needing to fix them in order to feel good about yourself. Turn them over to God, and get back into focus. "You will keep in perfect peace all who trust in you, whose thoughts are fixed on you." (Isa 26:3 NLT).

Ask God—then do what He says!

Survival Guide for **January 9**

**"DO YOU SEE WHAT THIS MEANS—ALL THESE PIONEERS
WHO BLAZED THE WAY, ALL THESE VETERANS CHEERING
US ON? IT MEANS WE'D BETTER GET ON WITH IT . . . "
HEBREWS 12:1**

A study of the lives of Bible heroes reveals two commonalities: they
struggled with failure, and they refused to let any single experience distort
their view of themselves. These characteristics are common not only to
Bible heroes but to many visionaries.

The Emperor Ferdinand told Mozart that his opera, The Marriage of
Figaro, was "far too noisy." Van Gogh sold only one painting during his
lifetime, yet his smallest one today sells for millions. Einstein's teacher
told him he would never amount to anything. They succeeded because
they refused to be limited by the opinions of others.

Author, Leo Buscaglia, was a great admirer of television cooking expert,
Julia Child. He wrote,

> "I just love her attitude. She says, 'Tonight we're
> going to make a soufflé.' Then she beats this, whisks
> that, drops stuff on the floor, and does all these
> wonderfully human things. Then she throws it into the
> oven and chats with you while it's baking. Finally,
> she says, 'Now it's ready.' But when she opens the
> oven, the soufflé just falls flat as a pancake. But does
> she panic or burst into tears? No! She just smiles and
> says, 'Well, you can't win them all. Bon appetite!'"

Our greatest regrets may be over the things we haven't done, rather than
the things we have, because mistakes are redeemable while lost
opportunities aren't.

Get on with it—the reward is worth running the race!

Survival Guide for **January 10**

**"SO DON'T LOSE A MINUTE IN BUILDING ON WHAT YOU'VE BEEN GIVEN, COMPLEMENTING YOUR BASIC FAITH WITH GOOD CHARACTER, SPIRITUAL UNDERSTANDING, ALERT DISCIPLINE, PASSIONATE PATIENCE, REVERENT WONDER."
2 PETER 1:5-6**

Learning to control your impulsive reactions instead of "mouthing off" with the first thing that pops into your head takes restraint: "Patience is better than strength. Controlling your temper is better than capturing a city." (Pr 16:32 NCV). Learn to respond with wisdom, instead of reacting with anger. The difference between responding and reacting is subtle, but crucial.

For instance, if your boss hands you a pink slip and your first reaction is to slug him, take ten, go for a walk, and realize you have better long-term options than punching out his lights. If you can keep your head above water during the flood, you might be able to negotiate severance pay, a letter of recommendation, or even a referral. And if you want to be a learner instead of a loser, find out why it happened and what you need to do differently next time. There's wisdom in any crisis—try to glean it! Be patient and remember faith is the bridge that will take you from where you are right now to where you need to be.

Don't overreact to a crisis, instead trust that God is working on angles you haven't even considered: "I would have lost heart, unless I had believed that I would see the goodness of the Lord in the land of the living. Wait on the Lord; be of good courage, and he shall strengthen your heart." (Ps 27:13-14 NKJV).

Exercise self-control in any crisis by learning to see beyond the eclipse of the present moment. The sun will shine again.

God has promised it, so count on it!

Survival Guide for January 11

"I WAS AFRAID I MIGHT DISAPPOINT YOU, SO I FOUND A GOOD HIDING PLACE AND SECURED YOUR MONEY. HERE IT IS, SAFE AND SOUND DOWN TO THE LAST CENT." MATTHEW 25:25

The parable of the talents teaches that the one who risks will be rewarded; but the one who plays it safe will lose. Jesus was not just talking about "the sweet by and-by." No, this principle also applies to the "here and now." Many failures usually proceed any success. If we let the fear of failure keep us from taking risks we will never do anything significant. Walking by faith involves taking risks and making mistakes.

One day a ceramics teacher divided her class into two groups. The first group was graded on the number of pieces they produced, and the second on the quality of the pieces they produced. The first group could earn an "A" for making 50 pieces, a "B" for 40, a "C" for 30, and so on. However, all the second group had to do was produce one piece—but it had to be as near perfect as possible to get an "A." The results were amazing. While the first group kept churning out pieces, getting better as they went, the second group just sat around waiting for inspiration, theorizing about perfection, and in the end, all they had to show for their efforts—was a pile of unused clay. The lesson is clear: Unless we overcome our fear of making mistakes, we will never make a difference in life.

Faith means following God to the very edge, knowing that when we do, He will either put solid rock under our feet, or He will teach us to fly!

Survival Guide for **January 12**

**"YOU NEED TO STICK IT OUT, STAYING WITH GOD'S PLAN
SO YOU'LL BE THERE FOR THE PROMISED COMPLETION."
HEBREWS 10:36**

Francis Cabrini applied to join a missionary order at age 18, but was
rejected because she was too sickly. She spent the next 6 years working in
an orphanage only 50 miles away from her home. Her Superior said to her
one day, "If you want to be part of a missionary order, you will have to
start one yourself." So she did. She spent the next eight years building
foundations in Milan, Rome and other Italian cities.

Finally she was given a mission assignment to, of all places, New York
City.

And even that was problematic. When she arrived, she was told that the
plans had fallen through and that she should go back home to Italy. But
she refused. Instead, she stayed, solved the problems and built a school
and an orphanage. It didn't matter what difficulties she faced, she believed
that with God on her side, she could overcome anything. And she did.

By the time she died at age 87, she had founded 70 hospitals, schools and
orphanages in America, Spain, France, England and South America. Her
impact was incredible. She was the Mother Teresa of her day—displaying
the same compassion, grit and leadership.

But she would never have made a difference if she had allowed her past to
hold her hostage. Instead of lamenting the loss of her dream and the hurts
of her youth, she moved on and did what she could where God put her.
You can do the same—if you "stick it out!"

Survival Guide for **January 13**

"NEVER WALK AWAY FROM SOMEONE WHO DESERVES HELP; YOUR HAND IS GOD'S HAND FOR THAT PERSON." PROVERBS 3:27

Beware of the "someday" trap—rationalizing inaction now by thinking: "Someday when I have the money or someday when I have the time or someday when I'm through with school." This is the trap Solomon describes in Prov 3:27-28 "Don't tell your neighbor, 'Maybe some other time' or 'Try me tomorrow,' when the money's right there in your pocket."

God pours His blessings into pipes, not pots. As long as we constantly dwell on what we don't have instead of what we do, we will never feel that we have enough to give to others.

Don't wait until you can afford a "big" gift. Instead, do what you can now. Take a box of groceries to a needy family. Turn the clutter in your cupboard into the answer to somebody's prayer. Better still, give away something you really want to keep. Generosity develops character, crucifies self-centeredness, and helps us become more like Jesus.

Instead of measuring your generosity with that of your peers measure it by the Macedonian church—the most impoverished in Europe. "Though desperately poor . . . they gave . . . far more than they could afford!— pleading for the privilege of helping out. . .this was totally spontaneous . . . and caught us completely off guard. What explains it was that they had first given themselves unreservedly to God and to us. The other giving simply flowed out of the purposes of God working in their lives." (2 Cor 8:3-5).

Turn "someday" into "today"—be generous with whatever you have.

Survival Guide for **January 14**

"BUT NOW THAT WE'RE NO LONGER SHACKLED TO THAT DOMINEERING MATE OF SIN, AND OUT FROM UNDER ALL THOSE OPPRESSIVE REGULATIONS AND FINE PRINT, WE'RE FREE TO LIVE A NEW LIFE IN THE FREEDOM OF GOD." ROMANS 7:6

Living "a new life in the freedom of God" is an antidote to stress. Although obeying God usually has its own reward, obeying the "still small voice of God" is especially rewarding. You see, when God speaks to us, it is usually more like a gentle prompting than like a hammer pounding us over the head. We can ignore His prompting, disobey it, argue with it, even try to postpone it until later. But when we take any of those options we always finish up under stress. After all, what is more stressful that knowing that things are not right between God and you?

The word obedience is a turn-off to many people. Right away, they think of God asking them for huge sums of money, or sending them to a mission field (horrors!) or telling them to do something they really don't want to do. Get real! If we won't listen to God when He tells us to turn off the TV and spend 10 minutes with Him in prayer, why would He want to send us on a mission?

Obeying God in little things—not big ones—is what lowers our stress level. For example, when He prompts us not to say another word and we keep right on talking—that's when we get into arguments and our stress level goes through the roof.

God's Word says, "If you will listen diligently to the voice of the Lord your God . . . you shall be above only and you shall not be beneath." (Deut 28:1,13 AMP). The difference between being under the situation or on top of it is usually found in one word—obedience.

Do what God prompts you to do and immediately you'll begin to lower your stress levels.

Survival Guide for **January 15**

"ABOVE ALL AND BEFORE ALL, DO THIS: GET WISDOM! WRITE THIS AT THE TOP OF YOUR LIST: GET UNDERSTANDING!." PROVERBS 4:7

Jimmy's mother said, "Get up, it's time for school." He didn't answer. Again she said, "Get up, it's time to go to school!" He said, "I am not going any more. There are 1500 kids in that school and they all hate me." Sharply she replied, "You've got to go to school!"

"I can't," he said, "even the teachers hate me. Give me one good reason that I should have to go through that misery?" Looking him in the eye, his mother said, "I'll give you two; first, you are 42 years of age and second— you're the principal!"

Life is a never-ending education. When he was 85, Pablo Casals, the great cellist, was asked why he still practiced five hours a day. He replied, "Because I think I'm getting better." What an attitude! Peter said, "Grow in grace and understanding of our Master and Savior, Jesus Christ . . . " (2 Pet 3:18). One of the toughest decision we all must make is whether to be content with who we are now—or to keep striving to reach our full potential.

Built into every painful experience is the wisdom to build a better future. All we need is the right teacher and the right textbook. When God found Gideon he was hiding in a cave, thinking, "There is nothing anybody can do." But God showed him that he wasn't a captive to the Midianites; he was a captive to his own inferior attitude, his own fear and the opinions of those around him. God had the power; He even had the plan; all He needed was Gideon to open his heart.

God has things He wants to teach you.

The question is: are you ready to go to school?

Survival Guide for **January 16**

"LISTEN FOR GOD'S VOICE IN EVERYTHING YOU DO, HE'S THE ONE WHO WILL KEEP YOU ON TRACK." PROVERBS 3:6

Insanity is "doing the same thing over and over again, hoping for different results." Think about that definition while you read this essay by Portia Nelson called, "Autobiography in Five Short Chapters:"

Chapter One.
> I walk down the street. There is a deep hole in the pavement. I fall in. I am lost. I am helpless. It isn't my fault. It takes forever to get out.

Chapter Two.
> I walk down the street; there is a deep hole in the pavement. I pretend I don't see it. I fall in again. I can't believe I am in the same place, but it isn't my fault. It still takes a long time to get out.

Chapter Three.
> I walk down the street. There is a deep hole in the pavement. I see it is there. I still fall in. It is a habit. But now my eyes are open. I know where I am. It is my fault. I get out immediately.

Chapter Four.
> I walk down the street. There is a deep hole in the sidewalk. I walk around it.

Chapter Five.
> I walk down a different street.

Now read this essay by Solomon in Proverbs 3:5 - 7:
> ". . . don't try to figure out everything on your own. Listen for God's voice . . . He's the One Who will keep you on track. Don't assume that you know it all. Run to God! Run from evil!"

Survival Guide for **January 17**

"GOD DEALS OUT JOY IN THE PRESENT, THE NOW. IT'S USELESS TO BROOD OVER HOW LONG WE MIGHT LIVE." ECCLESIASTES 5:20

Solomon says, "It is good for a man to enjoy his work whatever his job may be. . . . The person who does that will not need to look back with sorrow." (Ecc 5:18 - 20 TLB). Don't wish your life away by constantly thinking: "If only I had. . . a bigger house. . . a more understanding significant other. . . better grades . . . a better-paying job. . . a beautiful body. . . a higher IQ. . . the acceptance of a particular person. . . then I would be happy!"

Happiness doesn't work like that. David says: "This is the very day God acted—let's celebrate and be festive." (Ps 118:24). This very day, not tomorrow!

My mother is a great cook. When I was a boy, I loved to watch her bake. When I put my fingers in the bowl and smudged batter across my cheeks, I learned what took me years later to articulate—that life is good!

If you want to enjoy life to the fullest, don't wait for what's in the oven, take the bowl now and scrape it out. People who learn to scrape the bowl don't hunger for life because things that others ignore nourish them. Too many of us spend our lives waiting for the cake to come out of the oven and miss scraping the bowl—yet the bowl is often contains the best things life has to offer.

Jesus says, "Look at the birds . . ." (Matt 6:26 NIV). "See how the lilies of the field grow." (Matt 6:28 NIV). "Be content . . . " (Lk 3:14 TLB). What Jesus is simply saying is this, "Take the time to enjoy where you are, on your way to where you are going!"

My simple way of saying it is: Don't neglect scraping the bowl!

Survival Guide for **January 18**

"SO THE SISTERS SENT WORD TO JESUS, 'MASTER, THE ONE YOU LOVE SO VERY MUCH IS SICK.'"   JOHN 11:3

Mary and Martha sent someone to Jesus on behalf of Lazarus and, because they went, Jesus responded. The miracle wouldn't unfold for several days, but the timer was set when the appeal was made.

Ever wonder where your prayers go when they leave your lips?

". . . there was silence in heaven and another angel came and stood at the altar, holding a golden pan with the prayers of all God's people. The angel put this offering before the throne. The smoke went up to God with the prayers of God's people." (Revelation 8:1-4 NCV).

Why was there silence in heaven? Because Heaven pauses to hear the prayers of people like you and me: "the prayers of all God's people" went up to God. The awesome truth about prayer is that our words don't stop until they reach the heart of God.

Take note that the friend who went to Jesus on behalf of Lazarus said, "Master, the one You love so very much is sick." He didn't base his appeal on the imperfect love of the one in need, but on the perfect love of the Savior. He didn't say, "The one who loves You is sick." Instead, he said, "the one You love is sick." There is a huge difference there.

The power of prayer doesn't depend on the virtue of the one who prays, but on the unchanging love of the One who hears. Aren't you glad? It means that we may be deeply flawed; we may not understand the mystery of prayer, but prayer doesn't depend on our virtue but on God's love.

So pray with confidence that when you pray your prayers go to the heart of God.

Survival Guide for **January 19**

"I LOOKED FOR SOMEONE TO STAND UP FOR ME AGAINST ALL THIS, TO REPAIR THE DEFENSES OF THE CITY, TO TAKE A STAND FOR ME AND STAND IN THE GAP TO PROTECT THIS LAND SO I WOULDN'T HAVE TO DESTROY IT. I COULDN'T FIND ANYONE. NO ONE." EZEKIEL 22:30

Mr. Kimball, a Boston Sunday School teacher began visiting one of his students at the shoe shop where he worked as a clerk. Eventually, he led him to Christ. The year was 1898 and that student's name was Dwight L. Moody.

Twenty-one years later, D.L. Moody, now an evangelist, visited London and a great spiritual awakening took place. F. B. Meyer, a local pastor, went to hear Dwight L. Moody preach and his life was transformed. Later F. B. Meyer went to America to preach and in one of his meetings a student named J. Wilbur Chapman came to Christ. J.W. Chapman became active in the YMCA, where he met and discipled a former baseball player called Billy Sunday.

Billy Sunday became a great revivalist and, in one of his crusades in Charlotte, a group of businessmen came to Christ. A year later, they decided that their city needed another crusade, so they invited Mordecai Hamm to be their speaker. After 3 weeks Mordecai Hamm left town, discouraged because his crusade had yielded only had one convert—a 12-year-old boy named Billy Graham.

One Sunday school teacher just trying to be a good teacher of the Word started the chain that gave the Kingdom Billy Graham! One person—just one—can make all the difference in the world.

You can be that one!

Survival Guide for **January 20**

"I AM LADY WISDOM, AND I LIVE NEXT TO SANITY; KNOWLEDGE AND DISCRETION LIVE JUST DOWN THE STREET." PROVERBS 8:12

No matter how great our cause, when we push ourselves beyond the limits designed into us by God, we suffer the same results as those who burn out in any other pursuit. As a classic work-a-holic I have had to learn how to make stress work for instead of against me.

Here are a few insights I have gained along the way:

1. Many don't know how to handle life any other way. (When our only tool is a hammer, we tend to see every problem as a nail.) Acknowledge that stress is like emotional adrenaline to you—that is why you keep creating it.

2. When you sit in a chair and hear the legs crack, common sense tells you that if you don't take your weight off it you are going to end up on the floor. Use your common sense to heed the telltale signs of your health cracking and take the stress off before your health breaks or you will greatly diminish what you can do for God or anybody else.

3. Learn prudence.   The word prudence just means "careful management." The prudent person becomes a better manager of their time, their energy and their God-given gifts.

4. Recognize your "stressors." (I know a lot of mine! Do you know what yours are?) Change the ones you can and start accepting the ones you can't change—such as other people! You must learn to adapt to any "stressor" that can't be changed so that the stress they induce motivates you instead of pressuring you or burying you.

5. Most importantly, spend more time with the One Who said, "Come unto Me all you who . . . are over-burdened and I will . . . (relieve and refresh your souls)." (Matt 11:28 AMP).

Survival Guide for **January 21**

"...HE WHO WINS SOULS IS WISE." PROVERBS 11:30 (NIV)

Witnessing requires wisdom especially in three areas:

1. Don't assume people understand the Gospel, because they were raised in church and don't think they will catch your faith by osmosis, because you hang around them. "How can they believe in the One of Whom they have not heard? And how can they hear without someone preaching to them?" (Rom 10:14 NIV). Share your testimony—the short version. Forget the good advice, just give them the good news about God's love.

2. Be patient—sometimes you have to sow the seed and leave the rest to the Lord of the harvest. Don't try to corner them into a decision. Share the Word, leave the door open and trust the One Who said, "I am watching over My word to perform it." (Jer 1:12 NAS).

3. Be alert to opportunities—and don't be afraid to take them. R.A. Torrey tells of an experience that totally changed his attitude toward witnessing. While he was eating at a restaurant with some friends, he felt that he should witness to the waiter who looked very depressed. But he didn't. An hour later when the waiter didn't return, he inquired about him. The manager replied, "We just found him dead in the back of the restaurant. He hanged himself."

When God leads you to speak to someone about His Son—just do it!

Survival Guide for **January 22**

"ANYONE WHO MEETS A TESTING CHALLENGE HEAD-ON AND MANAGES TO STICK IT OUT IS MIGHTY FORTUNATE. FOR SUCH PERSONS LOYALLY IN LOVE WITH GOD, THE REWARD IS LIFE AND MORE LIFE." JAMES 1:12

Testing is a part of life. We are tested by major changes, delayed promises, impossible situations, unanswered prayers, undeserved criticism and seemingly senseless tragedies.

An important test is how we act when we don't feel God's presence. Hezekiah experienced this: "God withdrew in order to test him and to see what was really in his heart" (2 Chronicles 32:31 NLT). Hezekiah had enjoyed close fellowship with God, but at a crucial point God left him alone to test his character, reveal his weakness, and prepare him for greater blessing.

Could that be what is happening with you?

Viewing life as a test makes us realize that nothing is insignificant. Every day is an important day and every second a growth opportunity to deepen our character, demonstrate our love and make us depend more on God.

Are you in a time of testing? If so, take strength from the promise that God never allows the tests we face to be greater than the grace He provides: "He will not allow you to be tested beyond your power to remain firm; at the time you are put to the test, He will give you strength to endure it." (1 Corinthians 10:13 TEV).

Every time we pass a test, God notices and makes plans to reward us: "Blessed is the man who perseveres under trial, because when he has stood the test, he will receive the crown of life that God has promised to those who love him." (James 1:12 NIV).

So hang in there, God will bring you through this test and make you stronger and wiser.

Survival Guide for **January 23**

**"ABOVE ALL AND BEFORE ALL, DO THIS: GET WISDOM!. . ."
PROVERBS 4:7**

An old man came across a young lumberjack working feverishly to cut down a tree. "What are you doing?" he asked. "I am sawing down this tree," the young lumberjack replied. The old-timer said, "You look exhausted. How long have you been at it?" The young lumberjack replied, "Over five hours and I am beat."

Not yet ready to reveal that he, himself, had spent 30 years as a lumberjack, the older man said, "It looks as if your saw might be a bit dull." "It probably is," said the young man, "I've been sawing all day." "Then why don't you take a break and sharpen it?" the older man suggested. "The job will go a lot faster if you do." The young lumberjack replied, "I don't like sharpening, and anyway I don't have time right now, I am too busy sawing!"

It is one thing to work hard—it is another to work smart—working hard is sawing; working smart is taking time to sharpen your saw! Every five years, knowledge in most major fields doubles. That means if we don't stay sharp we soon find ourselves following those who have and eventually we find ourselves well qualified to live in a world that no longer exists.

To stay sharp spiritually, spend time with God, for nobody is sharper than He. Read His Word. Seek His guidance. Acknowledge Him in all you do. Don't get so busy (even doing good things) that you are too busy to sharpen your saw.

"Above all and before all, do this: get wisdom!. . ." (Prov 4:7)

Survival Guide for **January 24**

***

"TRUE, GOD MADE EVERYTHING BEAUTIFUL IN ITSELF AND IN ITS TIME—BUT HE'S LEFT US IN THE DARK, SO WE CAN NEVER KNOW WHAT GOD IS UP TO, WHETHER HE'S COMING OR GOING." ECCLESIASTES 3:11

We can see further than we can go because we are finite persons working with an infinite God. Because His Spirit resides in each of us that belongs to Him, there is more potential inside us than we have the life-span to realize. When we lay down our heads for the last time, we will still be dreaming dreams that we have never personally fulfilled.

Does that signal failure? No! There are things we were meant only to begin or continue. Like an athlete handing the baton to the next runner, we can say to our successors, as Jesus did to His disciples, "The person who trusts me will not only do what I'm doing but even greater things, because I, on my way to the Father, am giving you the same work to do that I've been doing. You can count on it." (Jn 4:12).

Like Moses, we stand on the top of Mount Nebo and see a land we will never personally enter, for our vision will always show us more road than our feet can travel in a lifetime. But, like Moses, we can enter on the feet of our Joshua, who goes on to possess the land.

In Genesis, God did not continue to create blades of grass every time He wanted a lawn rather He created the first of everything, put the seed of life into it and made it responsible for reproducing what came next.

Be a reproducer! If you are a Naomi, start looking for a Ruth. If you are a Paul, start looking for a Timothy. Pour into someone else the things God wants you to pass on to the next generation.

If you do that, God will extend your influence beyond your life!

Survival Guide for **January 25**

"THE LONGER THIS WAITING GOES ON, THE DEEPER THE ACHE. I SO WANT TO BE THERE TO DELIVER GOD'S GIFT IN PERSON AND WATCH YOU GROW STRONGER RIGHT BEFORE MY EYES!" ROMANS 1:11

Tamar, a Gentile, married Judah's son, Hur. When he died leaving her childless, custom dictated that his brother, Onan, marry her, give her a child and make her part of their family. That way Hur's inheritance could be passed on to her son.

However, on their first night together, instead of imparting his seed to her, Onan deliberately spilled it on the ground, and God killed him. Onan, it seems, was up for the stimulation but was not willing to be the agent of impartation. God wanted it the other way round. (Genesis 38).

Why do you attend Christian gatherings (church or campus ministry for example) for stimulation or impartation? What good is it if the choir or the Praise Band brings you to your feet and the pastor or campus pastor brings you to your knees, yet you keep going home—moved but not changed?

At some point, the Word we hear has got to be conceived in our heart and bring forth fruit. At some point, we have got to become so impregnated with divine purpose, that we begin imparting it to others. Otherwise, the story ends with us. The business world refers to this as "succession planning." We dare not die without imparting to others what has been imparted to us.

After Moses had met God at the burning bush, he sent back into Egypt and brought the people back to see what he saw and to touch what he touched. That is what we have been called to do too. There are places where God will take us so that we can go back and bring others there too.

If you have received an impartation from God—don't keep it to yourself!

Survival Guide for **January 26**

". . . MY PRESENCE WILL GO WITH YOU. I'LL SEE THE JOURNEY TO THE END." EXODUS 33:14

Knowing when to say "when" can save your life.

Self-deceit is the hallmark of those who esteem what they do to be more important than the one who does it. This is called "The Martyr Syndrome." As humbling as it maybe, the world will go on wonderfully well without you.

If you're going to survive, you've got to discover your own pace—not be driven by somebody else's! Look out! Fatigue is dangerous; when it walks in, faith walks out! Furthermore, when we're burned-out, we're attacked by old enemies we've already conquered.

The first to return is usually negativity; what we used to enjoy we now endure.

The second one to show up is inadequacy. That's because we try to carry the whole world on our shoulders. Give it back to God! Learn to take care of yourself like you would a valued friend. Know when to apply the brakes, for without times of rest and recreation, you'll never reach your highest potential!

We're conditioned to think of ourselves as weak or self-indulgent when we allow ourselves down-time. We push on, exhausted, wondering why we don't enjoy life more, when the truth is that we haven't really learned how to live.

Nurtured people are much more effective in every area. Their relationships with God are stronger; their families are happier; their health is better; they live longer than "martyrs." Why? Because they've found a place of "rest."

Have you?

Survival Guide for **January 27**

"THIS IS THE KIND OF LIFE YOU'VE BEEN INVITED INTO, THE KIND OF LIFE CHRIST LIVED. HE SUFFERED EVERYTHING THAT CAME HIS WAY SO YOU WOULD KNOW THAT IT COULD BE DONE, AND ALSO KNOW HOW TO DO IT, STEP-BY-STEP." 1 PETER 2:21

What does it mean to be "invited into the kind of life Christ lived?" Before you answer, read this story by Tony Campollo:

> Joe was a drunk, miraculously converted in a street outreach mission. Before his conversion he'd gained a reputation as a derelict and dirty wino for whom there was no hope. But following his conversion to Christ, everything changed. Joe became the most caring person at the mission. He spent his days there, doing whatever needed to be done. There was never anything he was asked to do that he considered beneath him. Whether it was cleaning up vomit left by some sick alcoholic, or scrubbing toilets after men had left them filthy, Joe did it all with a heart of gratitude. He could be counted on to feed any man who wandered in off the streets, undress and tuck him into bed, when he was too out-of-it to take care of himself.
>
> One evening, after the mission director delivered his evangelistic message to the usual crowd of sullen men with drooped heads, one of them looked up, came down to the altar and kneeled to pray, crying out for God to help him change. The repentant drunk kept shouting, "Oh God, make me like Joe! Make me like Joe! Make me like Joe!" The director leaned over and said, "Son, wouldn't it be better if you prayed 'make me like Jesus?'"
>
> After thinking about it for a few moments, the man looked up with an inquisitive expression and asked, "Is He like Joe?"

What does it mean to be invited "invited into the kind of life Christ lived?"

It means to love like Jesus loved.

Survival Guide for **January 28**

"HE GAVE THEM EXACTLY WHAT THEY ASKED FOR—BUT ALONG WITH IT THEY GOT AN EMPTY HEART." PSALM 106:15

Frank Sinatra sang, "The record shows, I took the blows and did it my way." Sometimes God will let us do things our way—then let us deal with the consequences. When we insist on having something that He in His wisdom has withheld, He steps back and says, "O.K., I've warned you, but have it your way."

> The Bible says that because the Children of Israel:
> a)   "forgot His works,
> b)   did not wait for His counsel,
> c)   lusted exceedingly,
> d)   tested God. . .

He gave them their request, but sent leanness into their soul" (Ps 106:13-15 NKJ).

That is the formula for spiritual barrenness.

When God called Moses to deliver the Children of Israel, he decided to do it his way. He saw an Egyptian beating a Hebrew slave, but instead of consulting God he took matters into his own hands by killing the abuser. Before he did, the Bible says he "looked this way and then that. . . " (Ex 2:12)—but he never looked up! He was more concerned about audience response than God response.

God had to teach Moses that his orders came from Him. After Moses dug a hole and tried to hide the work of his flesh, God allowed it to be exposed. Why? To show Moses that by doing things his way, he couldn't keep a single soldier buried in sand, whereas by doing things God's way, he was able to bury a whole army in the depths of the Red Sea.

Whose way will you follow today?

Make up your mind to do it God's way!

Survival Guide for **January 29**

"HE SAID WATCH ME AND DO WHAT I DO. WHEN I GET TO THE EDGE OF THECAMP, DO EXACTLY WHAT I DO."
JUDGES 7:17

Effective leaders understand that caring about workers is even more important than caring about work. They understand that happy people are more productive people. Three things set effective leaders apart:

> (1) They are facilitators. They realize that nobody is ever what they ought to be, until they are first doing what they ought to be doing and that the way to accomplish their own goals is to help others reach theirs.

> (2) They are courteous. They never look down or talk down. They don't have one set of manners for the important people and another for the less important. To them, everybody is important, because everybody has God-given potential. Servant-hearted leaders work hard to bring it out.

> (3) They are decisive. Joshua's challenge cut to the chase: "Choose for yourselves this day whom you will serve. But as for me and my household, we will serve the Lord." (Joshua 24:15 NIV). No waffling allowed! People need direction; therefore the good leader has to be decisive. Leaders are generally remembered for one of two things: the problems they caused through indecision, or the ones they solved through clear direction. The decisive leader sometimes has to go out on a limb, because that's where the fruit is.

As a Christian leader I often find myself praying this prayer, maybe it will be helpful to you as well:

> Lord it is not easy being in the spotlight. It is lonely and scary and often the last place I want to be. This task is so far beyond me that there is nothing I can do but throw myself on You. Help me to exercise my authority with grace. Keep me strong. Give me courage and wisdom. My desire is to lead with Your heart: give me the love it takes to lead well. In Jesus Name, Amen

Survival Guide for **January 30**

───

"GOD-LOYAL PEOPLE, LIVING HONEST LIVES, MAKE IT MUCH EASIER FOR THEIR CHILDREN." PROVERBS 20:7

In 1927, a Georgia real estate and insurance company folded, short-changing 500 stockholders. The owner, a man called Mercer, was a person of integrity who vowed if possible to repay every single penny. But despite his best efforts, his company never did make a comeback. After he died, his son remembered his father's vow and 28 years later deposited a check in a Savannah bank to reimburse every last stockholder.

That young man was the successful singer/songwriter, Johnny Mercer. One of the songs he wrote from which he earned the royalties to pay the stockholders was, "Accentuate the Positive." You've probably heard it.

When you go, leave your children—both biological and spiritual—something more important than money to remember you by; leave them a legacy of integrity: "God-loyal people, living honest lives, make it much easier for their children."

The person who can't be trusted on all counts, can't truly be trusted on any. Ethical principles are not flexible. A little white lie is still a lie; theft is theft, whether it's one dollar or one million. Character is made in the small moments of our lives when no one is there to check up on us.

Sociologists suggest that people of poor character might have been different if they'd grown up in a better environment. Character is a choice. Our circumstances are no more responsible for our character than the mirror is for our looks. What we see only reflects what we are—and what we are is what we have spent our life building.

Of course the choice I am talking about is that of making Jesus Lord—that is the foundation on which to build character!

Survival Guide for **January 31**

"NOW THAT I'VE PUT YOU THERE ON A HILLTOP,ON A LIGHTSTAND – SHINE! KEEP OPEN HOUSE; BE GENEROUS WITH YOUR LIVES. BY OPENING UP TO OTHERS, YOU'LL PROMPT PEOPLE TO OPEN UP WITH GOD, THIS GENEROUS FATHER IN HEAVEN. MATTHEW 5:16

Jesus said, "Let your light shine before men in such a way that they may see your good works, and glorify your Father Who is in heaven" (Matthew 5:16 NAS). What kind of good works? Patience and courtesy in stressful situations, gracious attitudes in the midst of difficulty, stopping and saying thank you, apologizing when wrong, taking time to help someone in need. Those are the kind of simple acts that make our Father look good.

Chuck Swindoll writes,

> I'm just maverick enough to say that I think fewer Christians ought to be going into the ministry, and more should be going into business and occupations that have nothing to do with vocational Christian service. I don't see life divided into public and private, secular and sacred. It's all an open place of service before God.
>
> Recently I had a delightful talk with a keen-thinking young man at our church. As we visited, I asked him about his future plans. 'Well, I've just graduated from Law School,' he said. When I asked how he hoped to use his training, he replied, "I want to be a man of integrity who practices law."

Whether you're a judge or a janitor, the same God who used David's sling, Moses' rod and the widow's mite will use you for His glory if only you will give yourself to Him fully, and determine to make Our Father look good in all you do.

Survival Guide for **February 1**

" . . YOU ARE ALL EQUAL. THAT IS, WE ARE ALL IN A COMMON RELATIONSHIP WITH JESUS CHRIST." GALATIANS 3:28

Spiritual advantage has nothing to do with the color of our skin and everything to do with the contents of our heart. It doesn't matter if our ancestors came over on the Mayflower or on a slave ship for "There is neither. . . slave nor free. . . you are all one in Christ Jesus." In Jesus' kingdom, social status doesn't count.

And He doesn't consider gender either, because "In Christ's family there can be no division into Jew and non-Jew, slave and free, male and female. . . we are all in a common relationship with Jesus Christ."

God doesn't even discount us because of our moral background. Rahab was a harlot until she exercised faith in God's Word. In fact, she is even mentioned alongside Sarah, Abraham's wife, because she believed and was blessed.

Faith is the only thing that creates true equality. When we have it, we can walk with our head held high in spite of our past failures. It doesn't matter what people say about us but what God says about us and consequently, what we say about ourselves is all that matters.

Jesus healed a woman who was stooped over with severe spinal curvature for 18 years. When He saw her Jesus said, "Woman you are free . . . and immediately she was able to stand up straight . . ." (Luke 13:12-13 NCV). When we place our complete faith and trust in Christ, we too find the power to stand up straight.

Once that happens—we can look around and see that we are all the same height before God!

Survival Guide for **February 2**

". . . IF MY GOAL WAS POPULARITY, I WOULDN'T BOTHER BEING CHRIST'S SLAVE." GALATIANS 1:10

We remain locked in a prison of our own making until we quit trying to please those who disapprove of us. Too many of us have made it our life's work to change somebody else's opinion of us. We are determined to prove to them that we are valuable.

Never allow somebody else's approval to become your goal. The truth is that some folks may never like you. They may never see your good qualities.

Any time we try to please somebody who rejects or abuses us, we put ourselves into bondage to them. By saying either in word or deed, "You were right to hit me, or leave me or hurt me," you are tying yourself up with their opinion rather than God's. Furthermore, when their opinion of you becomes your opinion, you have built a prison inside your soul with only one prisoner—you.

Are you prepared to accept that the person you have spent your life trying to impress may never be impressed? Even more importantly, are you prepared to accept that from God's perspective—it doesn't matter? To deal effectively with others, we must be able to work alongside them—without allowing ourselves to be controlled by their moods, or governed by their opinions of us. Most of all we must not let their opinions of us become the basis for our self-images. We must believe that God's opinion of us is all that matters.

When you believe that God's opinion of you is all that matters, you have taken the first step toward being a God pleaser—instead of a man pleaser.

Survival Guide for **February 3**

"AS A DEER PANTS FOR STREAMS OF WATER, SO MY SOUL PANTS FOR YOU, O GOD." PSALM 42:1 (NIV)

"Panting" is a word picture for longing, yearning, desiring. When we pant for something we seek it, long for it, thirst for it, wait for it, see it, know it, love it, hear it, and respond to it! "Panting" for God means desiring more of Him in our activities, thoughts, and desires. Most of all "panting" for God means that we want more of the company of God. Too often in our rush to perform for God, we fail to simply to enjoy His company. Yet we were created to be dissatisfied and incomplete with anything less.

In *Secrets of the Vine*, Bruce Wilkinson writes, I made three simple commitments to God:

> (1) To get up earlier and read my Bible.
> (2) To write a page in my spiritual journal.
> (3) To seek Him until I found Him.

> I still remember the first line of my spiritual journal: "Dear God, I don't know what to say to you." Each day I read what I'd written. On every page I saw why my busy Christian life left such a bland taste—I'd become an expert at serving God, but remained a novice at being His friend. But I stayed with it. By the middle of the second month, things started to shift. His presence entered my room. My rambling journal entries gradually began to change as I listened. His passion for me, His purposes for my life, began to rise from the pages of my Bible.

> That was more than 15 years ago. The pleasures of abiding —and the extraordinary benefits—have redefined God's work through me. I see fruit everywhere I turn. Yet none of it is a result of my working harder.

Fill up your soul today at the Fountain of God—only He can quench your thirst.

Survival Guide for **February 4**

"I'M NO LONGER CALLING YOU SERVANTS BECAUSE SERVANTS DON'T UNDERSTAND WHAT THEIR MASTER IS THINKING AND PLANNING. NO, I'VE NAMED YOU FRIENDS BECAUSE I'VE LET YOU IN ON EVERYTHING I'VE HEARD FROM THE FATHER." JOHN 15:15

Friendship with God is maintained through continual meditation. It is impossible to be God's friend apart from knowing what He says. We cannot love God unless we know Him and that is possible only through His Word: "He revealed Himself to Samuel through His word"(1 Samuel 3:21 NIV)

God still uses the same method.

While we can't spend all day studying the Bible, we can think it throughout the day, recalling verses we have read or memorized, mulling them over in our mind. This is called meditation. Meditation isn't some difficult, mysterious ritual, it is simply focused thinking—a skill anybody can learn.

Thinking about a problem over and over again is called worrying. Thinking about God's Word over and over again is called meditation.

If you know how to worry, you know how to meditate.

Simply switch your attention from the problem to the solution. The more we meditate on God's Word, the less we have to worry about. David said, "Oh, how I love Your law! I think about it all day long." (Psalm 119.97 NLT).

The more time we spend meditating on God's Word, the more we will understand its secrets: "Friendship with God is reserved for those who reverence Him. With them alone He shares the secrets of His promises" (Psalm 25:14 TLB).

To cultivate a friendship with God, start by practicing constant conversation with Him and continually meditating on His Word.

Survival Guide for **February 5**

"I'M NOT SAYING THAT I HAVE DONE THIS ALL TOGETHER, THAT I HAVE IT MADE. BUT I AM WELL ON MY WAY, REACHING OUT FOR CHRIST,WHO HAS SO WONDROUSLY REACHED OUT FOR ME." PHILIPPIANS 3:12

An Anglican Bishop buried in Westminster Abbey in 1533 had the following words are inscribed on his tomb:

> "In my youth, my imagination had no limits. I dreamed of changing the world. But as I grew older and wiser, I found that the world would not change, so I decided to change my country. But it, too, seemed immovable. So as I grew into my twilight years, in one last attempt, I settled for changing my family; but alas, they would have none of it.

> "Now on my death bed I realize that—if I had only first changed myself, then by example, I might have changed my family, and through my family changed my country, through my country changed the world."

Change must begin within. Maturity is a race with no finishing line. Paul wrote ". . . I keep working toward that day when I will finally be all that Christ . . . wants me to be." (Phil 3:12 NLT). Notice that the Apostle Paul felt he must "keep working" to accomplish his goal—should we expect anything else?

Don't have enough time? Then get rid of these three great time wasters:
1. Laziness: time put to no useful purpose, not even relaxation.
2. Procrastination: opportunities lost that can never be regained.
3. Sloppiness: lack of preparation resulting in time consuming mistakes.

Life is not a dress rehearsal, it is the real thing—so keep "reaching out!"

Survival Guide for **February 6**

"I HAVE CALLED YOU FRIENDS." JOHN 15:15(NIV)

We must be honest with God to build our friendship with God. He doesn't expect perfection, but He does expect honesty. If perfection were a requirement, no one would qualify.

God's friends, in the Bible, were not perfect but they were honest about their feelings, even complaining and arguing with Him, yet God didn't seem to mind. In fact, He encouraged it.

God listened patiently to David's accusations of unfairness, betrayal and abandonment. He didn't strike down Jeremiah for claiming He had tricked him. Job was allowed to vent his bitterness, and He actually defended him for being honest.

On the other hand, He rebuked Job's friends for faking it: "You haven't been honest either with Me or about Me—not the way My friend Job has. My friend Job will pray for you, and I will accept his prayer." (Job 42:7-8). God's friends should share their true feelings with Him, not what they think they ought to feel or say. Until we fully believe that God uses everything for good in our lives, we are likely to find ourselves harboring resentment toward Him over our looks, our ethnicity, our economic background, unanswered prayers, past hurts, and anything else we feel that we would change if we were God.

Actually, revealing our feelings and releasing our resentments are the first steps to true healing. Isn't it encouraging to know that God's closest friends felt just like we do? But instead of masking their feelings in pious clichés, they voiced them openly. And so should we. Why?

Because being honest with God leads to a new level of friendship with Him.

Survival Guide for **February 7**

"I'VE NAMED YOU FRIENDS." JOHN 15:15

Obedience is the way we build our friendship with God.

We normally think of obedience as a characteristic of our relationship to a parent, a boss or a teacher, not a friend. But Jesus said, "You are My friends if you do what I command." (John 15:14 NIV).

True friendship isn't passive; it is active. When Jesus asks us to love others, help the needy, give our finances, keep our lives clean, offer forgiveness, and bring others to Him—love motivates us to obey immediately.

Great opportunities usually come once in a lifetime, but small ones surround us every day. Through simple acts of obedience we bring a smile to God's face. God treasures obedience more than all our religious ritual: "What pleases the Lord more. . .sacrifices or obedience. . . It is better to obey." (1 Samuel 15:22 NCV).

At the beginning of Jesus' public ministry, God announced, "This is My beloved Son, and I am fully pleased with Him." (Matthew 3:17 NLT). What had Jesus been doing for 30 years that pleased God? The Bible says: "He was obedient." (Luke 2:51 NLT).

Thirty years of pleasing God were summed up in three words: "He was obedient"

Jesus is our model in all things.

The relationship Jesus had with His Father is the one we are to have as friends of God!

Survival Guide for **February 8**

"I HAVE CALLED YOU FRIENDS." JOHN 15:15 (NIV)

We must desire to build our friendship with God above all else.

David desired to know God above all else. He used words like longing, yearning, thirsting, hungering: "the thing I seek most of all, is the privilege of living in His presence every day of my life." (Psalm 27:4 TLB). David went so far as to say, "Your love means more than life to me." (Psalm 63:3 CEV).

Jacob's desire to know God was so intense that he wrestled with God all night: "I will not let You go unless You bless me." (Genesis 32:26 NIV). The amazing thing is that God, Who is all-powerful, let Jacob win. Why? Perhaps because wrestling requires personal contact, it brings us closer to Him.

Paul was another man who was passionate for friendship with God. Nothing mattered more: "[for my determined purpose is] that I may know Him—that I may progressively become more deeply and intimately acquainted with Him." (Philippians 3:10 Amp).

Friendship with God is a choice, not an accident. We must intentionally seek it.

That means answering these questions:

Do I value God's friendship more than anything else?
Is it worth giving up other things for?
Is it worth developing the habits and skills required?
Is it worth praying, "Lord, more than anything else, I want to know You?"

God's answer to our honest desire to be His friends has always been: "When you get serious about finding Me and want it more than anything else, I'll make sure you won't be disappointed."(Jeremiah 29:13).

Survival Guide for **February 9**

**"BUT BLESSED IS THE MAN WHO TRUSTS ME, GOD, THE
WOMAN WHO STICKS WITH GOD." JEREMIAH 17:7**

"Then (Delilah) called, 'Samson, the Philistines are upon you.' He awoke
from his sleep and thought, 'I'll go out as before and shake myself free.'
But he did not know that the Lord had left him. Then the Philistines seized
him." (Judges 16:20-21 NIV). Samson, a champion who once depended
on God for his every move, now says "I will just do what I have done
before." Where was his confidence?

Jesus said, ". . .Separated, you can't produce a thing." (John 15:5). Read
that again. He couldn't make it any clearer, yet we keep going out without
bending our knee or committing our way to the Lord, acting as if it all
depends on us and falling flat on our faces.

Dear God, will we ever learn where to put our confidence?

"Cursed is the one who trusts in man, who depends on flesh for his
strength and whose heart turns away from the Lord. He will be like a bush
in the wastelands; he will not see prosperity when it comes. But blessed is
the man who trusts in the Lord whose confidence is in Him. He will be
like a tree planted by the water that sends out its roots by the stream. It
does not fear when heat comes; its leaves are always green. It has no
worries in a year of drought and never fails to bear fruit." (Jeremiah 17:5-8
NIV).

Most of our internal agony, our struggling and frustration, comes from
misplaced confidence.

Before you go a step further today, pause and ask yourself, "Where have I
placed my confidence?"

Survival Guide for **February 10**

"ELIJAH SAID TO AHAB, 'UP ON YOUR FEET! EAT AND DRINK—CELEBRATE! RAIN IS ON THE WAY; I HEAR IT COMING.'"   1 KINGS 18:41

Are you going through a dry spell?   Are you busy encouraging others while your own life seems to be falling apart?   Maybe work or school has got you down, or you're facing some unexpected health concerns or family problems.

That is what happened to Elijah; this man who earlier called down fire from heaven suddenly found himself in the middle of a full-blown famine. So what did he do?

"Elijah . . . got down on his knees, with his face to the ground." (1 Kings 18:42 TLB).

Elijah chose to:
(a) shut out his surroundings for a while
(b) focus only on what God was saying
(c) keep praying.

And when he did, the Bible says he said "I hear it coming". What Elijah sensed inside was completely contrary to what was happening outside. His spirit sensed the rain—before a single drop fell.

God speaks in our spirit, not our flesh and what He says there, is more real than anything that's happening around us.   But be warned: what we sense in our spirit may go against what we actually have in the bank, or what is actually happening on the job or at school, or what is actually taking place at home, or what is actually happening in your body.

Elijah had to discount all the "no rain" weather reports he kept getting.   So will we.

When you know that God has promised you a certain thing, you must tune out all the negativity around you, reject your doubts and keep believing God!

Survival Guide for **February 11**

"THEN HE SAID TO HIS YOUNG SERVANT, 'ON YOUR FEET NOW! LOOK TOWARD THE SEA.' HE WENT, LOOKED, AND REPORTED BACK, 'I DON'T SEE A THING.' 'KEEP LOOKING,' SAID ELIJAH, 'SEVEN TIMES IF NECESSARY.'" 1 KINGS 18:43

As he prayed for rain, Elijah sensed something in his spirit that he wasn't seeing with his natural eyes. When he told his servant, "Look toward the sea", the same negative report kept coming back, "I don't see a thing." But Elijah kept believing. Finally, the seventh time his servant told him he saw, ". . . a little cloud rising from the sea." (1 Kings 18:44 NLT).

When you are a praying person, God will often show you the direction your answer is going to come from. But first you have to:

(1) Stop being influenced by others who don't share your vision. Amos 3:3 asks, "Do two people walk hand in hand if they aren't going to the same place?" When his servant didn't share his vision, Elijah sent him away. Allowing yourself to be influenced by those who aren't in sync with you spiritually can cost you dearly.

(2) Disregard conflicting voices. Elijah put his head down and tuned out every voice except God's. Learn to tune out the voices of confusion and doubt, until you hear only what God has promised.

(3) Get into birthing mode. Elijah went into "spiritual labor." That's what that phrase "travailed in prayer" means. The pain of labor is only worth it because of the joy of the new life it yields.

Today, if there is a storm in your spirit don't ignore it. Travail in prayer—if you don't push, it won't be born.

On the other hand when you do, God may send a NEW LIFE that will overwhelm you.

Survival Guide for **February 12**

"WHEN THE RAINBOW APPEARS IN THE CLOUD, I'LL SEE IT AND REMEMBER THE ETERNAL COVENANT BETWEEN GOD AND EVERYTHING LIVING, EVERY LAST LIVING CREATURE ON EARTH." GENESIS 9:16

When Noah preached about the coming rain, it was a symbol of judgment.

But after the flood God said, ". . . never again will (I) destroy all life. I will see the rainbow and remember My eternal promise to every living being." (Genesis 9:15-17 TLB). From that point on, rain became a symbol of blessing.

When God turns the thing that should have destroyed you into a blessing, you'll be able to look back and say, "The suffering You sent was good for me, for it taught me to pay attention to Your principles" (Psalm 119:71 NLT).

Without suffering, we would never discover:

(a) that isolation creates determination and makes us lay hold of God
(b) the power of prayer
(c) what God can accomplish in the face of adversity
(d) that God doesn't need our friends to support us in order to bless us
(g) that God alone brings us through suffering.

Suffering will come, but after the rain comes the rainbow.

God has a way of turning suffering into blessing.

Survival Guide for **February 13**

". . .IF IT SEEMS SLOW IN COMING, WAIT. IT'S ON ITS WAY. IT WILL COME RIGHT ON TIME." HABAKKUK 2:3

God sometimes post-dates His promises.

He takes His time getting us ready for our destiny even when we feel we're more than ready. Visionaries are usually impatient; the greater their vision, the more difficult it is for them to wait. Yet, paradoxically, waiting is an essential part of the process!

God finds some of His best people in some of the worst places. For example, He found Gideon hiding in a cave and Rahab working in a brothel. But no matter where He finds us it takes time to clean us up and get us ready. Then when we do catch the vision, we have to continue living among those who don't share it.

Take Joshua for example. Joshua went to the Promised Land and tasted its blessings. Then he had to go back home and live with people who had no idea (and probably in most cases, no interest) in what he was talking about.

Is that where you are today? Have you been asking, "Lord, how long will my passion be there, but my place be here? How long do I have to keep this promise in my heart and not have a soul to share it with?"

Don't despair! God sometimes post-dates His promises: "There has never been the slightest doubt in my mind that the God Who started this great work in you would keep at it and bring it to a flourishing finish . . . (Phil 1:6).

Even though your promise may be post-dated, remember Whose signature is on the check!

Survival Guide for **February 14**

"WE DON'T KNOW WHAT TO DO, WE'RE LOOKING TO YOU."
2 CHRONICLES 20:12

I don't have a twelve step program but here is a seven step one that has often helped me when seeking God's guidance:

(1) Clear the channel. Repent and receive forgiveness. Sin hinders communication with God. Confession and repentance shows our willingness to set aside our personal desires and be open to God.

(2) Be patient. "Don't be impatient. Wait for the Lord." (Psalm 27:14 TLB). ". . .No one whose hope is in you will ever be put to shame. . ." (Psalm 25:3 NIV). Don't give in to self-generated urgency. Wait for God to open the door.

(3) Beware of external pressures. These usually come from our present circumstances, or from those who are trying to impose their agendas on us. Sift all advice through God's Word.

(4) Watch out for internal pressures. These are triggered by old messages, and often manifest themselves as fear of loss, or exaggerated expectations.

(5) Persist in prayer. "Pray all the time" (1 Thessalonians 5:17). God's goal is to mold us into His Son's likeness, and prayer is one of the Potter's tools. Prayer is not for God's benefit; it is for ours. He already knows what we should do; as we persevere in prayer He will reveal it to us at just the right time (His, not ours!).

(6) Search the Scriptures. Read and digest God's Word. It is an unfailing source of wisdom. It cuts through the clutter and filters out whatever is not of God.

(7) Wait for peace. "Let the peace of Christ keep you in tune with each other, in step with each other." (Colossians 3:15). Peace is the deciding factor after going through the other steps. It is the verification that we are making the right decision, so don't go for it first or proceed without it.

Survival Guide for **February 15**

"WE ARE CITIZENS OF HIGH HEAVEN" PHILIPPIANS 3:20

Billy Graham writes,

> "I have a friend who during the Depression lost his
> job, his fortune, his wife, and his home. But he
> tenaciously held to his faith—the only thing he had
> left. One day he stopped to watch some men doing
> stonework on a huge church. One of them was
> chiseling a triangular piece of stone. 'What's that
> for?' asked my friend. The workman said, 'See that
> little opening way up there near the spire? Well, I'm
> shaping this down here so that it'll fit in up there.'
>
> "Tears filled the eyes of my friend as he walked away,
> for God had used this workman to help him understand
> the ordeal through which he was going. 'I'm shaping
> you down here, so that you'll fit in up there!'"

Paul writes, "We are citizens of high heaven." We are on earth on a
temporary visa—never forget that. Weigh your actions and your decisions
in the light of your ultimate destiny, not your immediate comfort. Get rid
of the idea that "thoughts of heaven are only the pleasantries of the
ageing." This life is the short story; heaven is the unending one. Tummy
tucks, face-lifts, liposuction, fame, fortune, and personal empire building
notwithstanding, our earthly suit isn't going to last forever. Before you
shed it, be sure you have fulfilled your destiny, and that you are ready to
hear the words: "Well done, good and faithful servant!" (Matthew 25:21
NIV).

One second after arriving in God's presence, what are you going to wish
you had not left undone?

How different each day of life would be if that question guided our actions
and attitudes.

Survival Guide for **February 16**

"A GIFT GETS ATTENTION; IT BUYS THE ATTENTION OF EMINENT PEOPLE." PROVERBS 18:16

It is what you believe about yourself not what others believe about you that matters—opinions can be changed. Jesus never begged anybody to believe in Him. He knew that integrity usually isn't proven, it is discerned. If you are struggling to find your place in life, maybe this story will help.

Sparky didn't have much going for him. In high school he flunked Latin, Algebra, English and Physics. He made the golf team but promptly lost the only important match of the season; then lost the consolation match. He was awkward socially—more shy than disliked. He never once asked a girl out on a date in high school. One thing, however, was important to Sparky—drawing. He was proud of his artwork even though nobody else appreciated it. He submitted cartoons to the editors of his high school yearbook, but they were rejected. Even so, he aspired to be an artist. After high school he sent samples of his work to the Walt Disney Studios—again he was rejected. But Sparky didn't quit. He decided to write his autobiography in cartoons. The popularity of his cartoon strip eventually led to countless books, television shows, and licensing opportunities.

Sparky, you see, was Charles Schulz, creator of the Peanuts comic strip, possibly the most famous cartoonist of all time. Like his main character, Charlie Brown, Schulz seemed unable to succeed at many things, but he made the most of his talent, refused to quit, and ended up on top.

Today believe in yourself, don't give up, and use whatever God has given you to His glory!

Survival Guide for **February 17**

"I WAS AFRAID I MIGHT DISAPPOINT YOU, SO I FOUND A GOOD HIDING PLACE AND SECURED YOUR MONEY." MATTHEW 25:25

If you weren't afraid of failing, what would you attempt today?

In Matthew 25:14-30, a wealthy businessman entrusted his entire estate to three key workers. He gave the first five talents, the second two talents and the third one talent.

In Bible times one talent is believed to have been about 1 years' salary. Knowing that helps us see what an opportunity this was. It was a defining moment that gave each of them the opportunity to
  (a) test their skills in the market
  (b) develop personal initiative
  (c) practice good judgment
  (d) profit from their investment.

Two men did exactly that; but the third was afraid of failing. He decided to play it safe, so he buried his talent. Playing it safe only got him called "wicked and lazy" (Matthew 25:26 Amp).

Fear of failure always make us play it safe. Without the courage to start—we are already finished. Everyone either overcomes their fears or gives in to them. Overcomers include: Moses, Gideon, Deborah, and Esther.

On the other hand:

—Fear of poverty made Jacob deceive his father.
—Fear of starvation made the Israelites want to run back to Egypt.
—Fear of their critics made the disciples forsake Jesus in His darkest hour, and that same fear made Peter deny Jesus three times.

Refuse to let fear stop you from making God a return on His investment in you. How we use the gifts God gives us is a matter of the utmost importance. Faithful living is risky living.

Failure is not fatal, but according to this parable, playing it safe can be!

Survival Guide for **February 18**

"WHAT MARVELOUS LOVE THE FATHER HAS EXTENDED TO US! JUST LOOK AT IT—WE'RE CALLED CHILDREN OF GOD! THAT'S WHO WE REALLY ARE." 1 JOHN 3:1

The most amazing thing about God's love is that it is unconditional.

God doesn't say, "I love you, if." There are no "ifs" in God's heart. His love for us doesn't depend on what we say or do, on our looks or intelligence, on our success or popularity, or even on our performance. His love for us existed before we were born, and it will exist after we are gone. His love is from eternity to eternity and is not bound by any time-related events or circumstances.

Does that mean that God doesn't care what we do or say? No! Loving without condition doesn't mean loving without concern. Sometimes we confuse unconditional love with unconditional approval. God doesn't approve of betrayal, selfishness, pride, resentment, or any other form of disobedience. These are opposite to the love God wants to instill in our hearts.

God loving unconditionally just means that He continues to love us even when we blow it. (I love saying that—because I blow it a lot) He continues to wait for us as the father waited for the return of the prodigal son. It is important that we hold to the truth that God never gives up loving us, even when He is grieved by what we do. Why is that so important?

Simply because God's love is the magnet that draws us back to Him over and over again.

Survival Guide for **February 19**

"SINCE THIS IS THE KIND OF LIFE WE HAVE CHOSEN. . . LET US MAKE SURE THAT WE DO NOT JUST HOLD IT AS AN IDEA IN OUR HEADS OR A SENTIMENT IN OUR HEARTS, BUT WORK OUT ITS IMPLICATIONS IN EVERY DETAIL OF OUR LIVES." GALATIANS 5:25

Christians today often seem to distinguish between one who is living "a Christian life" and one who is living "the life of the Spirit" or a "Spirit-filled" or "Spirit-led" life. However, this distinction seems to be foreign to what the Apostle Paul says about the Christian's life in the Spirit:

> "It is obvious what kind of life develops out of trying to get your own way all the time: repetitive, loveless, cheap sex; a stinking accumulation of mental and emotional garbage; frenzied and joyless grabs for happiness; trinket gods; magic-show religion; paranoid loneliness; cutthroat competition; all-consuming yet-never-satisfied wants; a brutal temper; an impotence to love or be loved; divided homes and divided lives; small-minded and lopsided pursuits; the vicious habit of depersonalizing everyone into a rival; uncontrolled and uncontrollable addictions; ugly parodies of community. I could go on. But what happens when we live God's way? He brings gifts into our lives, much the same way that fruit appears in an orchard—things like affection for others, exuberance about life, serenity. We develop a willingness to stick with things, a sense of compassion in the heart, and a conviction that a basic holiness permeates things and people. We find ourselves involved in loyal commitments, not needing to force our way in life, able to marshal and direct our energies wisely. Since this is the kind of life we have chosen, the life of the Spirit, let us make sure that we do not just hold it as an idea in our heads, or a sentiment in our hearts, but work out its implications in every detail of our lives." (Galatians 5:19-25).

Don't let Satan use semantics to keep you from the truth that living "the Christian life" and living "the life of the Spirit" are one and the same thing. Really, does the idea of a non-Spirit filled Christian even make sense?

Survival Guide for **February 20**

"BE EVEN-TEMPERED, CONTENT WITH SECOND PLACE, QUICK TO FORGIVE ANOFFENSE. FORGIVE AS QUICKLY AND COMPLETELY AS THE MASTER FORGAVE YOU."
COLOSSIANS 3:13

The power to forgive is the only power we have over anyone who hurts us.

When we say, "I no longer hold it against you," both sides are set free from the negative bond that exists between us. But there's more: we also free ourselves from the burden of being "the offended one." As long as we don't forgive those who have wounded us, we take them with us: we carry them like albatrosses around our necks. The great temptation is to cling to our anger toward our enemies, then define ourselves as being offended and wounded by them. Forgiveness not only liberates the other party, but it liberates us too. It is the way to true freedom.

Unfortunately, forgiving doesn't always mean forgetting. Though we forgive somebody, the memory might stay with us for a long time. We can even carry it in our bodies as a physical sign. But forgiveness changes how we remember. It converts the curse into a blessing. When we forgive our parents for their divorce or their lack of love, our friends for their unfaithfulness in times of need, or our counselors for their bad advice, we no longer have to suffer as victims of events over which we have no control.

Forgiveness allows us to take back our power and not let the events destroy us. It actually allows those experiences to deepen our wisdom and sharpen our discernment.

Today exercise the only power we have over anyone who has hurt you—forgive them.

Survival Guide for **February 21**

"LET'S JUST GO AHEAD AND BE WHAT WE WERE MADE TO BE . . . " ROMANS 12:6

Confront your defects of character to maximize your walk with God. Call them what they are—hindrances to a productive life in the Spirit—and begin to work on them one by one.

Here are six of the most common hindrances, some of which I know up close and personal!

(1) Pride.   Spiritual pride, social pride, racial pride. God hates any form of pride that looks down on others: ". . . with humility regard one another as more important than himself." (Philippians 2:3 NAS). Pride toppled Satan and it has toppled many Christians.

(2) Insecurity. Insecure people are generally unwilling to take risks. Really believing that God is with us is the key to overcoming insecurity.

(3) Moodiness. Moody people are like the wind: unstable. They tend to be undependable. Moodiness is hard to overcome, but confession and prayer helps.

(4) Perfectionism. Perfectionism is the obsessive need always to perform flawlessly. Perfectionists can't affirm themselves; therefore, it is difficult for them to affirm anybody else. Learning to accept the fact that God loves us "warts and all" is the key to overcoming perfectionism.

(5) Over-sensitivity. Overly-sensitive people are constantly licking their wounds and looking inward; they're totally unaware of the needs of others. A change of focus from inward to outward is they first step in increased sensitivity to others.

(6) Negativism. Negative people are depressing to be around. Their personality says "no" to life in general. Negativism is usually rooted in fear and the antidote to fear is faith.

Survival Guide for **February 22**

"BUT NOW YOU HAVE ARRIVED AT YOUR DESTINATION: BY FAITH IN CHRIST YOU ARE IN DIRECT RELATIONSHIP WITH GOD." GALATIANS 3:25-26

Not enough hours in your day? Join the club! Time has become our most precious commodity and it usually goes to the highest bidder.

In 1965, experts predicted that in 20 years we would be working a 22-hour week and retire by the age of 40 because computers would do most of the work. So here we are in the 21st century; computers are computing, faxes are faxing, beepers are beeping, but leisure time has shrunk by 37% and the average workweek has increased to 47 hours—for some of us that would be a short week!

What did the experts overlook? Appetites! The more we have, the more we want, and the more we want, the harder we work. So the vicious cycle continues, and the first casualty is our time with God.

To build a relationship with God, we must "add on a small room upstairs." (2 Kings 4:10), where we meet with Him daily. It is easy to fail at this, especially with unrealistic expectations like, "I will get up at 6 a.m. and pray for an hour," but by the third day we are exhausted. We are no longer under the law so it is not about following some regimented pattern; it is about a relationship. Daily devotions must be rewarding, otherwise you won't stick with them. So set a time that works for you.

Start each day with prayer then punctuate it with praise: "Seven times each day I stop and shout praises. . ." (Psalm 119:164).

If we can take time for coffee breaks, surely we can take time for "praise breaks."

We just have to want Him as much as we want caffeine!

Survival Guide for **February 23**

"GOD WILL LET YOU LAUGH AGAIN; YOU'LL RAISE THE ROOF WITH SHOUTS OF JOY." JOB 8:21

Nothing gets us through the tough times like a sense of humor.

Doctors say laughter is like "internal jogging"—it is good for you. It actually widens your arteries, de-stresses your heart and strengthens your immune system, enabling it to fight off disease.

The Bible agrees: "A cheerful disposition is good for your health. . ." (Proverbs 17:22).

A positive attitude will bring you more favor and cooperation than a negative one. When you keep adding to the heat and confusion of a crisis, people lose respect for your ability to handle things under pressure. But if you stay cool and maintain your sense of humor when things are falling apart, people will show their appreciation in better work and increased loyalty.

Jesus said, "The thief comes to steal and destroy; I have come that they may have life." (John 10:10 NIV). Don't let Satan steal your joy! Sure, some problems are serious, but nothing is gained by exaggerating their importance or dwelling on the bleak side of things. Instead, put the problem into God's hands and trust the results to Him.

Remember Job? Job says, "God will let you laugh again; you'll raise the roof with shouts of joy." If he could say that after everything he had been through—surely you can too!

"A cheerful heart brings a smile to your face; a sad heart makes it hard to get through the day." (Proverbs 15:13).

There is something to smile about in almost any situation—and you'll find it by remembering Who is on your side!

Survival Guide for **February 24**

"GOD, MY SHEPHERD! I DON'T NEED A THING." PSALM 23:1

Are you in the prison of "I want?"

Do you feel better when you have more and worse when you have less? Are you always wanting something bigger? Nicer? Faster? Newer? Is joy always one delivery away, one accomplishment away, one makeover away? Does happiness come from something you deposit, drive, drink, or dwell in? If so, you are in the prison of "I want."

When David wrote: "God is my Shepherd; I don't need a thing," he understood that what we have in God is greater than whatever we don't have in life. He had figured out two things that release us from the prison of "I want:"

(1) Your stuff isn't yours

When John D. Rockefeller died, someone asked, "How much did he leave?" His accountant replied, "Everything!" Everything in this life is temporary.

(2) Your stuff isn't you

Jesus said, "Life is not defined by what you have." (Luke 12:15). When God looks at us He sees our devotion and our faith, not our image or possessions.

Doug McKnight was diagnosed with multiple sclerosis at 32. Over the next 16 years, it would cost him his career, his mobility and eventually his life. But he never lost his sense of gratitude. When his church friends asked him to compile a list of prayer requests, he responded by sending them 18 blessings for which to be grateful, and 6 concerns for which to be prayerful. His blessings were three times greater than his needs. Doug McKnight had discovered that what he had in God was greater than whatever he didn't have in life.

He had been released from the prison of "I want."

Have you?

Survival Guide for **February 25**

"YOU HAVE BEDDED ME DOWN IN LUSH MEADOWS, YOU FIND ME QUIET POOLS TO DRINK FROM." PSALM 23:2

Sheep are the only creatures that have more trouble sleeping than people do. Everything must be just right: no wolves, no insect pests, and no hunger. Since sheep can't find pasture, spray insect repellent, or protect themselves, they need a shepherd. So do we.

Our Shepherd chooses the path, prepares the pasture, and protects the sheep. All we have to do is just follow, eat, rest, and stay close: "He makes me lie down in green pastures." (Psalm 23:2 NIV).

Of the ten commandments God gave to Moses, which one do you think required the most words? Adultery? Five words. Murder? Four words. Taking a day off each week—94 words! (Exodus 20:8-11). God knows us so well that He knew the storeowner would say, "Somebody's got to work that day; if I can't, my son will." So God said, "Nor your son." "Then my daughter will." "Nor your daughter." "Then an employee." "Nor your manservant."

I can imagine God saying, "One day a week you are to say "no" to work and "yes" to worship. You are to slow down, sit down, lie down and rest. After all, I rested on the seventh day and the world didn't crash. So, my child, repeat after Me, 'It is not my job to run the world.'"

Spurgeon said, "Even the sea pauses at ebb and flood; earth keeps the Sabbath of the wintry months and man must rest or faint, trim his lamp or let it burn low. In the long term, we shall do more by sometimes doing less."

At least once a week, say "It is not my job to run the world" and let God bring His Sabbath rest to your mind, your body and most of all your soul.

Survival Guide for **February 26**

"IF YOU WORK THESE WORDS INTO YOUR LIFE, YOU ARE LIKE A SMART CARPENTER WHO BUILT HIS HOUSE ON SOLID ROCK. RAIN POURED DOWN, THE RIVER FLOODED, A TORNADO HIT—BUT NOTHING MOVED THAT HOUSE. IT WAS FIXED TO THE ROCK." MATTHEW 7:24-25

While I would expect a multi-million dollar home to be of the highest quality, it isn't necessarily true. Michael Eisner, CEO of the Disney Corporation, had plans drawn up for such a house. When constructed one wall was so thin it almost buckled under its own weight. Bill Gate's house had pine paneling that rotted out before the house was even completed. Were these executives too busy to notice? No, according to many architects people find construction details boring; they only pay attention to the glitzy finishing touches.

Boring or not, it is the foundation that determines the integrity of the structure, and ultimately the value of the house.

Are you putting all your efforts into maintaining your image, but neglecting the foundational things of life, like attitude, integrity and sense of purpose? Jesus says, "These words I speak are foundational; work (them) into your life like a smart carpenter who built on solid rock. Nothing moved that house." (Matthew 7:24-25). Houses built on sand are quick, cheap and easy; they provide temporary comfort and instant gratification. But building on rock is hard: it takes time, effort, foresight and perseverance—but the results are worth it.

If you are not sure what kind of house you are building, watch and see what happens when the next storm hits. The house built on rock will withstand the same storm that levels all the others around it. There are no shortcuts. Successful Christian living is the result of commitment, consistency and building according to God's Word.

When commitment, consistency and God's Word are the foundation of your life, you will make it through any storm!

Survival Guide for **February 27**

"...YOU FIND ME QUIET POOLS TO DRINK FROM."
PSALM 23:2

God is in front of us clearing the path and showing us the way not behind us shouting, "Get going!" At the bend He says, "Turn here." At the rise He whispers, "Step up." At the pothole He warns, "Watch your foot." He tells us what we need to know, when we need to know it: "... we will find grace to help us when we need it" (Hebrews 4:16 NLT).

The operative word is, "When."

"I don't know what I will do if my husband dies." You will—when the time comes.

"I don't know how I will ever pay these bills." Jehovah Jireh, the Lord Who provides, will be there for you—when the time comes.

"I am not qualified to handle this, there is just too much I don't know." God will give you wisdom—when the time comes.

The point is we should meet today's problems with today's strength and leave tomorrow's problems in God's capable hands!

During World War II, Arthur Sulzberger, publisher of the New York Times, found it hard to sleep or rid his mind of fear, until he adopted these words from the hymn *Lead Kindly Light*: "I do not ask to see the distant scene; one steps enough for me." God does not show us "the distant scene." He promises a lamp for our feet, not a crystal ball for our future.

"He leads me" and that's enough for today!

And tomorrow? "... we will find grace to help us when we need it." (Hebrews 4:16 NLT).

Survival Guide for **February 28**

"TRUE TO YOUR WORD, YOU LET ME CATCH MY BREATH AND SEND ME IN THE RIGHT DIRECTION." PSALM 23:3

The theme song for *Monk* is "It's A Jungle Out There." I often can relate. Can't you?

You are in the "jungle" when you are out of ideas and energy, out of time and money, out of solutions and hope. The "jungle" is filled with aching hearts, broken promises, frightened minds, complaints and demands. Speaking of the "jungle," Max Lucado writes eloquently: "Our predators are creditors and the brush that surround us is the rush that exhausts us."

When we are in the "jungle" we need two things:

(1) The right person. Not just any person and not someone equally confused as we are. No, you need Someone who knows the way out; Someone to say to us, "Don't give up, there's a better place than this and I will lead you there." Our loneliness leaves because we have His constant companionship.

(2) The right direction. We need someone Who can heal our emotional wounds, release us from fear and give us hope. We need a new direction. And that is what our Shepherd provides. He diminishes despair by giving us a clearer understanding. He lifts our confusion and points us in the right direction.

When we get the right person and the right direction the "jungle" is still the "jungle;" it doesn't change—but we do!

If you're not in the "jungle" thank God but still prepare because one day soon you will be. You may be no more than one turn from a failure, an illness or a major life change. Although you may not need it now, you will need to know Who to turn to then—your Shepherd.

Don't wait until you're in the "jungle"—spend some time with The Good Shepherd today

60   *Timothy L. Hudson*

Survival Guide for **February 29**

"YOU SERVE ME A SIX-COURSE DINNER RIGHT IN FRONT OF MY ENEMIES." PSALM 23:5

When shepherds in Scotland find new pasture, one of the first things they must deal with is the adder, a small brown snake that can pop out of its hole, bite the sheep and kill them. Our Shepherd has dealt with Satan the old serpent and prepared for us "a six-course dinner right in front of my enemies."

He has done for us what He did for Peter, prepared for us a table and invited us to come and fellowship with Him in spite of our failures.

See the guy hiding in the shadows? That's Peter. Soon he will preach to multitudes, but tonight he is weeping. What is worse—that he denied Jesus, or that he swore he never would? One denial was bad—but three?

And we are just like him, aren't we? Listen to us: "I have given up all of that. No more messing around with the wrong people, pastimes, or pleasures. I have learned my lesson. Others might, but not me!" Oh, the level of our boasting and oh the heartache when we fall.

But there is good news: God permits U-turns!

Three days after His crucifixion when Jesus rose from the dead, the angel said, "Now—on your way. Tell his disciples and Peter that he is going on ahead of you to Galilee. . ." (Mark 16:7). Notice the "and Peter:" The biggest failure was the only disciple singled out by name.

Beaten and weary Peter returned to his former life as a fisherman. After a night's work he reached the shore where the fire was burning, the meal prepared and there was Jesus saying, ". . .Breakfast is ready. . ." (John 21:12).

Have you failed badly?

Jesus invites you to come to the table and be restored to fellowship with Him.

Survival Guide for **March 1**

"YOUR BEAUTY AND LOVE CHASE AFTER ME EVERY DAY OF MY LIFE." PSALM 23:6

David didn't say, "Maybe, possibly, or I've a hunch." No, "Surely goodness and mercy." With God it's a sure thing. James writes: ". . . with Whom there is never the slightest variation or shadow of inconsistency" (James 1:17 Phillips). Our moods may shift, our minds may change, our devotion may falter, but God never does: "If we are unfaithful, He remains faithful, for He cannot deny Himself" (2 Timothy 2:13 NLT).

On our worst days we can still say, "Surely goodness and mercy shall follow me . . . "

"All the days?" Think of the days ahead and what do you see? Days at home raising a family? Days at school in endless classes? Days of loneliness or poor health? Days spent caring for a sick loved one? "Surely goodness and mercy shall follow me all the days of my life." Goodness to provide, mercy to pardon; we never have a day without them.

"Shall follow me?" That sounds like another promise God made: "All these blessings will come down on you, and spread out beyond you . . ." (Deuteronomy 28:2). Note the words "come down on you, spread out beyond you." You can't get away from God's goodness. God's goodness followed Jonah to the bottom of the sea, Daniel into a lion's den, and John into exile and opened heaven for him. Stop and look back: think of the scrapes God has brought you through, the messes He has helped clean up, the doors He has opened for you and what do you see? Blessings undeserved, inescapable, and new every morning.

On those days when you don't feel God's presence just trust His promises!

Survival Guide for **March 2**

"I'M BACK HOME IN THE HOUSE OF GOD FOR THE REST OF MY LIFE." PSALM 23:6

Read this story that's floating around the internet:

> The bird's name was Pootsie. When nobody else claimed her, the Humane Society gave her to Sue. They became fast friends. One day, the little bird did something incredible; it perched on her shoulder and whispered, "1500 South Oneida Street, Green Bay." Sue was dumbfounded. She discovered that the address actually existed. She went there and found a man named John Stroobants. "Do you have a parakeet?" she asked. "I used to, I miss him terribly." When he saw Pootsie, he was thrilled. "You know," he said, "he even knows his phone number."

While this story is probably just another urban legend it may not be as wacky as you might think. After all we have an eternal address written in our soul: "He has also set eternity in the hearts of men." (Ecclesiastes 3:11 NIV). Deep down, we know we are not home yet, so be careful not to live as though you are. Would you hang pictures on the wall of an Amtrak Sleeper Car? Or set up house in a motel? It is a terrible thing not to feel far from home when you are, or to feel right at home when you are not. So remember your eternal address: "our homeland is in heaven." (Philippians 3:20 TLB).

When we are young, heaven has limited appeal. We have too many dreams like graduation, love, marriage, children, and career. But ageing is God's way of keeping us headed homeward. And death, for the Christian, is not when we get buried, it is when we get planted—like flower seeds awaiting spring. "Put in the ground weak, it comes up powerful." (1 Corinthians 15:43). At our home-going, an angel announces, "Watch, that one's just about to blossom!"

And then "I'm back home in the house of God for the rest of my life."

Survival Guide for **March 3**

**"THE LORD IS MY SHEPHERD, I SHALL NOT BE IN WANT."
PSALM 23:1(NIV)**

Sheep are dumb! Of all God's animals, sheep are least able to care for themselves. Ever see a sheep roll over and do tricks? They are defenseless. They have no fangs or claws so they can't bite or fight off their predators. They are dirty. A cat can clean itself, but sheep? They get dirty and stay that way.

Yet the Bible compares us to sheep: "We're all like sheep who have wandered off and gotten lost." (Isaiah 53:6). Even though I don't particularly like being compared to a sheep I get the point—we need a Shepherd because we are unable to care for ourselves. Think you are? Then take this simple test and see how you do:

(1) I can control my impulses.
(2) I never play the victim.
(3) I can't relate to Jekyll and Hyde.
(4) I am always upbeat and upright.
(5) I always make peace.
(6) Every relationship is harmonious; even old flames speak well of me.
(7) I love all and am loved by all.
(8) I have no fears.
(9) I don't need forgiveness.
(10) My life is an open book.
(11) I have never cheated, lied, or lied about cheating.

Unless you did a whole lot better than me on that test it looks like all of us need a shepherd to keep us from wandering off some cliff's edge or getting devoured by some wolf.

Today instead of saying, "The Lord is my shepherd," try saying, "The One who is my Shepherd, is also Lord over every area of my life."

Survival Guide for **March 4**

"HE RESTORES MY SOUL. HE GUIDES ME IN PATHS OF RIGHTEOUSNESS FOR HIS NAME'S SAKE." PSALM 23:3(NIV)

God hates arrogance. What do we have to be arrogant about anyway? Do art critics award the brush? Is there a Pulitzer Prize for ink? No, they're only tools. Why would God even use us? "For His name's sake"

There's only one name on the marquee: God! Does God have an ego problem? No, but we do. With the same intensity that He hates arrogance, God loves humility. "I live with people who are. . . humble" (Is 57:15 NCV). So here are a few tips on cultivating more humility:

(1) Evaluate yourself honestly: "Don't cherish exaggerated ideas of yourself . . . but try to have a sane estimate of your capabilities in the light of the that God has given you." (Ro 12:3 PHPS).

(2) Learn to celebrate others: "In humility consider others better than yourselves." (Phil. 2:3 NIV).

Every touchdown in life is a team effort. Be as excited about your part as the little boy who came home from the try-outs for the schools play and announced, "Mommy, I got the part. I have been chosen to sit in the audience and cheer."

(3) Don't announce your success before it occurs: "One who puts on his armor should not boast like one who takes it off." (1 Ki 20:11 NIV).

When one of Charles Spurgeon's students stepped up to preach with great confidence but failed miserably, Spurgeon told him, "If you had gone up the way you came down, you would have come down the way you went up."

God honors only what is done "for His name's sake."

Today remember that!

Survival Guide for **March 5**

"OUR FATHER IN HEAVEN" MATTHEW 6:9

When we say, "Our Father," we're acknowledging that we belong to God's family. Being a member of God's family means we are entitled to all the rights and privileges that go with it.

Have you discovered what they are yet?

"Daddy" is one of the most important words we learn to say because intimacy with our father helps us understand our identity. It is important for us to know who our father is and how he feels about us.

If you had an abusive father or an absentee dad, it will take you a while to believe and act on the fact that God as your heavenly Father is not like that. He is the Dad who loves you and that you can come to any time day or night knowing He will be there for you. When you finally accept that God is the Father you always wanted then prayer becomes simply talking to your Dad.

If God is our loving Father, why don't we spend more time with Him?

One reason is that while His love draws us, His holiness intimidates us. When Isaiah saw the Lord in the Temple, he cried, "Woe to me!" (Isa 6:5). Being in our Father's presence forces us to look more closely at ourselves to see how strong or weak the family resemblance is. That is why David said, "The Lord is like a Father to His children, tender and compassionate . . . for He understands how weak we are." (Ps 103:13 - 14 NLT).

All of us long to be understood. It is exhausting to be with people who audit our every move and constantly demand that we qualify every statement. But our Father is not like that. We don't have to try to get God to understand us. He knows what both our speech and our silence suggest, so sometimes the best thing to do is just crawl up into His lap, look into His face and just say—

"Our Father In Heaven."

Survival Guide for **March 6**

"DON'T BECOME SO WELL-ADJUSTED TO YOUR CULTURE
THAT YOU FIT INTO IT WITHOUT EVEN THINKING.
INSTEAD, FIX YOUR ATTENTION ON GOD. YOU'LL BE
CHANGED FROM THE INSIDE OUT. READILY RECOGNIZE
WHAT HE WANTS FROM YOU, AND QUICKLY RESPOND TO
IT. UNLIKE THE CULTURE AROUND YOU, ALWAYS
DRAGGING YOU DOWN TO ITS LEVEL OF IMMATURITY,
GOD BRINGS THE BEST OUT OF YOU, DEVELOPS WELL-
FORMED MATURITY IN YOU." ROMANS 12:2

If you are wrestling with a certain problem, thinking, "If I could just get
beyond this, everything would be alright." I have bad news for you: When
you have conquered this particular problem, God will reveal something
else that needs to be dealt with. So relax, you are always going to be
working on something!

Real change doesn't come through frustration, self-rejection, guilt or
white-knuckling human effort. Real change comes as a result of having
our mind renewed daily by the Word of God. As we agree with God,
believing that what He says is true, change automatically begins. We start
to think differently, then talk differently and finally act differently. Be
patient with yourself: it is a process that develops in stages.

Would you think there was something wrong with a child who couldn't
walk perfectly the first few tries? On the contrary, we are delighted each
time they take another step. When they fall we pick them up, comfort
them, bandage them if necessary, encourage them to try again, and keep
working with them.

Do you think God does less for His children?

God is not angry with you because you haven't "arrived;" He is pleased
that you are pressing on, trying to stay on the path. It is God's job to
". . . (cause [you] to be governed by the Holy Spirit)." (2 Corinthians 3:8
Amp).

If we could change all by ourselves, we wouldn't need God.

Instead of driving yourself harder and harder, try this: start leaning on
God more and more!

Survival Guide for **March 7**

"I REFUSE TO . . . LOOK AT CORRUPTING . . . DEGRADING THINGS." PSALM 101:3

Working with college students means working with the group most addicted to pornography. But they are not alone by any means. Yesterday I received more than 20 pornographic emails, and I have never logged onto a pornography website. Imagine the number coming to someone who has given into the temptation and "checked out" even one porno site on the internet. Our eyes are the windows of our soul. What we expose ourselves to influences our imagination, our actions and finally our character.

Here are three important things to know about pornography:

1. Pornography is addictive. Family counselor Gail Horne said, "Pornography is more addictive than drugs and, thanks to the First Amendment, it is getting bigger every day."

2. Pornography is selfish. It trains you to see people as playthings to be played with, all for one purpose—self-gratification. Intimacy, responsibility and commitment are not even in the picture (or the frame).

3. Pornography is shaming. It leaves you feeling cheapened and unclean. But even if you have fallen prey to pornography don't despair because there is good news. Every leper who came to Jesus was cleansed; and through His blood you can be cleansed too! The last pornography you looked at can be the last you ever look at because you can be empowered by God's Spirit to cast down every imagination and take every thought captive.

But it will take determination on your part. Paul wrote, "I'm staying alert and in top condition. I'm not going to get caught napping, telling everyone else all about it and then missing out myself." (1 Corinthians 9:27). Discipline, direction, and focus are necessary to fight the good fight of faith. Pornography destroys all three.

Today make this your pledge: "I REFUSE TO . . . LOOK AT CORRUPTING . . . DEGRADING THINGS."

Survival Guide for **March 8**

"LET'S JUST GO AHEAD AND BE WHAT WE WERE MADE TO BE, WITHOUT ENVIOUSLY OR PRIDEFULLY COMPARING OURSELVES WITH EACH OTHER, OR TRYING TO BE SOMETHING WE AREN'T . . ." ROMANS 12:6

It is easy to get lost in the maze of life. Pressure comes at us from every direction to keep others happy. We spend a ton of energy studying the important people in our lives, trying to decide what they want from us and in the process we lose ourselves.

Take a moment right now and ask yourself, "What am I living for? Why am I doing the things I do? What has God gifted and called me to do?" Those who succeed at being themselves don't allow others to control them. Instead they give that right to God alone.

Don't get mad because people place demands on you. That is the nature of modern life. Just realize that it is your life and take responsibility for it. In reality the pressures you are feeling may not be coming from others at all, they may be coming from your own fears and insecurities. Sure, there are times when we all do things we would rather not do. We do them because we love others and we love Jesus and that is what Jesus followers do--led by God's Spirit we serve others in need. But there is a difference in serving others out of selfless service to God and serving others because of our own insecurities.

Try to become everything to everybody and you will get lost in the process. Live for other's approval and you will risk forfeiting God's and it is His approval that you really desire, isn't it?

A good morning prayer is, "Lord, what will You have me do?" But be warned—only pray that prayer when you are ready to listen for the answer and once you have it to commit yourself to it fully, regardless of who does or doesn't agree.

Don't reach the finishing line only to discover you ran on somebody else's track.

Survival Guide for **March 9**

"WE HAVE DIFFERENT GIFTS, ACCORDING TO THE GRACE GIVEN US . . ." ROMANS 12:6 (NIV)

God created each of us to be different from one another. Each of us plays a unique role. When we struggle to be like someone else, we lose ourselves in the process. God wants us to fit into His plan, not feel pressured to fit into somebody else's.

My point is simple: It is all right to be different; being different is okay.

Find out what you are good at, throw yourself into it wholeheartedly and you will discover your highest level of joy. When we instead try to do what somebody else is good at, we generally fail. Why? Because we are not wired to do what they are doing or, at least, not in the way they are doing it. But that doesn't mean we are not good at anything, it just means we are not good at that one thing.

Here is a life lesson that has helped me through my years of ministry: focus on your potential, not your limitations.

We all have limitations and we must accept them. That is not bad, it is just a fact. Actually, it is wonderful to be different without feeling as if something is wrong with you. Secure people know that God loves them as they are and that they have a part to play in God's plan, so they are not threatened by the abilities or accomplishments of others. Actually, they enjoy what other people can do, because they enjoy what they themselves do. Paul writes, "Let us not become competitive envying (jealous of) one another." (Galatians 5:26 Amp).

In the end, what matters most is being able to say what Jesus said, "I have brought You glory on earth by completing the work You gave Me to do." (John 17:4 NIV).

Any time you can say that—you have grasped what it means to be uniquely you!

Survival Guide for **March 10**

"BLESSED ARE THE PEACEMAKERS, FOR THEY WILL BE CALLED SONS OF GOD." MATTHEW 5:9 (NIV)

Become a peacemaker if you want God's blessing.

Jesus didn't say, "Blessed are the peace-lovers", because everyone loves peace. Nor did He say, "Blessed are the peaceable" who are never disturbed by anything. No, He said, "Blessed are the peacemakers."

Peacemakers are rare because peace-making is hard work. But it is worth the effort.

Relationships are always worth restoring. God wants us to value our relationships instead of discarding them every time there's a problem. Paul wrote, "If you've gotten anything at all out of following Christ, if His love has made any difference in your life, if being in a community of the Spirit means anything to you. Agree with each other, love each other, be deep-spirited friends." (Philippians 2:1-2).

The ability to get along well with other believers is a mark of spiritual maturity. God wants His family to be known for their love of each other. Broken fellowship is a terrible testimony to others. That's why Paul was embarrassed when the members of the Church in Corinth started splitting into warring factions, even taking others to court. "Shame on you!" he wrote. "Surely there is at least one wise person who can settle a dispute between fellow Christians." (1 Corinthians 6:5 TEV). He was shocked that nobody was mature enough to resolve the conflict peacefully. So in the same letter, he wrote, "I'll put it as urgently as I can: You must get along with each other." (1 Corinthians 1:10).

That order that has never been rescinded!

Survival Guide for **March 11**

**"GOD BLESSES THOSE WHO WORK FOR PEACE, FOR THEY
WILL BE CALLED THE CHILDREN OF GOD."
MATTHEW 5:9 (NLT)**

Those who "work for peace" mend broken relationships.

Here are some steps to restoring broken relationships:

(1) Talk to God before talking to anybody else. If you pray about it, God
can either change your heart, or theirs. Most conflict is rooted in unmet
needs. Any time we expect others to meet a need that only God can meet,
we are setting ourselves up for trouble: "What causes. . .quarrels among
you? . . .You want something but don't get it. You do not have, because
you do not ask God." (James 4:1-2 NIV). Instead of looking to God we
look to others, then get angry when they fail us. James is revealing to us
an important principle for peacemaking: Go to God first!

(2) Plan a peace conference. Whether you are the offender or the offended,
God expects you to make the first move. Schedule a face-to-face meeting
as soon as possible. In conflict, time heals nothing; it only causes hurts to
fester. Furthermore, acting quickly reduces spiritual damage to us,
because bitterness blocks our fellowship with God and keeps our prayers
from being answered. Job's friends reminded him, "You are only hurting
yourself with your anger." (Job 18:4 TEV).

(3) Choose the right time and place. Don't try it when either of you is
tired, rushed, or will be interrupted. The best time is when both of you are
at your best.

If you're thinking "That sounds good but I'm not sure I can do it." then
you are thinking in the flesh not the Spirit because God has ". . . called us
to settle our relationships with each other." (2 Corinthians 5:18)

Survival Guide for **March 12**

"YOU'RE BLESSED WHEN YOU CAN SHOW PEOPLE HOW TO COOPERATE INSTEAD OF COMPETE OR FIGHT. THAT'S WHEN YOU DISCOVER WHO YOU REALLY ARE, AND YOUR PLACE IN GOD'S FAMILY." MATTHEW 5:9

Emotions are hard to understand. Try to accurately describe how you are feeling to a group of people and changes are you'll end up with as many different understandings as there are people in the group. So learn to sympathize with the other person's feelings, even if you don't understand them. Never try to talk someone out of how they feel. Just listen without being defensive. Nod to show you understand, even when you don't agree. Feelings aren't always true or logical. David said, "When my feelings were hurt, I was as stupid as an animal." (Psalm 73:21-22 TEV).

David is not alone is he? Most of us act badly when we are hurting. But Solomon says, "A man's wisdom gives him patience; it is to his glory to overlook an offence." (Proverbs 19:11 NIV).

Patiently listening to another tell how they feel says, "I care about our relationship more than our differences; you matter to me." Sure, it is a sacrifice to patiently to absorb someone's anger, especially when it is unfounded. But remember, that is what Jesus does for us!

If you have hurt someone's feelings confess your part (even if you didn't mean to do it). Jesus said, "First get rid of the log from your own eye; then perhaps you will see well enough to deal with the speck in your friend's eye" (Matthew 7:5 NLT). This verse shows that we all have blind spots, so don't be quick to dismiss another who says that you have hurt their feelings. Get a third party to help you evaluate your own actions if you can't be objective yourself. Then ask God, "Am I part of the problem? Am I unrealistic, insensitive to others, or too sensitive myself?" Confession is a powerful tool. When we admit our own flaws to one who is angry with us, it defuses the other person's anger, because they are expecting a defensive reaction. So don't make excuses or shift the blame, just acknowledge your part.

Is that easy to do? Of course not! But with God's help it is possible!

Survival Guide for **March 13**

"LOVE NEVER FAILS." 1 CORINTHIANS 13:8

Mature love—the kind that enables relationships to go the distance—is spelled out clearly in 1 Corinthians 13. We need to read it regularly. It tells us that:

(1) Mature love is tolerant. It knows that a relationship is a package deal—you enjoy what's good and develop patience by learning to live with what's still under construction.

(2) Mature love is never envious. It understands that real contentment comes from knowing that God has a plan for each of us —and what He has got for you, He will never give to anybody else.

(3) Mature love is courteous. In a world where good manners are in short supply, it knows that the value you place on something is evidenced by how you treat it.

(4) Mature love is not touchy. It knows that if you wear your feelings on your sleeve, you will go broke buying paper tissues
.

Here is how Paul describes mature love in the modern language version of the Bible . . . "The Message:" "Love never gives up. Love cares more for others than for self. Love doesn't want what it doesn't have. Love doesn't strut, doesn't have a swelled head, doesn't force itself on others, isn't always 'me first,' doesn't fly off the handle, doesn't keep score of the sins of others, doesn't revel when others grovel, takes pleasure in the flowering of truth, puts up with anything, trusts God always, always looks for the best, never looks back, but keeps going to the end." (1 Cor 13:4-8).

Today, ask God to give you mature love!

Survival Guide for **March 14**

"DON'T YOU SEE THAT CHILDREN ARE GOD'S BEST GIFT? THE FRUIT OF THE WOMB HIS GENEROUS LEGACY?" PSALM 127:3

I got to see all my grandsons, my daughters, and sons-in-laws this weekend. It was so good to see them all. Watching my grandsons being parented by them got me thinking of what a privilege and yet what a job it is to raise kids today. I once saw a cartoon depicting a mother hen with her chicks following her in a line. As she walked, she rolled her eyes upward and said, "Lord, grant me the patience to endure my blessings!" What parent amongst us hasn't felt like that sometimes!

But, "Children are God's best gift," and if you are currently parenting your kids that makes you God's steward of a most precious gift. As such it is your job to:

(1) Protect them: stay vigilant. Shield them from pornography, drugs, violence and negative influences. Insist on knowing where they go and who their friends are. Remember, "A child left to himself brings shame," but when you correct him he'll bring "delight to your soul." (Proverbs 29:15&17 NKJ).

(2) Nurture them: not just physically, but spiritually and emotionally. "Point your kids in the right direction--when they're old they won't be lost." (Proverbs 22:6). This means giving them something that is in short supply—time! If I had a chance to raise my daughters again. I would give them more quality time than I did as a young workaholic minister. I would try to be less serious and play with them more. I would do more hugging, cuddling, and kissing. I would build their self-esteem by trusting them more. I would try to show them more by example about the power of love, not just for them but for others. I offer this advice as one who has already had his chance!

(3) Release them. A parent's ultimate goal is to produce a responsible, well-adjusted adult who'll make a difference in the world. Letting go can be scary, but it is easier when you know you have done your best, you have covered them with prayer, and that you have placed them under God's divine protection.

My daughters are good mothers, like their mother.

That is the way it is supposed to work!

Survival Guide for **March 15**

"IT'S IMPOSSIBLE TO PLEASE GOD APART FROM FAITH."
HEBREWS 11:6

Peter walking on the water to Jesus is one of the great stories from the Gospels. It is good to remember that Peter didn't walk on water because Jesus lifted him out of the boat and moved his legs. Instead, that miracle happened because Peter believed Jesus' word and responded in faith.

Can we still "walk on water?" We can if we:
  (1) See Jesus in our storms
  (2) Respond to what He says to us
  (3) Refuse to be intimidated by our surroundings
  (4) Do what others in the boat are afraid to do
  (5) Choose what is possible, instead of settling for what seems rational.

All God needs to act is something to work with and someone to work through. If we are willing to give ourselves to God we can "walk on water." The only thing that can stop God is our unbelief: ". . .He didn't do many miracles there because of their hostile indifference." (Matt 13:58).

Since God can not be pleased without faith, each of us needs to make a quality commitment each day to develop our faith. When faith is developed and put to the test lives change forever.

One day, onboard a ferryboat, George Muller prayed, "Lord, lift this fog so that I can get to church on time to speak." As he said "Amen" and rose to his feet, the captain said in amazement, "Look, the fog's lifting!" Muller replied, "Just as I thought." Muller actually believed Jesus when He said: ". . . Whatever you ask for in prayer, believe that you have received it and it will be yours." (Mk 11:24 NIV).

Do you? If you do you can "walk on water."

Believe God today!

Survival Guide for **March 16**

"THE LORD SEES NOT AS MAN SEES." 1 SAMUEL 16:7

I received this "pulpit search committee report" in an email recently:

"In our search for just the right pastor, only one was found to have the qualities we need. After interviewing each of the candidates, here are their names, along with our comments:

Noah: A failure as a preacher; 120 years experience, but no converts.
Moses: Stutters and loses his temper.
Abraham: Got into trouble with the authorities and lied his way out.
David: Would make a good minister of music if he had better morals.
Solomon: A walking encyclopedia of wisdom, but doesn't practice what he preaches.
Elijah: Prone to depression; folds under pressure.
Hosea: Divorced and remarried to a prostitute.
Jeremiah: Too emotional and negative; a real alarmist.
Amos: A farmer, better suited to picking figs and raising cattle.
John: Says he's a Baptist, lacks tact and dresses like a hippie.
Peter: Bad tempered; denied Christ publicly.
Paul: Not good media material; too long-winded.
Timothy: Has potential, but much too young.
Jesus: Offends church members with his preaching, hangs out with questionable characters and upset the committee with His pointed questions!
Judas: Practical, cooperative, good with money, cares for the poor, well-dressed.

We all agree, Judas is the man!"

Doesn't this barbed little parable make you glad that, ". . . the Lord sees not as man sees; for man looks on the outward appearance, but the Lord looks on the heart" (1 Sam 16:7 AMP)?

Survival Guide for **March 17**

". . .JESUS CALLED OVER A CHILD, WHOM HE STOOD IN THE MIDDLE OF THE ROOM" MATTHEW 18:2

This story by James Dobson reminds us that life is not built on things, but on relationships.

> "Some time ago a friend of mine punished his three-year-old daughter for wasting a roll of gold wrapping paper. Money was tight, and he became upset when she tried to decorate a box to put under the Christmas tree.
>
> Nevertheless, the little girl brought the gift to her father the next morning and said, 'This is for you, Daddy.' He was embarrassed by his earlier over-reaction. But his anger flared again when he opened the box and found it empty. He yelled at her, 'Don't you know that when you give someone a present there's supposed to be something inside?' The little girl looked up at him in tears and said, 'Oh, Daddy, it's not empty. I blew kisses into it, I filled it with my love and I wrapped it up just for you.' He was crushed. Quickly he put his arms around her and begged for her forgiveness.
>
> My friend told me that he kept that gold box by his bed for years and whenever he got discouraged, he'd take out an imaginary kiss and remember the love of the child who'd put it there. In a very real sense, each of us as parents has been given a gold container filled with the unconditional love of our children. There's not a more precious possession anyone could hold."

Unconditional love is the greatest gift we can ever receive or give.

Like so many of God's gifts it often comes wrapped in the body of a little child.

Survival Guide for **March 18**

"... A FARMER PLANTED SEED" MATTHEW 13:3

The Sower (the Lord) never deviates from His job and the seed (God's Word) is always alive. The only variable is the soil. The soil ultimately determines if the seed will be productive. In the parable of the sower, Jesus describes three unproductive kinds of soil.

(1) Hard: In Bible times, hard-packed paths often ran alongside the farmers' fields. Any seed falling there just shriveled and died. Hard soil people have been walked on and disappointed. Hardened hearts develop a tough, impenetrable shield that makes it easy for Satan to come along and steal the seed before it has a chance to grow.

(2) Shallow: In Jesus' day, most farmland in the Holy Land was just a few inches of topsoil over rock, with nothing to sustain roots. Richard Foster writes: "Superficiality is the curse of the age. We live in a world of shallow relationships, superficial conversations, hurried moments of prayer. We bounce from one spiritual activity to another without any real root system." Those are the shallow soil people.

(3) Overgrown: Untended soil soon is so overgrown, there is no room for anything healthy to grow. The soil's nutrients are used up sustaining the weeds. Overgrown soil people are cluttered people. Clutter happens so easily that it takes no effort on our part. Our society bombards us with guarantees that things will bring happiness. Since the "thing" we just bought hasn't made us happy we must need another "thing." "Things" become clutter and soon we have no room left for the one thing that can actually produce happiness.

If one of these unproductive soils describes your heart the good news is that you can become productive soil for the seed the Sower wants to plant in you. If your heart is hard tenderize it. If your devotion is shallow deepen it. If your life is cluttered simplify it. Do a soil analysis today and weed out anything that is hindering your spiritual growth.

Prepare your heart to receive the Word and you will be amazed at what God can accomplish through you.

Survival Guide for **March 19**

". . .YOUR OLD MEN WILL DREAM, YOUR YOUNG MEN WILL SEE VISIONS." JOEL 2:28

God is the giver of new dreams and the mender of broken ones.

God loves dreamers.

When we dream, we move closer to the way God sees things. When we dream, we no longer are limited by. . . our faults. . . our lack. . . or our past. When we dream we begin to move from where we are to where God wants us to be. In other words, when we dream we catch a glimpse of our goals in their completed state. We catch a glimpse of "the Promised Land!"

Dreaming is good but to make our dreams come true takes action. The critical question is not do you have a dream, but do you have the courage to act on it? If faith without works is dead, then a dream without diligence is dead too. It is not enough just to dream, we have to wake up and do something about it. God won't miraculously lift us out of our dreams and set us down in the middle of their fulfillment. Thoreau said, "It's fine to build castles in the air, so long as you work to put foundations under them."

A Godly dream is the "Promised Land." The way to the "Promised Land" is always through the wilderness. The wilderness is where we learn to:

(a) trust God daily for what we need
(b) discover God's power to deliver us from our enemies
(c) learn how to be led daily by God
(d) keep our eyes on our destination and move steadily toward it
(e) refuse to be like those who complain.

Dreams keep us moving through the wilderness and focused on the Promised Land.

What dreams are you dreaming?

Survival Guide for **March 20**

"... I CAN MAKE IT THROUGH ANYTHING IN THE ONE WHO MAKES ME WHO I AM" PHILIPPIANS 4:13

Self-confidence had Paul write, "I can make it through anything."

God-confidence had Paul add, "in the one who makes me who I am."

Combining these two elements is the secret to an adventurous Christian life.

To release the strength of Christ within you, realize that:

(1) God's Kingdom must be our first pursuit.
   "Seek first His kingdom . . ." (Mt 6:33 NIV).

(2) God responds to our faith. So begin developing yours, even in small things.

(3) God can use every experience and gift He gives us.

(4) We need to look within ourselves and acknowledge what God has given us.

(5) It is not enough to acknowledge our gifts; we must make them available to God.

(6) God deserves all the glory! When praise comes, pass it on to Him.

One final thing—once you release the strength of Christ realize it is there for God's use!

Survival Guide for **March 21**

"THESE LAST WORKERS PUT IN ONLY ONE EASY HOUR, AND YOU JUST MADE THEM EQUAL TO US, WHO SLAVED ALL DAY UNDER A SCORCHING SUN." MATTHEW 20:12

Five different groups of workers are hired in this parable of the vineyard workers. The first group complains when those who work only the last hour get paid the same wages as themselves. These are performance-based believers. They think because they avoid certain sins, God is getting a good deal. Instead of rejoicing with those who come late to the Kingdom, they are resentful.

They are easy to spot because they have three characteristics:

(1) A complaining spirit. They overlook the good, magnify the bad, and seek out people who agree with them. The have a complaining spirit and it is deadly; it kills churches and hearts. The cure for a complaining spirit is to develop a spirit of continual gratitude for what God has and is still doing.

(2) A resentful spirit. Instead of resting in God's grace, they act like duty-bound soldiers—conscripts—not volunteers. They struggle constantly for God's approval, never seem to measure up, and their hostility prevents them from experiencing joy. The cure for a resentful spirit is to begin to reflect on God's love. It is hard to feel loved and resentful at the same time.

(3) A judgmental spirit. "It is unfair," they think. "I did the work and they get the credit!" They forget that God dispenses gifts—not wages. The cure for a judgmental spirit is to realize that God doesn't repay us "according to our iniquities" (Psalm 103:10 NIV), but lavishes us with love and mercy.

The last group of workers are grace-based believers. Latecomers with no contracts or guarantees, their relationship with God is based solely on grace. They are happy with whatever God is offering. They are humbled by His goodness, and motivated to work by overwhelming gratitude.

Are you a performance-based or grace-based worker?

Survival Guide for **March 22**

―――

"BUT EVERYTHING SHOULD BE DONE IN A FITTING AND ORDERLY WAY." 1 CORINTHIANS 14:40(NIV)

I used to be organized. But if you were to see my office today you would know why Good Housekeeping cancelled my subscription! Seriously, my biggest struggle is not to be decent; my struggle is to be orderly. I want to be better organized because I know that we waste valuable time and energy when we are disorganized and that God likes things done decently and in order.

If you are up to it here are ten questions to answer to test your orderliness. (And no, I'm not going to give you my answers!)

(1) How often do you lose things?
(2) Are you usually late or on time?
(3) Do you procrastinate?
(4) Are your big time-wasters telephone and television?
(5) Do you pay your bills on time?
(6) Do you return telephone calls and answer your mail promptly—or at all?
(7) Do you have lots of unfinished projects lying around?
(8) Can you locate important documents right away?
(9) Do you have a current will, in a safe place, where you can find it?
(10) Can you think things through?

Well, how did you do? If you really want to put order into your life, start by writing down the habits you need to work on. Don't announce, "Starting today, everybody around here is going to change!" Instead, work on yourself first and on only one or two things at a time. If you try to shoot at too many targets, you won't hit any and you will give up in discouragement.

And don't forget to pray. After all, it was our best efforts in the past that made us what we are today. So we all need God's help.

Reach for it, orderliness is out there!

Survival Guide for **March 23**

"BEFORE YOU KNOW IT, A SENSE OF GOD'S WHOLENESS, EVERYTHING COMING TOGETHER FOR GOOD, WILL COME AND SETTLE YOU DOWN. IT'S WONDERFUL WHAT HAPPENS WHEN CHRIST DISPLACES WORRY AT THE CENTER OF YOUR LIFE." PHILIPPIANS 4:7

Beverly LaHaye was terrified when her husband Tim began taking flying lessons. She wrote: "Right away I started giving God my opinion and drawing my own conclusions. Fear was controlling me."

Tim told her to pray about it and just be open to the Lord. "Let Him know you're afraid of flying, but that you're willing to be changed." She did—but there was no overnight miracle. She continually had to give her fear of flying to God. But it worked almost without her noticing.

Years later, when she was flying with her attorney through a violent storm in a small plane, he noticed that while he was sweating it out, she was fast asleep. When they landed, he asked her, "How could you sleep so peacefully?" She replied, "It's God; only He could have brought me to the place where I could fly through that and be at peace." Sometimes God calms the storm, but most of the time He lets it rage—and calms us.

"Casting all your cares (continually. . . the moment they raise their voices . . . before they take control of you) upon Him, for He cares for you." (1 Pet 5:7 paraphrased from NIV).

"Don't worry about anything; instead pray about everything. . . if you do this you will experience God's peace, which is far more wonderful than the human mind can understand. . . " (Phil 4:6-7 TLB).

Don't be discouraged when you have to turn your fears over to God, again and again.

For that as how we learn to trust.

Survival Guide for **March 24**

"I SAW THIS AND FAINTED DEAD AT HIS FEET. . ."
REVELATION 1:17

While the Apostle John was a prisoner on the Isle of Patmos, far from his loved ones, surrounded by the cries of abused captives, he had a vision of Jesus. The incredible Book of Revelation came to him amidst chaos and pain. Often that is the way it works.

The difficult circumstances of life can actually clear our perceptions, cause us to seek God's face as never before, and lead us to find real answers. John's predicament shows us that negative experiences don't hide the Lord—they reveal Him—if we are looking for Him..

Satan's attacks can actually take us to new spiritual heights. When he puts on the pressure, it stretches our faith. Stretched faith expresses itself in two ways: in deeds of faith and in perseverance of faith.

The Lord revealed Himself to Shadrach, Meshach, and Abednego in a furnace heated seven times over. In the midst of the fire they were safe with God. There is a place in God where the fire consumes everything except the desire to know Him. Though that place may sometimes escape your grasp, never let it escape your view. It was Paul's all-consuming goal: "I gave up all that inferior stuff so I could know Christ personally, experience his resurrection power, be a partner in His suffering, and go all the way with Him." (Philippians 3:9).

Paul lived with no reservations and no regrets; just a passion to know the Lord more intimately, and a commitment to "go all the way with Him."

Can you think of a better commitment?

Survival Guide for **March 25**

"GOOD PEOPLE WILL PROSPER LIKE PALM TREES."
PSALM 92:12

Be like the palm tree if you want to flourish in your faith:

(1) The palm tree can be cut without being cut off from its source. The minerals and nutrients most trees need to survive are found near their surface, just below the bark, so, when they are cut they sicken and may even die. But not the palm tree. Its life comes from within, so it flourishes, even under attack. The Christian's source is also within. That is why Paul refers to us as those who ". . . carry this precious Message around in the unadorned clay pots of our ordinary lives. . ." (2 Corinthians 4:7). Even though our earthen vessel without may be cut and wounded, the treasure within is secure, beyond the enemy's reach.

(2) The palm tree will bend, but seldom will it break. Tropical winds can blow most trees away, but not the palm tree. The stronger the wind, the further it bends—sometimes all the way to the ground. Yet when the storm ceases, it straightens up again and is actually stronger in the place where it bent. Christians were made to bend, but not break, because God gives us ". . . strength that endures the unendurable and spills over into joy" (Colossians 1:11).

(3) The palm tree's depth normally exceeds its height. While the roots of the average plant go only a few feet under the ground, the palm tree's roots can go down hundreds of yards in search of water. The Christian life is more about spiritual depth than accomplishment height. David described it well: "As the deer pants for streams of water, so my soul pants for you . . . " (Ps 42:1 NIV).

Flourish like a palm tree.

Go deep, bend but don't break, and make God your source.

Survival Guide for **March 26**

". . .HE'LL EXPOSE THE ERROR OF THE GODLESS WORLD'S VIEW OF SIN." JOHN 16:8

Change is God's job, not ours.

For years I tried to change people. I warned them of the wrath of God and tried to convict them of their sins. But, for the most part, the more I tried, the more they resisted me and the worse things got. Finally, God got through to me with this insight:

People can't change other people—only God can!

I wasn't being very successful because I was trying to do something I didn't have the power to do. My job as a Christian was just to love people, pray for them and then to let God change them. When I got out of His way, God did what I could not. Along the way I also learned that God doesn't work according to our plans or timetables. Only when I accepted that was I freed from obsessing over people.

Commit the people you love to God! Trust Him! Let God be God and stop trying to play God!

When we try to play God, everybody gets hurt. We get hurt because others can't or won't do what we want. They get hurt because our love comes with strings attached. And we are not doing God any favors either, for He is well able to speak for Himself.

". . . I'll be a personal guide to them, directing them through unknown country. . ." (Isa 42:16).

Straightening people out is God's job—let Him do it!

Survival Guide for **March 27**

". . .WITH GOD, ONE DAY IS AS GOOD AS A THOUSAND YEARS. . ." 2 PETER 3:8

A man read this verse and asked God, "If one day is as good as a thousand years, does that mean a million dollars is as good as a penny?" God said "Yes." The man continued, "Then give me a penny." God replied, "Sure, wait a minute!"

Think about it. . . ah, you got it! We want the prize but not the process. I have heard the ability to wait well called "the master attitude." Having it requires:

(1) Trust. Among trapeze artists, a special relationship exists between the flier and the catcher. Once the flyer lets go, he can't afford to flail about; he must wait motionless until the catcher grabs him. We must also learn to let go of whatever God tells us to relinquish and wait for Him to catch us, even when we don't feel His hand. Scary stuff!

(2) Humility. Did you ever wait so long to see your doctor, you felt like sending him a bill for your time? But you didn't because in life there is a correlation between status and waiting. Lower status people generally wait for higher-status ones and the wise learn to wait with grace. Waiting reminds us we are not in charge; it humbles us in ways we need to be humbled.

(3) Hope. Paul writes, "If we hope for what we do not yet have, we wait for it patiently." (Romans 8:25 NIV). When I read that verse I always think about Christmas morning as a kid. You know there is something great downstairs, but you have to wait because Mom and Dad said, "Don't wake us before 6 am!"

Learn to wait well, it is the master attitude.

Survival Guide for **March 28**

". . .BUT AFFLICTED WITH A GRIEVOUS SKIN DISEASE."
2 KINGS 5:1

An extraordinary leader, Naaman's impressive armor hid a lethal condition. He was: "afflicted with a grievous skin disease." The odds may all be in your favor: you may have already graduated or be ready to graduate from a great university, built a big ministry or made company CEO. Yet at some point you will have to deal with what you are hiding under your "armor."

Between ordinary and extraordinary lie obstacles to be overcome; nobody gets a free pass. Outstanding people in every occupation, particularly spiritual ones, all go through it. It is what sets them apart. It is what ushers them across the bridge from mediocre to exceptional. Overcoming obstacles lifts ordinary to extraordinary.

I am not talking about petty little problems. Rather, I am talking about issues so overwhelming you can't sleep; things so gut-wrenchingly perilous that they cause your heart to skip a beat and make you fear that this is the problem that is going to do you in. I am talking about the thing you pray about in secret; the thing you don't want people to see. The thing you hide under your "armor," then go home and agonize about in private.

God teaches some of His greatest lessons in the valleys of life. In the valley is where we learn to lie prostrate before Him, weeping and broken. In the valley is where we learn to pray, "God, don't let this thing destroy me; deal with it through the power of Your Spirit." This is the prayer of desperation that moves God's hand and brings about change.

The prayer of desperation is initiated by taking off our "armor" and baring our infected lives to God.

What are you hiding beneath your "armor."

Survival Guide for **March 29**

". . .HE LOOKED UP AND SAW THE PLACE IN THE DISTANCE"
GENESIS 22:4

God told Abraham, "Take your son. Sacrifice him on one of the mountains, which I will point out to you." (Genesis 22:2 NLT). Abraham didn't know exactly where he was going. But God showed him—because when we walk with God He directs our steps. He often even gives us hints about upcoming events. The problem is that we don't always hear what His Spirit is saying to us. God usually doesn't lead by theatrics; He is not in the wind, the fire and the earthquake. But when we listen, His still, small voice will tell us who we can trust, where it is safe to rest, and what to do next. Abraham didn't know exactly which mountain to head for, but the Bible says, "On the third day Abraham saw the place in the distance."(Genesis 22:4 NLT).

At that point, Abraham told his servants, "Stay here. The boy and I will (go and) worship, then we will come right back." (Genesis 22:5 NLT). There is a place in every trial where even those closest to you can't go; a place where worship becomes a sacrifice. To worship means to express the worth (worth-ship) of something. The truth is that worship is not really worship until we lay something we value before God.

Abraham said, "we will come right back." Anytime we can say, "I don't know how God is going to intervene, but when this is over, I am coming back," the battle is already won!

Survival Guide for **March 30**

". . .KEEP ON YOUR WATCH. CHALLENGE, WARN, AND URGE YOUR PEOPLE. DON'T EVER QUIT. JUST KEEP IT SIMPLE" 2 TIMOTHY 4:2

A World War II soldier was caught creeping back to his quarters from some nearby woods. Brought before his commanding officer and charged with communicating with the enemy, his defense was that he had just gone out to pray.

His CO growled, "Do you make a habit of spending hours alone in prayer?"

"Yes Sir," he replied.

"Then down on your knees and pray now," roared the officer, "for you have never needed more!"

The soldier kneeled and poured out his heart in prayer so powerfully that his CO shouted, "Enough, you may go! I believe you! If you hadn't been at drill so often, you couldn't have done so well at inspection."

Prayer is not like a spare tire; that we just leave in the car truck (or boot for my international readers!) and expect to be effective when we need to use it.   Paul wrote to Timothy, "Keep on your watch. Challenge, warn, and urge your people. Don't ever quit. . ." He wrote and exhorted the Roman Christians to, "never stop praying." (Romans 12:12 CEV).

The prayer goal for the believer is to live with a prayerful attitude, and to stay in contact with God at all times.

Why pray? Because prayer changes things when nothing else will. Prayer puts the situation into God's hands; otherwise it remains in ours—not a very comforting thought.

Perhaps most importantly, prayer changes us; in prayer we become like the company we keep.

Survival Guide for **March 31**

―――――――――――――――――――――――――――――――――――――――

"LET'S JUST GO AHEAD AND BE WHAT WE WERE MADE TO BE. . ." ROMANS 12:6

To avoid living a regretful life learn to recognize your dominant gifts and orient your life around it. David sensed that he was more than a shepherd or a singer, he was a leader-in-the-making. Killing Goliath just gave him a chance to demonstrate it. Had he failed to seize the moment, he would probably have stayed a shepherd.

Two things blind us to our dominant gifts:

 1) An obsession with our flaws. Instead of focusing on our strengths, we listen to our critics and rehearse the qualities that discourage us most. Always remember that the company we keep lifts us, lowers us, or limits us. This is especially true of those who resent accomplishment because it reminds them of their lack of it. (Joseph's brothers come to mind)

 (2) Admiring the gifts of others. While it is right to appreciate others, we should not try to duplicate them and create something God doesn't need one more of. Instead of living in another's shadow stand on their shoulders. Be an Elisha and ask God for twice the impact of your mentor. Uncommon people are simply common people who recognized their dominant gift and put it to work.

One more thought: your gift can be taken away if you don't use it. Jesus said, " Take the thousand and give it to the one who risked the most. And get rid of this 'play-it-safe' who won't go out on a limb. Throw him out into utter darkness." (Matthew 25:28-30).

Today, ask God to help you discover your dominant gifts.

Then dedicate them to His highest service!

Survival Guide for **April 1**

"... TAKE YOUR DEAR SON ISAAC WHOM YOU LOVE AND
GO TO THE LAND OF MORIAH. SACRIFICE HIM THERE AS A
BURNT OFFERING ..." GENESIS 22:2

The purpose behind many of God's tests is to prove that when the heat is
on and our back is to the wall—you will still do God's will. Furthermore,
testing times let us know we are stronger than we thought we were. A
look at past trials survived shows us that God has enabled us to withstand
the same trials that have broken others.

When Abraham took his son Isaac up Mount Moriah, it is important to
note that Isaac wasn't a child. He was a young man walking beside an old
one; he could have resisted. But instead, in submission to his father's will,
he was prepared to lay down his life.

When we belong to God, we no longer belong to ourselves, and trust
becomes a form of worship where we say, "Have Your own way Lord. I
don't know Your plan, but I trust Your faithfulness."

Just as Abraham laid Isaac on the altar and tied him down, today God may
be tying you to some things you would rather escape: like that marriage
you think is hopeless, or those roommates who constantly irritate you, or
that job or class you hate. He is tying you down and holding you together
with His grace, even though your flesh is rebelling.

But just as Abraham was raising his knife, God said, "Stop! You pass the
test. You have proven that I can trust you, even when it hurts you to do
My will. You have proven that you are faithful, even when you are
maligned and misunderstood. You have proven that you stand fast, even
though you want to run."

That is the purpose of the test—to do God's will regardless!

Survival Guide for **April 2**

". . .YOUR LIFE IS A JOURNEY YOU MUST TRAVEL WITH A DEEP CONSCIOUSNESS OF GOD" 1 PETER 1:17

Imagine being an ambassador in a hostile nation. You would need to learn its language and adapt to its customs. You couldn't isolate yourself. To fulfill your mission you would need to be in constant contact with and learn to relate to those around you. But what if you fell in love with that country, preferring it to your own? Your loyalty and commitment would be compromised. Instead of representing your country, you would now be acting like a traitor.

"We are Christ's ambassadors." (2 Corinthians 5:20 NLT).

Don't get too attached to the world around you, your residence there is temporary: "Those in frequent contact with the things of the world should make good use of them without becoming attached to them, for this world and all it contains will pass away" (1 Corinthians 7:31 NLT). Take advantage of it—but don't fall in love with it.

The fact that this world is not our ultimate home helps explains why we experience difficulty, sorrow, and rejection. It also helps explains why some promises seem unfulfilled, some prayers unanswered, and some circumstances unfair. Our sojourn in this world is not the end of the story. In order to keep us from becoming too attached to this world, God allows us to feel a certain amount of discontent—longings that will never be fulfilled this side of heaven.

We are not completely happy here because we are not supposed to be. We won't be in heaven two seconds before we cry out, "Why did I place such importance on temporal things? What was I thinking?"

As Christ's ambassadors in this world the truth is that at death our tour of duty is over and we go home!

Survival Guide for **April 3**

"THERE WERE MANY LEPERS. THE ONLY ONE CLEANSED WAS NAAMAN." LUKE 4:27

It is easy to believe God for something we have already seen Him do before. Naaman's circumstances, however, were unique. Not only did he have leprosy, but nobody he knew had ever been healed of it. He had no point of reference to look back on and boost his faith.

Are you being tested today because of a unique situation in your life? Your marriage? Your relationships? Your job? A class at school? A chronic illness? One you are afraid even to talk about because you don't know anyone who has ever beaten your particular problem? If so, stop focusing on the circumstances and start focusing on God. Maybe God is preparing to make you exceptional.

"Naaman was a great man." (2 Kings 5:1 NIV). But God was about to make him an exceptional one!

God makes us exceptional by allowing us to get into predicaments without human solutions. When He wants us to have extraordinary influence, He often permits extraordinary affliction. It is how He moves us from being impressive to being truly exceptional.

But when God delivers you from a seemingly hopeless situation, be careful. Those around you will begin to ask, "How did you do it?" They will admire your status and your stamina, when all the time it was your exceptional affliction that God used to make you into the person you have become.

To become exceptional, we must develop a faith that believes God for the impossible and trusts what He says, regardless of the pain or the odds.

Survival Guide for **April 4**

"...URGING THEM TO STICK WITH WHAT THEY HAD BEGUN TO
BELIEVE AND NOT QUIT..." ACTS 14:22

Few athletes have had more fans than basketball superstar Michael Jordan.
Yet when a reporter asked him why he liked his Dad to attend his games,
Jordan replied, "When he is there, I know I have at least one fan!"
Everybody needs encouragement!

It wasn't his lofty title or great accomplishments that brought about
Naaman's healing. Rather, it was the encouragement of two of his
servants who got close enough to see his real problem, then introduced
him to a God who had the solution.

There is an important lesson here: often when God puts us close to
someone and makes us privy to certain information, He does it so that we
can use our "... well-taught tongue, So I know how to encourage tired
people." (Isaiah 50:4). God has placed us where we are to make a
difference; perhaps as in Naaman's case, a difference in whether someone
lives or dies.

We read that Paul and Barnabas encouraged the believers. We are not
called to judge or convict people—that is God's job. Our job is to pray for
them and keep on encouraging them.

In this remarkable story, God used a cleaning maid to save a dying
general. But what if she had rebelled against making beds and washing
dishes in Naaman's house? Or decided to go out and gossip about the
problem instead? Today, you have a vital role to play in God's plan. His
hand is on you to serve where He has placed you. Catch the vision, there
is no room for mediocrity.

God has called you to serve with excellence, so start doing it!

Survival Guide for **April 5**

"ABRAHAM LOOKED UP. HE SAW A RAM CAUGHT BY ITS HORNS IN THE THICKET. ABRAHAM TOOK THE RAM AND SACRIFICED IT AS A BURNT OFFERING INSTEAD OF HIS SON." GENESIS 22:13

God always has a plan—always.

While Abraham was climbing one side of the mountain, the ram was climbing the other. That is how it is with God's provision; we can't always see it coming and we don't necessarily understand how God is going to do it, but each step brings us closer to the provision He has planned for us. When we get to where God wants us to be, God's provision is waiting.

Today, God knows what you are going through and He has already prepared your provision. He has made provision for every struggle, every trial and every problem. Just look up and you will see it: "Abraham looked up and saw a ram caught by its horns. He took the ram, and sacrificed it instead of his son." (Genesis 22:13 NIV).

When God promises something He will do it. When we obey Him, He promises to, ". . . open up heaven itself to you. . ." and pour His blessings into our lives. (See Malachi 3:10).

Not only was the ram in the right place at the right time, it was also "caught" there. God will hold your provision in place until you arrive. He will tie you to a provision that nobody can take from you.

Our God is Jehovah-Jireh, the Provider!

Survival Guide for **April 6**

"IT'S NOT RIGHT TO TAKE BREAD.AND THROW IT TO DOGS" MATTHEW 15:26

Desperation puts us in situations where we have nothing to lose. When our pain level gets high enough, we will do whatever it takes to find relief.

Jesus told a Canaanite woman who asked Him to heal her daughter, "It's not right to take bread and throw it to dogs." She could have flown into a rage and said, "Who are you calling a dog!" But instead she replied, "Master, (even) beggar dogs do get scraps from the master's table." (Matthew 15:27). As a result, the girl was healed. The mother humbled herself and refused to be offended. Are you willing to do that?

Because Naaman was an important leader, his pride almost cost him his life. First: he got angry because Elisha sent his servant, instead of coming out to talk with him personally. Second: when the prophet instructed him on how to be made clean he "went away in a rage." (2 Kings 5:12 TLB). Can't you hear him? "I don't take orders from anyone!"

Self-importance will rob you of what God has for you. It will circumvent your potential and ruin your effectiveness. Don't let your pride rob you of the prize. While in the battle, stay low and keep your head down; holding it up when you are in the crossfire can cost you your life. The Bible says, "So be content with who you are, and don't put on airs. God's strong hand is on you; he'll promote you at the right time." (1 Peter 5:6).

Let God do the exalting; don't try to do it yourself!

Survival Guide for **April 7**

"TO CARE FOR THE NEEDS OF ALL WHO MOURN IN ZION, GIVE THEM BOUQUETS OF ROSES INSTEAD OF ASHES, MESSAGES OF JOY INSTEAD OF NEWS OF DOOM, A PRAISING HEART INSTEAD OF A LANGUID SPIRIT. RENAME THEM 'OAKS OF RIGHTEOUSNESS' PLANTED BY GOD TO DISPLAY HIS GLORY." ISAIAH 61:3

Surviving a crisis and turning it into growth takes an attitude adjustment, and the adoption of a new perspective. It may be painful to delve into the facts of the crisis, but just as lancing a boil is a necessary first step to healing, facing the facts is the first step toward becoming whole again.

Those who grow through a crisis learn which hopes, dreams and expectations were violated by the event. First they identify where the repair work is needed, then they develop a road map for the future.

Often a crisis leaves us with the feeling that "nothing will ever be the same again." That's normal. And there is often an element of truth to the feeling. A crisis can force us to make adjustments in how we work, how we spend our leisure time, and even how we relate to family and friends.

The nature of a crisis is that it shakes up our stable world. But a crisis also forces us to reach deep within ourselves, to find streams of hidden strength, courage, and hope we never knew existed. You may not feel courageous or hopeful right now, but that doesn't mean those things aren't there just waiting to be tapped during a time of crisis.

For the Christian the news is even better: we don't have to rely only on our hidden strength but we can call on the One Who is the author of all strength: "The Lord is my Rock, my Fortress, and my Deliverer; my God, my keen and firm Strength in Whom I will trust and take refuge." (Psalm 18:2 AMP).

Inner healing begins when we give up hope for a better yesterday and take the first step toward making a better tomorrow.

Survival Guide for **April 8**

"I WILL SPRINKLE CLEAN WATER ON YOU, AND YOU WILL BE CLEAN; I WILL CLEANSE YOU FROM ALL YOUR IMPURITIES AND FROM ALL YOUR IDOLS" EZEKIEL 36:25 (NIV)

Whatever takes God's place in your life is an idol.

That includes family idols. When Gideon tore down the altar his father had built to pagan gods, his family wanted to kill him. Why? Because he was upsetting the way things had always been done in his family. Sound familiar? If "the way things have always been done" in your family excludes God, it has to be changed. Those who do not acknowledge God, end up playing God!

The rich young ruler wasn't lost because he had money—he was lost because money had him. It gave him his security and his self-worth. None but God can reliably give security and self-worth.

And that includes relationships. The Bible says;

> "Don't become partners with those who reject God. . ." (2 Corinthians 6:14). You can't put an ox and a donkey in the same harness and get any plowing done, because their natures are different. When God tells us to let someone go but we hold on to them—it is idolatry (and insanity).

God wants to cleanse us of all our idols. The weaning process may be painful, because we all want what we want, when we want it. It takes real trust to believe that whatever we give up God will replace with something better.

Whether it is a job, a relationship, a ministry or a poor career-choice, our Father wants to wean us from the lesser and give us the greater.

His plans are so much better than ours that—whatever it costs—it is worth the pain to get rid of all our idols!

Survival Guide for **April 9**

**"CHRIST'S DEATH WAS ALSO A ONE-TIME EVENT, BUT IT
WAS A SACRIFICE THAT TOOK CARE OF SINS FOREVER.
AND SO, WHEN HE NEXT APPEARS, THE OUTCOME FOR
THOSE EAGER TO GREET HIM IS, PRECISELY, SALVATION."
HEBREWS 9:28**

When Dwight Eisenhower was President of the United States he was
vacationing in Denver and was told about six year-old Paul Haley, who
was dying of an incurable cancer. Paul had one great dream—some day to
meet the President. "Let's go see him," President Eisenhower said to one
of his aids. So they drove over to the boy's house.

The flags on the bumper were flying that Sunday afternoon, as the big
black limousine rolled up. Out stepped the president with his bodyguards
and knocked on the door. Paul's father answered, wearing old jeans, a
grubby shirt and a full day's growth on his beard. "Can I help ya?" he
asked. President Eisenhower responded, "Is Paul here? Tell him the
President of the United States would like to meet him." Thrilled, little
Paul Haley walked around his father's legs and stood looking up into the
face he admired most. The President kneeled down, hugged him, and took
him out to sit in the presidential limousine. Before they said goodbye they
shook hands, then just as suddenly as he appeared—he left.

The neighbors still talk about that day. But one man was not entirely
happy about it, that was Paul's dad, Donald Haley, who said: "I will never
forget standing there in those old jeans, a dirty shirt and a grubby beard to
meet the president. If only I had known he was coming."

He just wasn't prepared. Are you?

"He will appear a second time to those who are waiting for Him."
(Hebrews 9:28 NIV).

If you are "waiting for Him," you won't be unprepared!

Survival Guide for **April 10**

"DON'T BAD-MOUTH EACH OTHER, FRIENDS. IT'S GOD'S
WORD, HIS MESSAGE, HIS ROYAL RULE, THAT TAKES A
BEATING IN THAT KIND OF TALK. YOU'RE SUPPOSED TO BE
HONORING THE MESSAGE, NOT WRITING GRAFFITI ALL
OVER IT." JAMES 4:11

I read this account of two cats online. It is interesting:

> "We share our home with two sibling cats or, more accurately,
> they share their home with us! Delaney's a quiet affectionate
> soul, while O'Malley's a predator and a world-class backbiter!
>
> For reasons known only to God and himself, he waits until
> Delaney's back is turned, then he pounces on her and bites her.
> Like all seasoned backbiters, he . . . acts without warning . . .
> his attacks are unprovoked . . . his victims can't defend
> themselves. . . and he does it to get attention."

Backbiting—how often have you engaged in it and afterwards wished you
hadn't even opened your mouth? When we backbite, others may listen to
what we have to say, but they will never trust us with anything important.
Why not? Because they know that what a backbiter says to them, they will
also say about them. When we hurt someone by gossip and innuendo, it
says much more about our character than theirs!

"Who may worship in Your sanctuary, Lord? Who may enter Your
presence? Those who refuse to slander others or harm their neighbors or
speak evil of their friends. . . such people will stand firm forever." (Ps
15:1-5 NLT).

If you want to pray with more confidence . . . If you want to freely enter
into God's presence . . . then . . .

Don't backbite!

Survival Guide for **April 11**

"EVERYTHING DAVID DID TURNED OUT WELL. YES, GOD WAS WITH HIM." 1 SAMUEL 18:14

Do you want your relationships to turn out well? Then:

(1) Show appreciation. If somebody has helped or enhanced you, always acknowledge it. An attitude of "I don't expect it, so I don't give it" will close doors to your future. Never take others for granted and never forget to say, "Thank you."

(2) Carry your own weight. Avoid doing things that can be construed as opportunistic. Look for ways to make your presence a benefit, not a liability. Life owes you nothing except an opportunity to learn and grow.

(3) Be open and direct about what you want. Rambling speeches and ulterior motives that assume that the other person is somehow less intelligent than you—that can be lethal. Be clear about what you want to walk from the relationship. After all, if you don't know where the goalposts are, how can you score?

(4) Have a clear understanding of the relationship. Just because others know someone well enough to call him by his first name, doesn't mean you should. Err on the side of the formal, not the familiar. If somebody says, "Hello, my name is Charles," don't reply, "What's up, Charlie?" Be respectful—don't try to change the protocol to suit the environment you are used to. Observe boundaries. Respect the relationship.

And one more thing—lack of knowledge just requires learning, but lack of wisdom can be fatal!

Survival Guide for **April 12**

"SO WATCH YOUR STEP. USE YOUR HEAD. MAKE THE MOST OF EVERY CHANCE YOU GET. THESE ARE DESPERATE TIMES! DON'T LIVE CARELESSLY, UNTHINKINGLY. MAKE SURE YOU UNDERSTAND WHAT THE MASTER WANTS. DON'T DRINK TOO MUCH WINE. THAT CHEAPENS YOUR LIFE. DRINK THE SPIRIT OF GOD, HUGE DRAUGHTS OF HIM." EPHESIANS 5:15-18

In Ephesians 5, Paul gives us the formula for a happy, fulfilled life:

(1) "Watch your step" (v.15). Other translations say "Walk circumspectly." The word circumspect means "to be disciplined in your thoughts, speech, actions and motives." Watching our step means our wandering phase has to come to an end. Only then can we enter the Promised Land, drive out the enemy and take what belongs to us.

(2) "Make the most of every chance you get" (v.16). We make the most of every chance we get by not wasting our time on worthless diversions. Get serious! Begin each day by praying, "Father, thank you for this day. Some were alive yesterday, who didn't live to see this one. I accept it as a gift from You and commit myself to maximizing every moment, for Your glory."

(3) "Understand what the Master wants" (v.17). The word understand here means "to make sense of." Often people say to us, "Hey, what's happening?" That's because most of the time they don't know. But we do—not the details but we know that our steps are guarded, guided and governed by the Lord.

(4) "Drink the Spirit of God" (v.18). "Sing hymns instead of drinking songs! Sing songs from your heart to Christ." (Eph 5:19). All Christians are indwelled by the Holy Spirit. Drinking in the Spirit of God is, however, not automatic. We must intentionally invite the Holy Spirit to fill us up and use us to God's glory. When that happens we want to sing. When it is not appropriate to sing out loud, "sing songs from your heart to Christ."

There is the formula for a happy fulfilled life—put it into practice today.

Survival Guide for **April 13**

"PETER REMEMBERED WHAT JESUS HAD SAID: "BEFORE THE ROOSTER CROWS, YOU WILL DENY ME THREE TIMES." HE WENT OUT AND CRIED AND CRIED AND CRIED." MATTHEW 26:75

". . . the cock crowed, and Peter remembered his words to Jesus, 'Even if I have to die with You, I will never disown You.'" (Mk 14:31 NIV). Peter wasn't alone when he made his proclamation: "All the others said the same." (Mk 14:31 NIV).

The moment of truth came for Peter and he failed. The moment of truth eventually came to each of the other disciples. That moment of truth will come for each of us as well. When it does sometimes the very point where you thought you were strongest will show up as your point of hidden weakness.

Maybe you were raised to act like you always have it together. When the moment of truth comes our image gets tested and if we are wearing a mask it gets stripped away.

Hebrews 12 says God is going to do ". . . a thorough housecleaning, getting rid of all the junk so that the unshakeable essentials stand clear and uncluttered." (Heb 12:27). Only "a thorough housecleaning" will prepare our hearts for God to start laying a true foundation for our future. Often a moment of truth experience is where God's housecleaning begins. In that moment we have to come to terms with the fact that we can do nothing of real value in our own strength or, like Peter, we will fail. It is a painful lesson, but it can be life changing.

Peter was never the same after his moment of truth experience. He was humbled and open to "a thorough housecleaning." Now God could use him. The lesson was burned into his conscience, now he could write, ". . . be down to earth with each other, for—God has had it with the proud, But takes delight in just plain people" (1 Pet 5:5).

Have you faced your moment of truth?

Survival Guide for **April 14**

"IT'S NOT GOING TO BE THAT WAY WITH YOU. LET THE SENIOR AMONG YOU BECOME LIKE THE JUNIOR; LET THE LEADER ACT THE PART OF THE SERVANT." LUKE 22:26

In these Survival Guides I write often about goal-setting, perseverance, motivation and purpose. That's because I believe that without a goal, a strategy and a committed heart, we will never fulfill our purpose for living. And even though these are the same qualities that lead to a successful life that is not why I write often about them. At least not success the way the world measures it.

Jesus gives us a new way of measuring success: "Normally, the master sits at the table and is served. . . but not here! For I am your Servant" (Lk 22:27 NLT). The occasion for those words was Jesus washing the feet of His disciples.

In Jesus' day, the washing of feet was a task reserved not just for servants, but for the lowest of them. Every circle has its pecking order and the circle of household servants was no exception. The servant at the bottom was expected to be the one on his knees, with the towel and the basin. What a sight it must have been to see that the one on his knees with the towel and the basin was Jesus. The hands that shaped the stars, now wash filthy feet. The fingers that formed the mountains, now dry the feet of crude Galilean fishermen.

Hours before His death, His concern is singular: to let His disciples know that in His Kingdom, the way up is down, the way to the top is not through ambition or manipulation, but through humility and service to others. Living this way is not natural, it is supernatural; we can do it only as we surrender daily to the indwelling power of God's Spirit.

Jesus measures success by servanthood.

How successful are you?

Survival Guide for **April 15**

"CROWDS WENT AHEAD AND CROWDS FOLLOWED, ALL OF THEM CALLING OUT, 'HOSANNA TO DAVID'S SON!' 'BLESSED IS HE WHO COMES IN GOD'S NAME!' 'HOSANNA IN HIGHEST HEAVEN!'" MATTHEW 21:9

I have often wondered how many of the people who enthusiastically cried, "Hosanna!" on Palm Sunday shouted, "Crucify Him! Crucify Him!" a few days later. Some may have been keenly disappointed, even angry, that Christ didn't use His miraculous power to establish an earthly kingdom. Hadn't He created a golden opportunity to rally popular support by parading into Jerusalem and offering Himself as King?

Many of those present when Jesus rode into Jerusalem failed to recognize that before Jesus would openly assert His sovereignty He had to rule in their hearts. Their greatest need was not to be freed from Caesar's rule but to be released from the chains of pride, self-righteousness, and rebellion against God. They wanted the visible kingdom prophesied in the Old Testament with all its material benefits. But the Messiah first had to die for the sins of mankind and rise again to establish the basis for a spiritual rule.

The issue is the same today. Christ does not offer immunity from life's hardships, a cure for every disease, or the promise of financial success. What the King offered then is what He offers today—Himself as the sacrifice for our sins, and a challenge to serve Him. If we accept His offer, we will not be disappointed.

> There's no disappointment in Jesus,
> He's all that He promised to be;
> His love and His care comfort me everywhere;
> He is no disappointment to me.
> —Hallett

Putting Christ first brings satisfaction that lasts.

Survival Guide for **April 16**

". . .DON'T BE AFRAID. DON'T LOSE HEART."
DEUTERONOMY 1:21

Yesterday I went to the celebration of the life of good friend who died last week. It stirred lots of feelings in me: joy for Jay, sadness for Nancy, concern for their children, and fear for myself. What made me fearful is that Jay and I were in college together and if he could die so can I. Sure, I know that we are all terminal, but his death made me realize death can come sooner instead of later. So, I am feeling fearful and a bit discouraged today. How about you? If so keep reading.

When we are feeling fearful or discouraged God's Word says to us:

". . . fear not: stand still (firm, confident, undismayed) and see the salvation (deliverance) of the Lord, which He will work for you today. . . " (Exodux 14:13 AMP).

When we are weak, cowardly, and alone God's Word says to us:

"Be strong, courageous and firm; fear not nor be in terror before them, for it is the Lord your God Who goes with you; He will not fail you or forsake you." (Deuteronomy 31:6 AMP).

When we feel that you just can't cope anymore God's Word says to us:

". . . do not look around in terror and be dismayed, for I am your God. I will strengthen and harden you to difficulties, yes, I will help you; yes, I will hold you up and retain you with my (victorious) right hand. . . " (Isaiah 41:10 AMP).

When we long for peace of mind God's Word says to us:

"Do not fret or have any anxiety about anything, but in every circumstance. . . continue to make your wants known to God. And God's peace. . . which transcends all understanding, shall garrison and mount guard over your hearts and minds. . . " (Phil 4:6-7 AMP).

There, I feel better! If you don't, go back and read these Scriptures again. then repeat this truth—"God has everything under control, no matter how I feel about it!"

Survival Guide for **April 17**

―――

**". . .I CAME SO THEY CAN HAVE REAL AND ETERNAL LIFE,
MORE AND BETTER LIFE THAN THEY EVER DREAMED OF."
JOHN 10:10**

Do you want to experience "more and better life?" Jesus gives us the
formula:

> "Unless a grain of wheat is buried in the ground, dead to the
> world, it is never any more than a grain of wheat. But if it is
> buried, it sprouts and reproduces itself many times over. In the
> same way, anyone who holds on to life just as it is, destroys that
> life. But if you let it go, reckless in your love, you'll have it
> forever, real and eternal." (John 12:24-25).

Paul knew "death to the flesh" was so crucial to living "real and eternal
life" that it became the cry of his heart: "I gave up all that inferior stuff so
I could know Christ personally, experience His resurrection power, be a
partner in His suffering, and go all the way with Him." (Philippians 3:10).

To "experience His resurrection power" we must willingly lay down our:
 (1) will
 (2) desires
 (3) pride
 (4) independence.

We must reach the place where the only thing that matters—is what God
wants. We must do what is the exact opposite of all your natural instincts.
This is "dying to self."

How will you know when you have died to self? You can criticize a dead
man, walk on him, neglect him, abuse him, and generally treat him any
way you like, and he is not affected by it because he has moved to a
different dimension. That's how you will know.

"Real and eternal life" can only begin when we die to the flesh and
experience the resurrection to life in the Spirit of God.

Survival Guide for **April 18**

"GOD, GOD, A GOD OF MERCY AND GRACE, ENDLESSLY PATIENT—SO MUCH LOVE, SO DEEPLY TRUE." EXODUS 34:6

God loves each of us perfectly just as we are!

Do you think God's love for you would be stronger, if your faith was stronger? It wouldn't. You are confusing God's love with human love. Human love increases with performance and decreases with mistakes. But not God's love; He loves you just as you are right now.

Do you have trouble accepting that?

Maybe that is why God introduces himself this way: "I am the Lord, the merciful and gracious God. I am slow to anger and rich in unfailing love and faithfulness." (Ex 34:6 NLT). Isn't that awesome?

In spite of his terrible failures (or maybe because of them), David could say, "Your love, GOD, is my song, and I'll sing it! I'm forever telling everyone how faithful you are." (Ps 89:1).

And if you need more to convince you, Paul (formerly Saul, the persecutor of Christians) writes, "God showed His great love for us by sending Christ to die for us while we were still sinners." (Rom 5:8 NLT).

Get rid of your do-it-yourself approach to salvation. Salvation is not Do! Do! Do! It is Done! Done! Done! It is a finished work. We can add nothing to it. We stand before God in Jesus' name and in His righteousness—not ours. The righteousness we do now, we do in gratitude to Him and by His grace—not to earn God's love. God loves us just as we are, but He loves us too much to let us stay just as we are.

Perhaps you are saying, "It sounds too easy." Wrong! There was nothing easy about it. The cross was heavy, the blood was real and the price was staggering. It would have bankrupted you and me, so He paid it for us.

Call it simple, call it a gift, but don't call it easy.

Call it what it is—call it grace!

Survival Guide for **April 19**

"WHO GOT THE LAST WORD, OH, DEATH? OH, DEATH, WHO'S AFRAID OF YOU NOW?" 1 CORINTHIANS 15:55

There are at least 27 people banking on life after death. They are all members of the Alcor Life Extension Institute, where their bodies will be frozen in liquid nitrogen at death. They are waiting for science to solve the problem of death. One Alcor member says he plans to try it because, "I like living and I don't want to die." Unfortunately for him, the company Chief Executive says, "We don't even know if it will work."

I have good news for them—It doesn't matter! Jesus has already overcome death. He arose from the grave with a glorious new body—and all who put their trust in Him will do the same. Jesus, and Jesus alone, is the only sure thing when it comes to eternal life: ". . . Christians who have died will be raised with transformed bodies, then we who are living will be transformed so that we will never die. For our perishable earthly bodies must be transformed into heavenly bodies. O death, where is your victory? O death, where is your sting?" (1 Corinthians 15:52-55 NLT).

There's no record of Jesus ever preaching a funeral sermon. Perhaps because He is ". . . the Resurrection, and the Life." (John 11:25). In fact Jesus broke up every funeral we know he attended. Death cannot coexist with Him. When the dead heard His voice they sprang to life. And they will again. No wonder the song writer wrote:

> Death is vanquished, tell it with joy, ye faithful.
> Where is now thy victory, boasting grave?
> Jesus lives, no longer thy portals are cheerless.
> Jesus lives, the mighty and strong to save!

Easter is about The Empty Tomb—but so is everyday for the Christian!

Survival Guide for **April 20**

"AND THE FATHER WHO KNOWS ALL HEARTS KNOWS WHAT THE SPIRIT IS SAYING, FOR THE SPIRIT PLEADS FOR US BELIEVERS IN HARMONY WITH GOD'S OWN WILL." ROMANS 8:27

If your faith is on trial today, rejoice, you have a great Lawyer—the Holy Spirit.

If you have been praying for God to move the mountains of opposition out of your way but they haven't moved maybe it's because He wants to give you grace to endure instead of a strategy for escape. Sometimes God moves the mountains and sometimes He wants to demonstrate His strength through our weakness (see 2 Corinthians 12:9).

So if you are asking, "Lord, how much longer do I have to go through this?" remember that when God doesn't deliver you immediately, He will be your thermostat in the furnace of trial. If God was not regulating the heat, you would have burned up long ago, but each time you reached your breaking point and thought you couldn't take it another day, God put a hold on the Enemy and said, "Cool it! Give him a little grace today."

Paul wrote, ". . . we don't even know what we should pray for. But the Holy Spirit prays for us. And the Father knows . . . what the Spirit is saying, for the Spirit pleads for us." (Romans 8:26-27 NLT). Our prayers keep coming through because we have an Advocate in heaven, pleading our case. our Lawyer is on the job during all those sleepless nights and depressing days. We are here today only because of Him and we can trust Him to keep on defending us.

Continue to trust your Advocate and when the trials are over, you are going to come out the winner.

Job gives us this assurance: "But he knows where I am going. And when he has tested me like gold in a fire, he will pronounce me innocent." Job 23:10 (NLT)

That is a promise!

Survival Guide for **April 21**

"BY THE SEVENTH DAY GOD HAD FINISHED HIS WORK. ON THE SEVENTH DAY HE RESTED FROM ALL HIS WORK."
GENESIS 2:2

Are you having trouble keeping up the pace? Is the strain showing up in your relationships, your health and your attitude? Do you feel guilty and unproductive when you try to relax? If so, here are a few suggestions for you to consider:

(1) Take time out when you need it. Refuse to be intimidated by the opinions of others. People have a tendency to think they know what's best for you. They don't—only you know when you need a break.

(2) Your loved ones would choose having less over not having you. The trouble is, we don't give them a choice. If you have children realize that your lifestyle is your child's blueprint. If you neglect them now, don't be upset when they neglect you later, because they will just be following your lead.

(3) Don't use work as a narcotic. Workaholism, like any other addiction, only masks the real problem. There is an emptiness inside us that only God can fill. And He will, if we let Him.

(4) Effort without reward eventually destroys motivation. Whether it is you, your significant others, your classmates, or your co-workers everybody needs time to recharge their batteries. If you work hard, play hard.

The truth is rest time is the best time to assess our life, our dreams, our heartaches and our faith.

The power of rest is what allows us to enjoy the journey—not just the destination.

22222222222

Survival Guide for **April 22**

"CELEBRATE GOD ALL DAY, EVERY DAY. I MEAN, REVEL IN HIM!" PHILIPPIANS 4:4

If you feel that circumstances have you locked in today, read this: "About midnight, Paul and Silas were praying and singing hymns to God. . . . Suddenly there was such a violent earthquake that the foundations of the prison were shaken. At once all the prison doors flew open and everybody's chains came loose." (Acts 16:25-26 NIV).

The same power that opened every door for Paul and Silas that night is available to us today. It is the power of praise. Any time we praise God in spite of the circumstances, the forces of heaven come to our aid.

Can you imagine how God feels as He watches us on the battlefield, wielding our swords, shouting, "I praise You Lord. I know You're going to bring me through this victoriously." That is battle praise and when God hears it, He responds to it.

But what if we don't feel like praising God? Do it anyway as an offering to God: ". . . offer to God a sacrifice of praise. . . " (Heb 13:15 NIV). Anybody can praise God in the good times, but when we have to sacrifice to do it—that is when it is most effective.

The Battle of Jericho teaches us that sometimes we have to shout when:

(1) it makes no sense
(2) it seems as if we are just going in circles
(3) the enemy stands over us mocking
(4) our rational mind says, "This is no way to fight a war"
(5) it is the last thing on earth we feel like doing.

If you want to see the doors open and the walls come down today—start praising the Lord!

Survival Guide for **April 23**

". . .WE ARE TRANSFIGURED MUCH LIKE THE MESSIAH, OUR LIVES GRADUALLY BECOMING BRIGHTER AND MORE BEAUTIFUL AS GOD ENTERS OUR LIVES AND WE BECOME LIKE HIM." 2 CORINTHIANS 3:18

There are no cookie cutter Christians. Contrary to popular belief becoming like Christ does not mean losing your personality or becoming a mindless clone. God created each of us unique, so He certainly is not out to destroy that. Christ-likeness is about the transformation of character, not personality.

Paul writes, ". . . take on an entirely new way of life—a God-fashioned life, a life renewed from the inside and working itself into your conduct as God accurately reproduces His character in you" (Ephesians 4:23-24).

Whenever we forget that character, not comfort, is God's first priority in our lives, we open ourselves to frustration and begin to wonder, "Why is all this happening to me?" Abundant living is not the absence of adversity, rather it is growth in the midst of it and victory over it.

"As the Spirit of the Lord works within us, we become more and more like Him. . . " How does this happen in real life? Through the choices we make—we choose to do the right thing and then trust God's Spirit to give us the power, love, faith and wisdom to do it. Since His Spirit lives inside us, these things are available just for the asking.

When Joshua stood at the Jordan River, its floodwaters receded only after he stepped in. Obedience unlocks God's power. God waits for us to act first.

Don't wait until you feel capable or confident. Just move ahead in your weakness, doing the right thing in spite of your fears. That is how you cooperate with the Holy Spirit.

That is the path to Christ-like character being developed in you.

Survival Guide for **April 24**

". . .WE ARE TRANSFIGURED MUCH LIKE THE MESSIAH, OUR LIVES GRADUALLY BECOMING BRIGHTER AND MORE BEAUTIFUL AS GOD ENTERS OUR LIVES AND WE BECOME LIKE HIM." 2 CORINTHIANS 3:18

The Bible compares spiritual growth to a seed, a building and a child. What these disparate objects have in common is that each requires our participation. Seeds must be planted. Buildings must be built. Children must nurtured..

Effort has nothing to do with our salvation, but it has everything to do with our spiritual growth. Eight times in the New Testament, we are told to "make every effort" toward becoming like Jesus. We aren't to just sit around and wait for growth to happen.

Paul lists three responsibilities that must be shouldered in order for us to become more like Christ:

(1) Choosing to let go of our old ways. : ". . . everything connected with that old way of life has to go. It's rotten through and through. Get rid of it!" (Ephesians 4:22).

(2) Changing the way we think. "Let the Spirit change your way of thinking" (Ephesians 4:23 CEV). ". . . be transformed by the renewing of your mind.' (Romans 12:2 NIV). (The Greek word for transformed—metamorphosis—is used today to describe the amazing changes that a caterpillar goes through to become a butterfly. And it is a beautiful picture of what happens to us when we allow God to direct our thoughts. As we take on the beauty of Christ's character, we are set free to soar to new heights.)

(3) Clothing ourselves with the character of Christ. "Put on the new self, created to be like God in true righteousness and holiness." (Ephesians4:24 NIV).

We become more like Jesus by developing new habits.

Our character is made up of the sum of our daily habits.

Godly habits create Godly character.

Survival Guide for **April 25**

**". . .WE ARE TRANSFIGURED MUCH LIKE THE MESSIAH,
OUR LIVES GRADUALLY BECOMING BRIGHTER AND MORE
BEAUTIFUL AS GOD ENTERS OUR LIVES AND WE BECOME
LIKE HIM." 2 CORINTHIANS 3:18**

God uses His Word, His people and circumstances to mold us into
Christ's likeness.

God's Word provides the truth we need.

God's people provide the support we need.

Circumstances provide the environment we need to show Christ-likeness.

When we apply God's Word, connect regularly with other believers, and
learn to trust God in every circumstance—we become more like
Jesus—obedience pays dividends.

I know that some days you wonder if you will ever get there, at least I sure
do. That is because spiritual maturity is neither instant nor automatic.
Rather it is a gradual, progressive development that will continue as long
as we are alive: "This will continue until we are mature, just as Christ is."
(Ephesians 4:13 CEV).

So relax; we all are works in progress!

A lot of students talk to me about their fear of choosing the right career. I
tell them that what matters most is that whatever you do, you do in a
Christ-like manner. God is more concerned about our character than our
career, because we take our character into eternity, not our career.

"Don't become so well-adjusted to your culture that you fit into it without
even thinking. Instead, fix your attention on God. You'll be changed from
the inside out. Unlike the culture around you, always dragging you down
to its level of immaturity, God brings the best out of you, develops well-
formed maturity in you." (Romans 12:2).

Every day we must make a counter-cultural decision to focus on becoming
like Jesus. When we do, the Spirit of God empowers us to follow it
through.

Have you made your decision today?

Survival Guide for **April 26**

"PEOPLE WITH THEIR MINDS SET ON YOU, YOU KEEP COMPLETELY WHOLE, STEADY ON THEIR FEET, BECAUSE THEY KEEP AT IT AND DON'T QUIT." ISAIAH 26:3

Most people are driven by something. What drives you?

(1) Guilt? Guilt-ridden people are manipulated by their memories. They allow their past to control their future. They unconsciously sabotage their own happiness by thinking, "I don't deserve this.." We are all products of our past, but we do not have to be prisoners of it. God says, ". . . do not dwell on the past." (Isaiah 43:18 NIV). So stop!

(2) Anger and resentment? Instead of releasing the pain through forgiveness, those driven by anger and resentment rehearse it in their minds. Those who have hurt us can only keep hurting us if we hold on to the pain through resentment. For your own sake, forgive, learn from it and move on.

(3) Fear? Many of our fears are the result of a traumatic experience, unrealistic expectations, growing up in a high-control home, or genetic predisposition. Regardless of the cause, fear is a self-imposed prison that keeps us from becoming what God intends us to be. Rise up; move against it with the weapons of faith and love, for "Well-formed love banishes fear." (1 John 4:18).

(4) Materialism? Possession driven people think that if they have more, they will be more important. This is the philosophy of consumerism. But it is dead wrong. Net-worth doesn't bring self-worth. Our value is not determined by our valuables. The most common lie about money, is that having more of it increases security. The truth is that real security can be found only in what can never be taken away—our relationship with God.

So what drives you? There is an alternative to being driven—to be called.

Answer the call to give your life over to the control and direction of God's purposes and join the ranks of the called—instead of the driven!

Timothy L. Hudson

Survival Guide for **April 27**

"...OUR FATHER IN HEAVEN..." MATTHEW 6:9

When Jesus was asked by His disciples, "Lord, teach us to prayer." He responded with The Model Prayer that we call The Lord's Prayer. For the next few days the Survival Guides will explore the elements of this Model Prayer.

The name used for "Father" is "Abba," which simply means, "Daddy." No Jew of Christ's day dared address God that way, yet Jesus did it constantly. And He invites us to do it too.

Max Lucado writes:

> "One afternoon in old Jerusalem, as my daughter Jenna and I were exiting the Jaffa Gate, we found ourselves behind a Jewish family—a father and his three little girls. The four year-old fell a few steps behind and couldn't see him. "Abba!" she called. He stopped immediately. Only then did he realize they were separated. "Abba!" she called again. immediately he extended his hand and she took it. I made mental notes. I wanted to see the actions of an "Abba." He held her hand tightly as they descended the ramp. When they stopped at a busy street, she stepped off the curb and he pulled her back. When the signal changed, he led her and her sisters through the busy intersection. In the middle of the street, he reached down, swept her up into his arms and continued their journey."

We all need an "Abba" Who hears when we call... Who takes our hand when we are weak... Who guides us through the hectic intersections of life... Who swings us up into His arms and carries us home.

The good news is—we have one.

No matter what you face today, all you have to do is pause, reach up and whisper, "Abba," and God will be there for you!

Survival Guide for **April 28**

". . .HALLOWED BE YOUR NAME. . ."   MATTHEW 6:9(NIV)

Yesterday we saw God as a child sees her daddy. But with the words "hallowed be Your name" we are reminded of the fact that our intimacy with God is a gift from a transcendent God. With these words we move from the family room into the throne room where we are awed and silenced by God's majesty and power.   This is an important balance—intimacy and reverence!

Moses stood before a burning bush and heard: "Take off your sandals, for the place where you are standing is holy ground." (Exodus 3:5 NIV). The word for such moments is reverence.

As we read further we discover that no time is spent convincing Moses what Moses can do, but much time is spent explaining to Moses what God can do. My approach to enlisting Moses to lead the Israeli exodus from Egypt would have been the opposite. I would have explained to Moses how he was ideally suited to return to Egypt. After all, who better understood the culture of the palace? Then I would have reminded him how perfectly suited he was for wilderness travel. Who knows the desert better than a shepherd?   Then I would have spend time reviewing his résumé and strengths.

But God doesn't do any of that. The strength of Moses is never considered. Not one word is spoken to recruit Moses, but many words are used to reveal God. Why? Because the strength of Moses is not the issue; the strength of God is.

Repeat that last sentence and replace "Moses" with your name: Today, the strength of _____ is not the issue; the strength of God is.

The phrase "Hallowed be Your name" takes the focus off ourselves, and places it where it should always be—on God!

Survival Guide for **April 29**

"YOUR KINGDOM COME. YOUR WILL BE DONE ON EARTH, AS IT IS IN HEAVEN." MATTHEW 6:10 (NIV)

Each time we obey God, God's kingdom is operating in us just as it does in heaven. Can you imagine anybody in heaven responding to a command from God by saying, "Let me think about it." Or turning a deaf ear whenever God speaks? The last resident of Heaven to try that was Lucifer.

"Your kingdom come. Your will be done . . ." simply means, "Be fully in control. My steps are ordered by You. My decisions are based on Your approval alone. My choices are subject to Your veto. If You are not Lord over all, then You are not Lord at all."

Be honest; when you examine your greatest mistakes, whose will were you following—His or yours? Did you even consult Him? Did you linger in His presence long enough to hear what He had to say? Or did you not like the direction He gave you, and just launched out on your own?

God's will can be painful, because He has only one plan for our fallen human natures—death. Paul understood this when he wrote, " I look death in the face practically every day I live. . ." (1 Corinthians 15:31). Paradoxically the end result of dying to self is abundant living.

When we pray, "Your will be done," we are seeking the reign of God in our life. This is another way of acknowledging that Jesus is Lord.

The Lordship of Christ is what this section of the model prayer is all about.

When you pray, "Your kingdom come. Your will be done on earth, as it is in heaven," rest assured, that is a prayer God will answer!

Survival Guide for **April 30**

**"KEEP US ALIVE WITH THREE SQUARE MEALS."
MATTHEW 6:11**

Paul says that a man who won't feed his own family is worse than an unbeliever (see 1 Timothy 5:8). As our Heavenly Father surely God holds himself to a higher standard than that. After all, how can we fulfill our mission unless our needs are met? How can we teach, or minister, or influence others, if we ourselves are not provided for? Scripture promises that "God will give you every good thing you need so you can do what He wants." (Hebrews 13:20-21 NCV).

We pray "Give us this day our daily bread" only to find our prayer already answered. Here is what I mean. A high school student (secondary school pupil to my international readers) decides to go to college, then learns the cost of tuition fees. He says to his dad, "I'm sorry to ask so much, but I have no one else to turn to." His father smiles and says, "Don't worry, son. The day you were born I began saving for your education. I have already provided everything you need." Our Heavenly Father also has anticipated our needs and made provision to meet them.

At some point, it should occur to us that somebody else is providing our needs. Indeed, we take a giant step in maturity when we agree with David's words: "Everything we have has come from You." (1 Chronicles 29:14 NLT).

We may pay for the food and prepare the meals, but there is more to putting food on the table than that. What about the seed, the soil, and the sun? Who created animals for food and minerals for metal? Long before we knew we needed someone to take care of us—God already had.

God is committed to each of us. He lives with the self-assigned task of providing for His own.

Today, ask God for what you need with the assurance that if you really need it He has already provided for it.

Survival Guide for May 1

"KEEP US FORGIVEN WITH YOU AND FORGIVING OTHERS."
MATTHEW 6:12

Does someone owe you an apology? An explanation? A thank you? A second chance?

What are you going to do about it? Hold on to resentment? Talk to others about it? Get even?

Picture this: a big grizzly bear feeding alone on some discarded food. No other creature dares come close. But after a few moments, a skunk walks over and takes his place next to him and the grizzly doesn't object. Why? Because he knows the high cost of getting even.

We would be smart to learn the same lesson.

Ever notice in western movies that bounty hunters travel alone? Who wants to hang out with a guy who settles scores for a living? Or risk getting on his bad side and catching a stray bullet? No, debt-settling is a lonely occupation.

We describe those who bother us as "a pain in the neck." Yes, but whose neck? Not theirs. We are the ones who suffer. If you are out to settle a score you will never rest. How can you? Your enemy may never pay up. As much as you think you deserve an apology, they may not agree. You may never get a penny's worth of justice and, if you do, will it be enough? What's the answer? "Keep us forgiven with you and forgiving others."

Would you like some peace? Then stop giving others such hassle. Want to enjoy God's generosity? Then let others enjoy yours. Would you like the assurance that God forgives you?

You know what to do, don't you?

Do it.

Survival Guide for **May 2**

"KEEP US SAFE FROM OURSELVES AND THE DEVIL."
MATTHEW 6:13

Satan's power can be exercised at God's discretion.

Of course, Satan would rather we never learn how often God uses him as an instrument to:

(1) Humble us. Even the meekest among us tends to think too highly of ourselves. Paul did. But God protected him from his own pride, using Satan to do it: "To keep me from becoming conceited because of these surpassingly great revelations, there was given me a thorn in my flesh, a messenger of Satan, to torment me." (2 Corinthians 12:7 NIV).

(2) Awaken us. When dealing with two disciples who had made shipwreck of their faith and negatively influenced others, Paul wrote: "I have given these men over to Satan, so they will learn not to oppose God." (1 Timothy 1:20 CEV). Some of us respond to a tap on the shoulder, others need a kick in the seat of the pants.

(3) Teach us. Jesus told Peter, "Satan has asked" (notice that he needed permission) "to test all of you. I have prayed that you will not lose your faith!" (Luke 22:31-32 NCV). The Good Shepherd will permit the attack only if, in the long term, the pain is worth the gain.

Satan can be used as God's instrument to provide a testimony to God's saving and keeping power in our life.

That is why we are to pray, "Keep us safe from ourselves and the Devil."

Survival Guide for **May 3**

"FOR YOURS IS THE KINGDOM, AND THE POWER, AND THE GLORY, FOR EVER. AMEN." MATTHEW 6:13 (NAS)

Jesus points out three things that are God's, not ours: "the kingdom, the power, and the glory."

The disciples had no difficulty understanding this. They had just watched Jesus calm the worst storm they had ever been through. In a moment, they watched the sea go from a churning torrent to a peaceful pond. Immediate calm! Not even a ripple. And what was their reaction? "They were in absolute awe, staggered. 'Who is this, anyway?' they asked." (Mark 4:41).

They had never met anyone like Jesus. The waves were His subjects and the winds were His servants. And there was more to come; soon they would see fish jump into the boat, demons dive into pigs, cripples turn into dancers, and corpses become living, breathing people. Never had they experienced such power, never had they seen such glory.

Face it, we were not meant to run the kingdom; nor are we expected to be all-powerful. And we certainly can not handle the glory. Some of us think we can. We like to think of ourselves as self-made men or women. Instead of bowing our knees, we just roll up our sleeves and put in another 12-hour day. That may work when it comes to making a living, but when we face our own guilt or our own grave, our own power will not do the trick.

Jesus ends His model prayer with a message we must never forget: "Yours, not mine, is the kingdom. Yours, not mine, is the power. Yours, not mine is the glory."

Remember that—and your life will fall into place.

Forget it—and you are in for a very frustrating life!

Survival Guide for **May 4**

"BACK AND FORTH THEY TALKED. 'DIDN'T WE FEEL ON FIRE AS HE CONVERSED WITH US ON THE ROAD, AS HE OPENED UP THE SCRIPTURES FOR US'?" LUKE 24:32

Are you struggling to know God's will?

If so, take another look at the two confused disciples on the road to Emmaus. They thought they had seen the death of Jesus and His movement. Deeply discouraged, they packed their bags and headed home. Suddenly, Jesus appeared to them. This encounter gives us a model of how Jesus reveals His will to us. You might be surprised at the simplicity of the process:

(1) Through other believers. They should have paid more attention the words of their fellow disciples: "Today some women among us amazed us. Early this morning they went to the tomb, but they did not find His body there. They came and told us Jesus was alive." (Luke 24:22-23 NCV). God's method hasn't changed. He still speaks to believers through other believers. That is why we need to be honest with each other.

(2) Through the Scriptures. "Then starting with what Moses and all the prophets had said about Him, Jesus began to explain everything that had been written about Himself in the Scriptures." (Luke 24:27 NCV). Jesus used the Scriptures to quell their fears. The answer to knowing God's will is simple and at your fingertips—check your Bible. God still speaks through His Word.

(3) Through a burning heart. "They said to each other, 'It felt like a fire burning in us when Jesus talked to us.'" (Luke 24:32 NCV). God revealed His will to them by setting their hearts on fire. What ignites your heart? Forgotten orphans? Untouched nations? The inner city? Singles? The University campus?

Whatever it is—heed the fire within you!

Survival Guide for **May 5**

"SEE WHAT I'VE GIVEN YOU? . . . PROTECTION FROM EVERY ASSAULT OF THE ENEMY." LUKE 10:19

Are you easily intimidated? Do you suffer from a "no can do" attitude? If so, do I have good news for you!. God has already given you power over the Enemy. Start using it and see your life go from "no can do" to "can do."

Dr. Vincent Muli Wa Kituku writes:

> In physics class in Kenya I learned that AC meant alternating current. So when I came to America and bought a car with a button marked AC, I was afraid to press it. In summer I sweat a lot and drove with the windows open, or used a handheld fan. One day a friend asked me why the air conditioner wasn't on. I said, "I don't have one." She laughed, pushed the AC button—and my life changed forever. Relief had been at my fingertips all along! I wonder how many talents and gifts come and go from this world, locked up within people who never discover and use them? What is stopping you from pressing the buttons of spiritual development and growth? Loyalty to the past or to others? Fear of the unknown? Self-devaluation?

"I have given you (physical and mental strength) over all the power that the enemy (possesses) nothing shall harm you" (Luke10:19 Amp).

God has already given us the power. We just need to believe it and act on it. Once we recognize who we are in Christ, our outlook will change—from "can't do" to "can do."

Today is a good day to start demonstrating a "power conscious" attitude, and begin walking in the promises of God—they are, after all, already yours!

Survival Guide for **May 6**

". . . OFFER YOURSELVES TO THE WAYS OF GOD . . ."
ROMANS 6:16

Surrender isn't just the best way to live—it is the only way that works. All other approaches lead to frustration, disappointment, and self-destruction. Paul calls surrender, " the best thing you can do for him" (Romans 12:1).

Our wisest moments are those when we surrender to God.

Sometimes it takes years, but eventually we discover that the greatest hindrance to God's will in our life—is us! We cannot fulfill God's purposes for our life while focusing exclusively on our own plans. If God is going to do His deepest work in us, we must surrender to Him.

Give God your past regrets, your present problems, your future ambitions, your fears, dreams, weaknesses, habits, hurts, and hang-ups. Put Jesus in the driver's seat—and take your hands off the wheel. Don't be afraid; nothing under His control can ever be out of control. Mastered by Christ, you can handle anything.

Through the Jesus Film Project, Campus Crusade Founder Bill Bright has presented the gospel to four billion people. When asked why God used him so much, Bright replied: "When I was a young man I made a contract with God. I literally wrote it out and signed my name at the bottom. It said, 'From this day forward I am a slave of Jesus Christ.'"

Today make this your contract with God!

Survival Guide for **May 7**

_____

"SO LET GOD WORK HIS WILL IN YOU." JAMES 4:7

There are three great benefits of surrender:

(1) Peace. "If you agree with Him, you will have peace at last, and things will go well for you." (Job 22:21 NLT).

(2) Freedom. "Offer yourselves to the ways of God and the freedom never quits." (Romans 6:19 TM).

(3) Power. Stubborn temptations and overwhelming problems are given over to the power of Christ, the moment we surrender them to God. As Joshua approached the walls of Jericho he encountered God, fell down in worship, surrendered his plans and cried, "What orders does my Master have for his servant?" (Joshua 5:14).

Joshua's surrender led to a spectacular victory. One of the great paradoxes of faith is that victory comes through surrender. Surrender to God does not weaken, it strengthens. When we surrender to God, we don't have to fear or surrender to anything else. William Booth, founder of The Salvation Army, said: "The greatness of a man's power, is in the measure of his surrender."

Eventually everyone surrenders to something. If not to God, we surrender to the opinions or expectations of others, to money, to resentment, to fear, or to our own lusts or ego. We are free to choose what we surrender to, but once we have made our choice we are not free from the consequences of that choice. E. Stanley Jones said, "If you don't surrender to Christ, you surrender to chaos."

The supreme example of surrender is Jesus. The night before His crucifixion, He surrendered Himself to God the Father saying, "I want Your will, not mine." (paraphrased).

Following Jesus' example of surrender will yield peace, freedom, and power.

Surrender to God today!

Survival Guide for **May 8**

"HE KNEW WHAT THEY WERE MADE OF; HE KNEW THERE WASN'T MUCH TO THEM." PSALM 78:39

We all have weaknesses, but the ones we refuse to deal with:
    (a) draw us magnetically toward the wrong things
    (b) give Satan a foothold, which quickly becomes a
        stronghold
    (c) schedule tragedy down the line.

Be warned: a weakness left unmastered can emerge at any time, from college to retirement. What we fail to master now will master us later. No wonder David prayed, "But don't turn me out to pasture when I'm old or put me on the shelf when I can't pull my weight." (Psalm 71:9).

The Holy Spirit will repeatedly convict us of our need to deal with our weakness before it grows into a destructive force! Jesus told Peter: "Satan has asked to have all of you, to sift you like wheat. But I have pleaded in prayer for you, Simon, that your faith should not fail. So when you have repented and turned to Me again, strengthen and build up your brothers." (Luke 22:31-32 NLT).

God continues to use us even while our weakness grows within us because He is long-suffering and merciful. He provides opportunity after opportunity to reach for His help. Jesus warned Jerusalem ". . .how often I have longed to gather your children together but you were not willing. Look, your house is left to you desolate." (Matthew 23:37-38 NIV). God's mercy never ends but if we repeatedly reject God's mercy—eventually we must face the inevitable consequences.

Turn to God with your weakness. God is neither shocked by it nor unwilling to help you overcome it. Confess your inability to conquer your weakness on your own. Ask the Holy Spirit to empower you.

The Holly Spirit can not only deliver us but show us that our weakness is an opportunity for us to see God at work transforming our lives.

Survival Guide for **May 9**

"SO DON'T YOU BE SLOVENLY AND CARELESS. JUST WHEN YOU DON'T EXPECT HIM, THE SON OF MAN WILL SHOW UP." LUKE 12:40

Chuck Swindoll writes,

> "I once worked in a machine shop alongside a fellow named George. His job was to sweep out the shavings underneath the huge lathes we were running. George loved the subject of Bible prophecy. I remember him singing hymns as he worked: hymns such as, 'In The Sweet By And By' and 'When The Roll Is Called Up Yonder, I'll Be There.'

> "Late one Friday afternoon, about ten minutes before finishing time, I looked at George and said, 'George, are you ready?' He said, 'Uh-huh.' But he was all dirty. He obviously wasn't ready. In fact, he looked as if he was ready to keep on working. 'Aren't you ready to go home?' I asked. 'Yeah,' he said, 'I'm ready.' I said, 'Look at you! Man, you're not ready, you've gotta go clean up.' 'No,' he said, 'let me show you something.' Quickly he unzipped his overalls and underneath was the neatest, cleanest clothes you can imagine. All he did when the whistle blew was just unzip, step out of his overalls, walk up, punch the clock and he was gone. 'You see,' he said, 'I stay ready, to keep from gettin' ready—just like I'm ready for Jesus!'"

Without exception, when the Second Coming of Christ is mentioned in the Bible, it is followed by a call to godly living. If we see the call to be ready when Jesus comes as a giant bogey man to scare us into living right we have missed the whole idea.

The promise of the Second Coming should create in us a desire to maximize each moment, and to live it in the light of His coming soon!

Survival Guide for **May 10**

"MOST OF ALL, LOVE EACH OTHER AS IF YOUR LIFE DEPENDED ON IT . . ." 1 PETER 4:8

Napoleon conquered the world, yet when he died in exile on the island of St. Helena, he was alone and forsaken by all who knew him best. His wife went back to her father. His best friend deserted him without even saying goodbye, returning to become a captain in Louis XVIII's guard. Two of his most trusted marshals openly insulted him, even the faithful servants who'd slept outside his bedroom door left him. Why? Because he was totally self-centered—the only one he loved deeply was himself.

The people around him felt used, but never appreciated.

We need to learn this lesson: people are for loving not using. Our culture encourages us to think "I can do it better myself . . . I don't need others . . . I don't have time to waste on people." But if we reach all our goals, but lose the people who matter most in the process, what have we gained? The reality is that what we deposit into our relationships today is all we'll have to draw on later.

Imagine having a story to tell, but nobody to listen; or something to celebrate, but nobody to celebrate it with; then worst of all, imagine your influence ending at your death because you failed to deposit into others the things that God invested into you. I don't want that to happen to me and I bet you don't want it to happen to you either!

Loving deeply means "Pouring yourselves out for each other in acts of love" (1 Pet 4:9).

Max Lucado writes:
"Arrogance is a dog that turns on its owner.
Selfishness is a fire that consumes the one who started it.
Bitterness is a trap that ensnares the hunter.
But love is the choice that sets them all free."

"Love each other as if your life depended on it . . ." today!

Survival Guide for **May 11**

"MARTHA WAS PULLED AWAY BY ALL SHE HAD TO DO IN THE KITCHEN. . . ONE THING ONLY IS ESSENTIAL, AND MARY HAS CHOSEN IT—IT'S THE MAIN COURSE, AND WON'T BE TAKEN FROM HER." LUKE 10:40,42

Sometimes we need to move from Martha to Mary. From striving and serving, to sitting quietly at His feet so that we can be molded by His presence and instructed in His Word. Why? Because: "Martha was pulled away by all she had to do . . ." That is so easy to let happen!

Martha is having Jesus over for dinner. She wants to serve Him. Nothing wrong with that! But then something happens: her performance becomes more important than His presence. What begins as an attempt to serve Him, slowly and subtly becomes a way of displaying her talents. Those of us involved in God's work, face this danger every day.

Mary knew that Jesus wouldn't go hungry, for He could turn water into wine and stones into bread. She also knew that she might never have this life-changing moment of intimacy with Him again, so she seized it.

Some of the busiest people I know are also the most spiritually barren. Unfortunately, I have to put myself in that group sometimes. On the other hand, some of the most blessed people I know refuse to let anything rob them of the privilege of just sitting quietly in God's presence each day. I've found that if I do that, then my busyness doesn't produce spiritual barrenness. Why? Because: "Now you've got my feet on the life path, all radiant from the shining of your face. Ever since you took my hand, I'm on the right way." (Ps 16:11).

Do you need to move from Martha to Mary today?

Then do it!

Survival Guide for **May 12**

"IF A MAN'S GIFT IS. . . ENCOURAGING, LET HIM ENCOURAGE" ROMANS 12:6 (NIV)

There's no better exercise for strengthening your heart than stooping to lift somebody else's.

Your best friends are the ones who encourage you. Who wants to hang around somebody who always puts you down? Encouragement is a wonderful gift both to get and to give.

Dr Maxwell Maltz interviewed the son of a successful businessman. The boy had refused to take over the family business after his dad's death, even though it would've made him wealthy. He explained, "You don't understand the relationship I had with my father. He was a driven man who came up the hard way. His objective was to teach me self-reliance and he thought the best way to do it was never to encourage or praise me. Every day we played catch in the yard. The idea was for me to catch the ball ten straight times. I'd catch it eight or nine times, but always on that tenth throw he'd do everything possible to make me miss it. He'd throw it on the ground or over my head, so I had no chance of catching it."

He then paused tearfully and said, "That's why I have to get away; I want to catch that tenth ball!" This young man grew up feeling he could never measure up, never be perfect enough to please his father. Sound familiar?

William James said, "The deepest principle in human nature is the craving to be appreciated." Most of us think wonderful things about people, but neglect to tell them. Praise becomes valuable only if you impart it.

Today go out of your way to encourage somebody.

Survival Guide for **May 13**

". . .CHOOSE FOR YOURSELVES THIS DAY WHOM YOU WILL SERVE . . ." JOSHUA 24:15 (NIV)

In order for our lives to glorify God and bless others there are seven choices we must make:

1. Choose love
   No occasion justifies bitterness. (1 Corinthians 13:3-8).
2. Choose joy
   Since God directs our steps, we must resist the temptation to be negative or fearful. (Psalm 37:23).
3. Choose patience
   Instead of cursing the one who breaks into line, we can invite him to go ahead of us. Instead of complaining that the wait is too long, we can be grateful for a moment to pray. (Romans 5:3-4).
4. Choose kindness:
   Be kind to the poor, for often they are alone. Be kind to the rich, for often they are afraid. Be kind to the unkind, for that is how God treats us. (Colossians 3:12).
5. Choose goodness
   Be quicker to confess than to accuse, to be overlooked than to boast, to go without, than to accept anything dishonest. (Isaiah 3:10).
6. Choose faithfulness
   Keep our promises so that our creditors will never regret their trust, our friends question our word and our families doubt our love. (1 Corinthians 4:2).
7. Choose gentleness
   Nothing is won by force. If we raise our voices, let it be in praise. If se clench our fists, let it be in prayer. If we make demands, let them first be on ourselves. (James 3:17).

Make the right choices, live according to these principles and when your head hits your pillow tonight you will get a good night's sleep.

"CHOOSE FOR YOURSELVES THIS DAY . . ."

Survival Guide for **May 14**

"THE LORD WILL GUIDE YOU ALWAYS . . ."   ISAIAH 58:11

Can you imagine Sir Edmund Hillary being asked how he climbed Mount Everest and answering, "Well, my wife and I just went out for a walk one afternoon and, before we knew it, there we were on top of the mountain?" You know better!

First he studied the mountain. Then he developed a plan to climb it. Then he developed a budget. Then he recruited expert guides. Then he set a schedule for each day. Then he made sure he had adequate supplies. Above all, he understood that it would take perseverance to get to the top.

In his book, *Dare to Succeed*, Van Crouch says he came home from work one night, and his dad said to him, "What have you been doing all day?" He replied, "Nothing much." His dad asked, "Then, how did you know when you were finished?" Good point! Without goals to reach for or measure by, how can we evaluate the worth of anything we are doing?

Not all our goals are from God but when God gives us a goal, He supplies all that's required for us to reach it. Nehemiah said: "By day the pillar of cloud did not cease to guide them, nor the pillar of fire by night to shine on the way they were to take. You gave your good Spirit to instruct them. You did not withhold manna from their mouths and you gave them water for their thirst. For forty years you sustained them in the desert; they lacked nothing." (Nehemiah 9:19-21 NIV).

That is the God we serve!

His goals come with His sustenance!

Survival Guide for **May 15**

"WHAT YOU SAY ABOUT YOURSELF MEANS NOTHING IN GOD'S WORK. IT'S WHAT GOD SAYS ABOUT YOU THAT MAKES THE DIFFERENCE." 2 CORINTHIANS 10:18

A reporter once asked opera singer Marian Anderson to name her greatest achievement. Was it in 1955, when she became the first black soloist in the New York Metropolitan Opera? Or when she became a delegate to the United Nations? Or when she performed for visiting royalty at the White House? Or when she received The Presidential Medal of Freedom in 1963?

The accolades were endless, but she chose none of them. Instead, she told the reporter that her greatest moment came when she went home one day and told her mother that she no longer had to earn a living by taking in washing. How is that for humility?

Most of the people we admire in Scripture came from humble and flawed backgrounds. Rahab came out of Jericho's red-light district. Gideon came from a family of idol-worshippers. Samson had multiple relationships and struggled with lust.   Jacob the businessman had more angles than a pyramid. What a cast—but God used them because they were:
   a. humble
   b. available
   c. dependent on Him

In God's kingdom, the way up—is down. Paul says, "The person who wishes to boast should boast only of what the Lord has done. When people boast about themselves, it doesn't count for much. But when the Lord commends someone, that's different!" (2 Cor 10:17-18 NLT).

Today walk in humility and let God do the bragging!

Survival Guide for **May 16**

"WORK FROM THE HEART FOR YOUR REAL MASTER, FOR GOD." COLOSSIANS 3:23

A major insurance company conducted a work-study during which they discovered that 20 percent of their employees did 80 percent of the work; which meant the other 80 percent only did 20 percent of the work. And they found something even more interesting—the 20 percent at the top produced 16 percent more than the 80 percent at the bottom. The difference was not that that the top 20 percent were 16 times smarter or more experienced than the bottom 80 percent. The difference was that the ones at the top had made a conscious decision to be the best by committing to excellence on the job.

Which group includes you? What kind of worker are you? Do you pull your weight? Are you a clock-watcher? Do you depend on others to carry you? Do you think that tough working conditions give you the right to be a slacker?

Like it or not the New Testament scriptures are not silent about being a Christian in the workplace:

1. Obey and respect your boss as you would the Lord. (Ephesians 6:5).
2. Do it, even when he isn't watching. (Colossians 3:22).
3. Make sure your work ethic adds credibility to your testimony. (1 Timothy 6:1).
4. Do your best, even when your work environment is difficult. (1 Peter 2:18).

Jesus clearly taught excellence in the workplace: "In a word, what I'm saying is, grow up. You're kingdom subjects. Now live like it. Live out your God-created identity. Live generously and graciously toward others, the way God lives toward you." (Matt 5:48).

Work is a self-portrait of the one who does it, so, today, autograph it with excellence!

Survival Guide for **May 17**

". . . THE KIND OF PEOPLE THE FATHER IS OUT LOOKING FOR: THOSE WHO ARE SIMPLY AND HONESTLY THEMSELVES BEFORE HIM IN THEIR WORSHIP." JOHN 4:23

Worship is a universal urge, built by God into every fiber of our being—it is as natural as breathing. If we fail to worship God, we always find a substitute, even if it ends up being ourselves.

"The Father seeks worshippers." (John 4:23 NAS). We hear much about worship these days, but much of what we hear falls short of what constitutes true worship. It seems to me that most of us need to expand our understanding of worship. For example:

(1) Worship is far more than music. I often hear people say, "At our church, we have the worship first, then the teaching." I understand what they mean but the truth is that both singing and teaching done for God's glory are worship. If worship is just music, then a lot of us who can't carry a tune in a bucket are poor worshippers.

(2) Worship is not a style. The music style we prefer says more about us, than it does about God. One group's music style may sounds like noise to another. But not to God who is the creator of variety, so He enjoys it all when done to His glory.

(3) Worship is not for our benefit. When we say, "I didn't get anything out of the worship today," we are really confessing our failure as worshippers. We are focusing in the wrong place. Sure, there are benefits to worship, but we don't worship to please ourselves. Our motive should be to glorify God—in whatever we do.

(4) Worship is not confined to a "church service." Martin Luther said, "A dairymaid can milk cows to the glory of God." The secret of true worship is doing everything "as unto the Lord." Worship should be a lifestyle not a weekly exercise.

If you want to be a true worshipper: "Take your everyday, ordinary life—your sleeping, eating, going-to-work, and walking-around life—and place it before God as an offering." (Romans 12:1).

Survival Guide for **May 18**

"DAY AND NIGHT I'LL STICK WITH GOD . . ." PSALM 16:8

Frank Laubach's life began to fall apart when his plans to evangelize the Maranao people of the Philippines were rejected. Then after losing three children to malaria, his wife and remaining child moved away. In despair, Laubach climbed a mountain to seek God.

Later he wrote:

> My lips began to move and it seemed God was speaking: "You've failed because you don't really love these people. You feel superior. because you're white. Forget your skin-tone; think only about how much I love them and they'll respond." I answered, "God, I don't know whether you spoke through my lips, but I know it was the truth. My plans have all gone to pieces. Drive me out of myself, take possession, think Your thoughts through my mind."

Laubach immediately made a decision to live focused daily on God's presence. He makes these recommendations:

> —Practice "double-vision:" See others not as they are, but as God sees them.

> —Problem-solving? You'll think more clearly by including God in the process.

> —At mealtime, put an extra chair at the table to remind you that He is always present with you.

> —Set a picture of Jesus or a Scripture text where you will see it as you are falling asleep and waking up.

David said, "Day and night I'll stick with God . . ." David knew that what we focus on becomes the dominant influence in our life.

Laubach wrote books, led worldwide literacy crusades, and became an advisor to kings and presidents. All of these accomplishment were by-products of his practice of the art of focusing on Jesus.

Today practice the art of focusing on Jesus.

Survival Guide for **May 19**

". . . WE'VE BEEN SURROUNDED AND BATTERED BY TROUBLES, BUT WE'RE NOT DEMORALIZED . . ."
2 CORINTHIANS 4:8

Resistance to change creates ulcers, sleeplessness and stress. The following attitudes are counter-productive. Here are suggestions for adjusting them:

—Thinking like a victim. Stop expecting others to reduce your stress levels and get behind the wheel of your own life: "we can do everything with the help of Christ." (Philippians 4:13 NLT). Everything!

—Deciding not to change. Instead of banging your head against the wall of hard reality, invest your efforts into changing what you can—your attitude and your approach. It takes more energy to hang on to old habits and beliefs than it does to embrace new ones.

—Trying to play the new game by the old rules. When a car that is stuck in second gear keeps trying to do 100 mph, guess what happens—meltdown. If you don't want to burn out, learn to change gears. Figure out how the game has changed. Learn to play by the new rules, otherwise you will keep losing.

—Trying to control the uncontrollable. When the music changes, it is time to learn some new steps, otherwise you'll finish up sitting on the sidelines.

We don't have to like change, but we do have to accept it, adapt to it, pray for grace, and not get demoralized!

Survival Guide for **May 20**

". . . I'VE NAMED YOU FRIENDS BECAUSE I'VE LET YOU IN ON EVERYTHING I'VE HEARD FROM THE FATHER."
JOHN 15:15

A friend is not a casual acquaintance, but a close, trusted, relationship. In ancient times it referred to a king's inner circle. In royal courts, the servants had to keep their distance; but the inner circle enjoyed:
(a) close contact
(b) direct access
(c) confidential information.

How do friends of God then behave? They stay in close contact with God. His friends carry on open-ended conversations with Him throughout the day, talking with Him about whatever they are doing at that moment.

God wants more than a weekend visit, or even a brief appointment every day. He wants to be included in every activity, every conversation, every problem, every thought.

In his classic book, *Practicing the Presence of God*, Brother Lawrence, a humble cook in a French monastery, wrote:

> "The key to friendship with God is not changing what you do, but changing your attitude toward what you do. What you normally do for yourself, you now begin doing for God, whether it is eating, bathing, relaxing, or taking out the rubbish."

Some people seem to think that if they could just get away from their daily life pressures they would then experience intimacy with God. The opposite is the truth—intimacy comes as we learn to "practice His presence" in all things. No place is closer to God than where you are right now

In Eden there were no rituals—just a simple loving relationship between God and the people He created. Unhindered by guilt or fear, Adam and Eve delighted in God and He delighted in them. Is such a relationship possible today? Absolutely! It is called friendship with God and Paul reveals to us this wonderful news in Romans 5:10 (NLT): ". . . we were restored to friendship with God by the death of His Son."

Survival Guide for **May 21**

". . .WE'VE BEEN SURROUNDED AND BATTERED BY TROUBLES, BUT WE'RE NOT DEMORALIZED. . .'"
2 CORINTHIANS 4:8

Change and stress are both inevitable, but here are some steps you can take to help you cope with them:

—*Choose your battles.* Do you instinctively give in to fear and oppose change, even when it might benefit you? Do you think no issue is too small to be ignored? Do you keep throwing yourself across the tracks, hoping to stop the freight train of reality? If so, you need to choose your battles because waging war on too many fronts results in battle-fatigue. Choose battles only big enough to matter.

—*Work at becoming more adaptable.* What is your most common response to change? Dragging your feet? Assuming a "have to" attitude? Doing only what is necessary? Once we stop caring, life loses its sparkle and, ironically, we become even more stressed. Become resilient! Paul said, "I've learned (and he didn't learn it overnight) by now to be quite content whatever my circumstances" (Philippians 4:11).

—*Welcome new experiences.* When we move forward, our surroundings constantly change. Clinging to the familiar just buys comfort today at tomorrow's expense. Plunge into life instead of always testing the water.

—*Learn to live with uncertainty.* Always struggling to stay the same in a constantly changing world is like sweeping water uphill—as soon as you stop, you lose it. Learn to live with uncertainty; wing it a little more, instead of struggling to make sure that life always happens on your terms.

Survival Guide for **May 22**

"... WE'VE BEEN SURROUNDED AND BATTERED BY TROUBLES, BUT WE'RE NOT DEMORALIZED ..."
2 CORINTHIANS 4:8

Most people want to live stress-free without having to work at it, but it can't be done.

Here is a "Top 10 List" of things to do to make your life better:

1. Take time each day to pray and read God's Word: it will transform your outlook..

2. Take a vacation. If you look like your passport photo, you probably need one!

3. Develop better time-management habits.

4. Make room in your life for fun.

5. Maintain your sense of humor: "A cheerful disposition is good for your health; gloom and doom leave you bone-tired." (Proverbs 17:22).

6. Start counting your blessings: "I am overcome with joy because of Your unfailing love." (Psalm 31:7 NLT).

7. When you talk to yourself, say nice things.

8. Develop a sense of purpose by obeying God's Word.

9. Forgive; grudges are too heavy to carry: "If you refuse to forgive others, your Father will not forgive (you)." (Matthew 6:15 NLT).

10. Read the end of the book—God wins!

Survival Guide for **May 23**

"I'M AWAKE ALL NIGHT—NOT A WINK OF SLEEP; I CAN'T EVEN SAY WHAT'S BOTHERING ME." PSALM 77:4

When you can't sleep (even if it is because of chronic insomnia, like mine) —it's time to stop counting sheep and start talking to the Shepherd.

Here are some Biblical stress-relievers to live by:

—*Let go of what no longer works.* Hebrews 12:1 (NLT) says: ". . . let us strip off every weight that. hinders our progress . . ." The trouble is that we hate giving up what we do well. So, we focus on doing things right and end up failing to do the right things. Then we wonder why we don't succeed. There are limits to what anyone can carry. Letting go of what doesn't work frees us up to focus on what does.

—*Don't let change paralyze you.* In new situations for most of us our first inclination is to slow down, play it safe and buy ourselves some time. Sometimes that is wise but most times we just fall further behind. Being overly cautious can freeze us like a deer caught in the headlights. The Bible says that God ". . .gives power to the faint, and strengthens the powerless" (Isaiah 40:29 NRS). So trust Him and move forward, instead of giving in to the impulse to stand still and do nothing..

—*Approach the future with confidence.* Trying to figure out the future tends to put everybody on edge, but as children of God we can say, "I can lie down and sleep soundly because you, Lord, will keep me safe." (Psalm 4:8 CEV).

Stress is never relieved by giving in to fear.

The only way to prepare for tomorrow is by faithfully living fully today!.

Survival Guide for **May 24**

"BE QUICK TO GIVE A MEAL TO THE HUNGRY, A BED TO THE HOMELESS—CHEERFULLY." 1 PETER 4:9

A family who had guests over for dinner one evening asked their five-year-old to say grace. Puzzled, the child asked, "What should I say?" Her mother replied, "Just say what I always say". So, bowing her head, the little girl prayed, "Dear God, why did I invite these people to dinner anyway?"

The truth in that little joke is simple: hospitality is hard work. Hospitality involves sacrifice. Nevertheless, we are to "be quick to give a meal to the hungry . . . cheerfully."

Paul writes: "Make a habit of hospitality" (Romans 12:13 NAS).
Peter writes: "Be hospitable with brotherly affection for unknown guests, foreigners, the poor and all others." (1 Peter 4:9 Amp).

Had any unknown guests, foreigners, or poor folk over to dinner lately?

A man conducting a church survey wrote a letter to Dear Abby, (for international readers, "Dear Abby" is the pen name of a newspaper advice columnist) saying, "Of the 195 churches I visited, I was spoken to in only one by someone other than an 'official greeter'—and that was to ask me to move my feet!" How sad!

It is easy to extend hospitality to people we know, but Jesus said, "If all you do is love the loveable anybody can do that." (Matthew 5:46). So, how about those we don't know? Or those who don't fit our social circle? Sure, we can find excuses for being inhospitable: we are too busy, we don't have time to get involved, we are uncomfortable with strangers. But God says we are to be hospitable ". . . cheerfully". That elevates hospitality to a new level. It means it is worth the sacrifice of our personal agendas; it is worth giving our time and money to help people; it is worth going out on a limb for people—even those we don't know—and those we don't like.

True hospitality takes seeing others through God's eyes.

Are you hospitable?

Survival Guide for **May 25**

"EVERYTHING GOT STARTED IN HIM AND FINDS ITS PURPOSE IN HIM." COLOSSIANS 1:16

Since you didn't create yourself, there is no way you can tell yourself what you were created for. Only God can tell us that. Forget about self-actualization; it doesn't work. Life is about letting God use you for His purposes, not using Him for yours.

How can we discover God's purpose for our life? The Word says "It's in Christ that we find out who we are and what we are living for. Long before we first heard of Christ.[He] had designs on us for glorious living, part of the overall purpose He is working out in everything and everyone." (Ephesians 1:11).

Notice three things from these verses:

　　—We discover life's purpose only through a relationship with Christ
　　—God determined life's purpose before we existed—without our input.
　　—Your purpose fits into a much larger purpose.

Andrei Bitov, a Russian novelist, grew up under an atheistic, communist regime, but God got his attention. He wrote:

> "One dreary day while riding the Metro in St. Petersburg, I was overcome with a despair so great that life seemed to stop at once, preempting the future entirely, let alone any meaning. Suddenly, all by itself, a phrase appeared: without God life makes no sense. Repeating it in astonishment, I rode the phrase up like a moving staircase, got out of the Metro and walked into God"s light."

Are you looking for a greater sense of purpose?

Then give your life to Christ, because "Everything got started in Him and finds its purpose in Him."

Survival Guide for **May 26**

". . . SON, YOU DON'T UNDERSTAND. YOU'RE WITH ME ALL THE TIME, AND EVERYTHING THAT IS MINE IS YOURS."
LUKE 15:31

The prodigal son broke his dad's heart by leaving home, squandering his inheritance and living with pigs. Later, when he came back asking to live in the barn and work as a farmhand, he found that his father had left the porch light on and kept him a place at the table. In fact, he was so glad to see him that he threw a party.

But big brother wasn't about to celebrate little brother's return: "I have served and obeyed your commands. But you never gave me a feast. Your other son, who wasted money on prostitutes, comes home, and you kill the fat calf.." (Luke15:29-30 NCV).

The big brother is representative of those who lift themselves up by putting other people down.

Both sons did time in prison. One in the prison of rebellion, the other in the prison of resentment. One came home to a welcome, the other stayed home and wallowed in self-pity.

Because of jealousy he missed the party. Bitterness incarcerates us along with all those other victims of betrayal, abuse, the system, who have chained themselves to the walls of their prisons. Hurt held too long turns to hate. Let it go. Never forget that you are God's child and nothing can ever change that. Go to the feast. There is a seat reserved for you.

If you listen you can hear our Father saying to you, "Son, you're with Me all the time, and everything that is mine is yours."

Don't let a lousy attitude rob you of what God has in store for you today!

Survival Guide for **May 27**

―――

"BE GENTLE WITH ONE ANOTHER, SENSITIVE. FORGIVE ONE ANOTHER . . ." EPHESIANS 4:32

Henri Nouwen writes,

> We've all been wounded. Who wounds us? Those we love and those who love us. When we feel rejected, abandoned, abused, manipulated or violated, it's usually by people close to us: our parents, our friends, our marriage partners, our children, our teachers, our pastors. This is what makes forgiveness so difficult. It's our hearts that are wounded! We cry out, "You, who I expected to be there for me, have failed me. How can I ever forgive you for that?" Though forgiveness may seem impossible, nothing is impossible with God! The God Who lives within us will give us the grace to go beyond our wounded selves and say, "In the name of Christ, I forgive you."

There are two sides to forgiveness: giving and receiving. Although at first sight giving forgiveness seems harder, often we are not able to offer forgiveness—because we have not fully received it ourselves. Only as people who have tasted the joy of forgiveness can we find the inner motivation to give it.

Why is receiving forgiveness so difficult? Because it is hard to acknowledge, "Without your forgiveness, I am still affected by what happened between us. I need you to help set me free and make me whole again." That requires not only a confession that we have been hurt, but also the humility to admit our dependency on the very one who hurt us.

Only when we are able to receive forgiveness can we truly extend it to others.

Survival Guide for **May 28**

"(WE) HAVE RECEIVED THE SPIRIT OF ADOPTION BY WHICH WE CRY OUT 'ABBA! FATHER.'" ROMANS 8:15 (NASB)

Adoptive parents understand these words written by the Apostle Paul: "(We) have received the spirit of adoption by which we cry out 'Abba! Father.'" (Romans 8:15 NASB). They know what it means to have an emptiness in their hearts which causes them to set out on a mission hunting for a child to love. And when that child is found they take responsibility for the child regardless of a spotted past or a dubious future.

That is what God did for us. Knowing full well the trouble we would be and the price He would pay, He sought us, found us, paid an awesome price, signed the papers, gave us His name, took us home and gave us the right to call Him "Abba," which literally means, "Daddy." How can you help but love a God like that?

Adoption isn't something earned. Adoption is a gift received. Imagine prospective parents saying, "We would like to adopt little Johnnie, but first we want to know if he has a house for us to live in, money for college tuition, a ride to school in the morning and clothes to wear every day?" No agency would stand for such talk. They would rightfully say: "Wait a minute, you don't adopt little Johnnie because of what he has, you adopt him because of what he needs. He needs a home."

Paul didn't say we have earned the spirit of adoption. He said we have received it. That is important because, if we can't earn it by our stellar efforts, we can't lose it through our poor performance. How reassuring!

Why do any parents want a child? To love and to share their life with.

That is how God feels about each one of his adopted children today!

Survival Guide for **May 29**

"HE CREATES EACH OF US BY CHRIST JESUS TO JOIN HIM IN THE WORK HE DOES, THE GOOD WORK HE HAS GOTTEN READY FOR US TO DO, WORK WE HAD BETTER BE DOING" EPHESIANS 2:10

Here are a dozen principles to help get us doing the "work he has gotten ready for us to do:"

(1) Reject your sin, but never yourself.

(2) Be quick to repent. Unconfessed sin is like a ball and chain; holding you back.

(3) Be honest with God and yourself, about yourself.

(4) When God gives you light, walk in it. He will never command what He will not enable you to do.

(5) Stop putting yourself down, true humility is not self-deprecation.

(6) Never have an exaggerated opinion of your own importance.

(7) Do not always assume that when things go wrong, it is your fault. Admit when you are wrong; learn from it, then go on to become stronger and wiser.

(8) Beware of having yourself on your mind too much. Do not obsess over what you have done, right or wrong; either way you make yourself the center of your attention: "People with their minds set on you, you keep completely whole. . ." (Isaiah 26:3).

(9) Take care of yourself physically. Do the best you can with what God gave you, but do not be excessive or vain about your appearance—it is temporal at best.

(10) Do not allow your education to become a point of pride, or your lack of it, a source of shame. God does not use you because of your I.Q., He uses you because of your "I will."

(11) Your talents are a gift from God, not something you manufactured yourself, so do not look down on people who cannot do what you do.

(12) Do not despise your weaknesses—they keep you dependent on God.

Survival Guide for **May 30**

"YOU'VE ALL BEEN TO THE STADIUM AND SEEN THE ATHLETES RACE. EVERYONE RUNS; ONE WINS. RUN TO WIN." 1 CORINTHIANS 9:24

In life, you get to only run once, so run to win, To avoid stumbling and losing your place, don't look back. We can't change the past, but thank God we can learn from it and leave it behind. Don't be anxious about the next lap; focus only on the next step. After all, every fall starts with the next step.

Focus on one step after the other and before you know it, you will soon have more laps behind you than ahead of you. Make every lap count: "Let us run the race that is before us and never give up. We should remove from our lives anything that would get in the way and the sin that so easily holds us back." (Hebrews 12:1 NCV).

Many of us carry the weight and worry of burdens which older and wiser people understand are of no real importance. We spend our energies extinguishing fires that, if left alone, would burn out on their own. Time is our most valuable resource; using it wisely increases our assets and decreases our liabilities.

Get rid of the baggage of old relationships, pointless fears and false indebtedness to those who seek to manipulate you. There are enough painful trials in life; why endure the ones you can lay aside? When blind Bartimaeus heard that Jesus was within reach, he threw off his coat (lest it trip him up) and ran toward Him.

Today is a good day for each of us to do the same.

Survival Guide for **May 31**

"AND YOU PASSERSBY, LOOK AT ME! HAVE YOU EVER SEEN ANYTHING LIKE THIS?" LAMENTATIONS 1:12

A little girl was found dead in a big city housing project. Her mentally-ill mother had starved her to death, because she said she heard "voices" telling her that her child was "evil."

When police asked neighbors if they had seen anything unusual, they said they had noticed the child missing from the school bus, missing from the playground, even missing from Sunday school.

In fact, the people next door having heard her crying for days, turned their radio up to drown out her sobs! None of them did anything because nobody wanted to risk getting involved.

"Is it nothing to you, all you who pass by?" (Lam 1:12 NIV).

To the man who lay dying on the Jericho Road, the church folk who passed him by were worse than the robbers who beat him up, because more was expected of them.

Ultimately, we won't be judged by the degrees we have earned or the reputations we have built, but by our compassion: "Then those 'sheep' are going to say, 'Master, what are you talking about?' Then the King will say, 'I'm telling the solemn truth: Whenever you did one of these things (showing love and kindness) to someone overlooked or ignored, that was Me—you did it to Me.'" (Matt 25:34-40).

Is it risky to get involved? Absolutely. It is also costly. But somewhere between caution and indifference there must be a place for compassion. After all, if the world can't find mercy among those who call themselves "followers of Christ," where are they going to find it?

"And you passersby, look at me! Have you ever seen anything like this?" (Lam 1:12).

Survival Guide for **June 1**

"MAKE IT YOUR AMBITION TO LEAD A QUIET LIFE."
1 THESSALONIANS 4:11(NIV)

When Paul wrote, "Make it your ambition to lead a quiet life," he wasn't kidding—being quiet is hard work that doesn't just happen—we have to make it our ambition. But the result is worth the effort. The philosopher Plutarch wrote, "The first evil that attends those who know not how to be silent is that they hear nothing."

One of the kindest things you can do for anybody is—to listen.

People go to therapists and pay $100 an hour mostly for somebody to sit and listen to them. Once they feel they have been heard, they often can move quickly from the problem to the solution.

The trouble is that most of us are just too busy these days to listen. Unless the person who is talking to us has their thoughts already well put together we lose interest and mentally move on. It is amazing how many leaders and academic-types also fall into this category. How about you?

There are three major benefits that come from really listening to others:

(1) The more we listen, the less alone or unique we feel, for the truth we have more in common than we have differences.
(2) The more we listen, the better our assessment of any situation will be. Solomon says, "He who answers before listening—that is his folly and his shame." (Prov 18:13 NIV). Ouch!
(3) The more we listen, the more we understand, it is pretty much a given that we are not learning while we are talking. Again, Solomon says, "The heart of the discerning acquires knowledge; the ears of the wise seek it out." (Prov 18:15 NIV).

"Make it your ambition to lead a quiet life" includes working on controlling our tongues, opening our minds and developing better listening skills.

Make a "quiet life" your ambition today!

Survival Guide for **June 2**

"BE BRAVE. BE STRONG. DON'T GIVE UP. EXPECT GOD TO GET HERE SOON." PSALM 31:24

"The Serenity Prayer" is more than just pretty words:

> "God grant me the serenity
> to accept the things I cannot change,
> the courage to change the things I can,
> and the wisdom to know the difference."

Living by these principles will get us through suffering, keep us from growing sour and getting ulcers; it might even extend our lives.

A national study was done on the mortality rate among 4500 widowers within six months of the death of their wives. Compared with other men of the same age, these men had a 40 percent higher mortality rate. Why? Because they didn't accept the thing they could not change and gave up on life.

Howard Kushner, a medical officer and P.O.W. in Vietnam for five years, wrote about a marine who survived a Viet Cong prison camp for two years, because the camp commander promised to release him if he cooperated. Since this had been done for others before him, he actually became a model prisoner. But gradually, when he realized they'd lied to him, he became like a zombie. He refused to work, wouldn't eat and lay on his bed all day, sucking his thumb. In a matter of weeks he was dead. The VC abused him but they didn't defeat him—he defeated himself by giving up hope.

Even when the enemy destroyed King David's home and took his family prisoner, he "strengthened himself with trust in his God" (1 Sam 30:6). That is what it takes. "Be brave. Be strong. Don't give up. Expect God to get here soon." (Psalm 31:24)

So long as God is alive and we are still breathing, any situation can either be changed or accepted—by the grace of God!

Survival Guide for **June 3**

"... JUST SAY YES OR NO ..." JAMES 5:12

The most difficult word in the English language is "No."

It is easy enough to pronounce—it is just hard to say. Especially if we have been brought up to believe that good Christians, responsible parents, supportive spouses and dedicated workers never say "no."

We feel guilty when we say "No." We worry that people won't like us. And the truth is—some of them won't. But that is OK. Jesus said, "If the world hates you, keep in mind that it hated Me first." (John 15:18 NIV).

The truth is, the only way to avoid criticism is to say what everybody wants to hear. But the only way to do that is to either have no thoughts of our own or to live a falsehood.

When someone keeps abusing your kindness and all you say by word or deed is, "I don't mind, it is all right"—you are not telling the truth. It is not all right! You do mind! You are living a lie! Yes, people are speaking well of you; but if they're also stealing the life out of you, the price of their acceptance is too high.

Each time we say "yes" when we really mean "no," three not-so-good things happen to us:

1. We lose self-respect.
2. We harbor anger and often end up displacing it on those who don't deserve it.
3. We "stuff" our feelings and get depressed and isolated.

Refuse to live that way another day!

"Just say a simple yes or no, so that you will not sin." (Jas 5:12 TLB).

Survival Guide for June 4

"... I'VE OPENED A DOOR BEFORE YOU THAT NO ONE CAN SLAM SHUT ..." REVELATION 3:8

Today, God is giving you another chance at life—seize it! It is a day full of potential for good or evil, gain or loss. Either way, when the clock strikes midnight, it will be gone.

One open door God sets before us is the door of opportunity. Life's opportunities come at the speed of light, at 186,000 miles per hour and they can pass us by before we can understand where they went.

Opportunities begin with "daybreak:" "But Jacob stayed behind by himself, and a man wrestled with him until daybreak." (Gen 32:24). When the sun rose over his tent, Jacob discovered that God was offering him a new start, a new identity and a new way of living. He didn't have to go back to the way things were anymore.

Neither do we.

Each day God gives us another chance to right our wrongs, overcome our obstacles and embrace His will. Go through the door. Open it, then run—don't walk—through it. Get your running shoes and be ready, for opportunity won't wait for any of us—if we are not looking, we will miss it.

And whatever happens after you go through the door, remember, you had your chance. That is right—you had your chance to profess your love to a loved one, to answer the knock at the door, to say, "I am sorry" or "I forgive you" or "I am available, Lord."

So go ahead, walk through the open door, exercise your option and live each day to the max. Then before you go to bed each night you can look in the mirror and say, "God gave me this day of life and by His grace I lived it to the fullest."

Any day we can say that, has been a successful day!

Survival Guide for **June 5**

"GOD'S GLORY IS ON TOUR IN THE SKIES . . ." PSALM 19:1

Take a minute to reflect on God's celestial workshop. If you do your concept of Him will grow and your faith in Him will increase.

Look at the sun. Every square yard of it radiates 130,000 horsepower of energy—the equivalent of 45 eight cylinder engines. Yet, it's only one of millions of stars in the Milky Way. If the sun moved just two degrees without divine permission, it would mean catastrophe for us all.

Look at the earth. Weighing 6,000,000,000,000,000,000,000,000 (six sextrillion) tons and tilted at exactly 23 degrees—just right! Even one degree off and the seasons as we know them would disappear and we'd all drown in a colossal polar meltdown.

We are passengers on Planet Earth, an orb that has been traveling faster than the speed of sound for thousands of years, without once breaking down, blowing up or tumbling out of orbit. Ponder the intelligence that put it all together.

Then ponder these questions:

(1) If God is able to put each star in its own place, don't you think He is able to show you where you belong?

(2) If He is big enough to ignite the sun, isn't He big enough to light your pathway?

(3) If He can keep this incredible Planet Earth suspended on nothing (Job 6:27), could you have a problem for which He doesn't already have a solution?

Look around you at the creation that declares the glory of God and experience God tapping you on the shoulder and saying, "If I can do all this, don't you think I can handle your problems?"

Survival Guide for **June 6**

"A GOOD LIFE GETS PASSED ON TO THE GRANDCHILDREN." PROVERBS 13:22

Life is an investment. We can't squander it now, and still have what we want in the end.

Solomon wrote these strong words: ". . . look at an ant. . . let it teach you a thing or two. . . All summer it stores up food. . . it stockpiles provisions. So how long are you going to laze around doing nothing?. . . A nap here, a nap there, a day off here, a day off there, sit back, take it easy—do you know what comes next? . . . a dirt-poor life. . . " (Prov 6:6-11).

Waste your now, and you will end up in the winter of your life depressed and resentful, cursing a wasted youth. Ants stockpile. Birds build nests. All creation prepares, delaying gratification in the interests of a better future. I believe part of our fallen nature is our strong desire for instant gratification regardless of the consequences. The Bible calls it lust.

Prosperity and piety can abound in the same life. Indeed they should, for visions die for lack of funding.

". . . My chosen ones will long enjoy the works of their hands." (Isa 65:22 NIV).

"A good man leaves an inheritance for his children's children . . . " (Prov 13:22 NIV).

Certainly enjoy every moment of your now, but don't fail to invest for your future. Never forget that the future doesn't just happen—it comes from our now. Ask God to add days to your life, and life to your days.

Strive to leave a legacy that is a witness to our Heavenly Father, and an inheritance that blesses those who come after you.

Survival Guide for **June 7**

"STAY WHERE YOU WERE WHEN GOD CALLED YOUR NAME." 1 CORINTHIANS 7:20

This Survival Guide is for all my discontented single readers.

Learn to enjoy being single.

Instead of constantly struggling with your singleness, or trying to change it, discover its advantages. Here are three you might not have considered:

(1) You can hang out with your Christian friends every night of the week, or pray out loud at 3:00 o'clock in the morning, and nobody can tell you, you can't.

(2) You can cling totally to a God who can do everything instead of clinging to a person who can do some things.

(3) The greatest visitation of the Holy Spirit in history happened to a single girl named Mary.

Before you ask God for another partner, learn to minister to the One you have. If you can't treat the perfect Partner right, how would you handle an imperfect one? There is nothing wrong with wanting to be married; just learn to take care of the Lord while you are waiting.

When God picks a partner for us, He always picks from among those who are faithful to Him. When you have proven you can keep your vow to Him, maybe He will trust you to keep it to somebody else. Commit yourself fully to God today. Bond with Him. Learn to relate to Him as the Lover of your Soul.

When you can do that, single or not, you will be whole.

Survival Guide for June 8

───

"... WATCH YOUR STEP. USE YOUR HEAD." EPHESIANS 5:15

If we don't "watch your step" we will end up wandering in the wilderness, delaying our growth, avoiding our calling, denying who we really are, and focusing on lesser things instead of lofty things. This wandering around is not the walk we are called to; it is not worthy of who we are, or what we are supposed to be as those who walk with Jesus! Our mandate is to be light, to expel the darkness, and to bring healing to the hurting. But to do that, we have to walk God's way, not our own.

Here are some guidelines for walking with God to think about today:

1. Walking with God is a responsible walk. We are supposed to bring honor to the One who saved us by staying on the path He has designated for us in order to demonstrate His character and compassion to all we meet. Are you walking responsibly?

2. Walking with God is a Spirit-empowered walk. We must continuously rely on God's ability, and not our own, in order to succeed. If by nature you're self-sufficient, you will have to work on having a Spirit-empowered walk each day.

3. Walking with God is a Word-directed walk. It is not based on our ideas or perceptions, but on the very mind and heart of God, which He has revealed to us in His Word. Are you walking a Word-directed walk?

4. Walking with God is a relational walk. Not one of us is walking alone—we are walking hand in hand with Jesus and our brothers and sisters in God's family. A relational walk is what gives us the collective power to reach and transform this world.

The truth is, our walk can bring results and rewards which reach far beyond our own little sphere of influence—in this life, and in the one to come.

No wonder we are told to "... watch your step. Use your head."

Survival Guide for **June 9**

". . . DON'T FORGET A SINGLE BLESSING!" PSALM 103:2

Over 10,000 people a day are told that their condition is terminal.

The testimony most common to those who have been told the stark truth that their life will soon end is "Things I've taken for granted, like my health, my family, and my friends, have suddenly become all-important to me. Trivialities no longer matter."

It shouldn't take a death sentence for us to make us stop taking the really important things in life for granted. David wrote, ". . . don't forget a single blessing!" (Ps 103:2).

We all have so many things we take for granted!

If you woke up this morning, you are ahead of the million people who didn't survive the week. If you sat down, read the paper and drank a cup of coffee, you're better off than the 500 million men, women and children around the world who are presently experiencing the horrors of war, the loneliness of imprisonment, the agony of torture, or the pangs of starvation.

If you attended church Sunday without threat, you exercised a freedom envied by two billion others who gathered together under threat or who had no church available to them. If you have food, clothes, and a roof over your head, you're richer than 75% of the earth's inhabitants. (Actually, our garbage can eats better that most of the people in the world!)

If you have money in the bank, you are among the world's top 8 percent financially. If you have a Bible, you are better off than the 1.5 billion people who have no Bible available in their own language.

If you are reading this you are ahead of one-third of the people on the planet who are illiterate.

If you have fallen into the trap of expecting much but appreciating little, now is the time to remember, repent, and gain a little perspective!

Survival Guide for **June 10**

". . . GOD'S PEOPLE SHOULD BE BIG-HEARTED AND COURTEOUS" TITUS 3:2

I like the story of the two taxidermists who stopped to look at an owl on display in a window. Immediately their criticisms started. Its eyes weren't natural; its wings weren't in proportion to its head; its feathers weren't properly arranged. Then just as they started to walk away—the owl turned its head and winked at them!

Before you criticize, ask yourself these questions:

  a. Have I waited long enough to get all the facts? What do I not know yet?

  b. Am I relying strictly on what I have heard? Am I eager to believe the best, or think the worst?

  c. If mistakes have been made, do I feel that gives me the upper hand? If so, what am I going to do about it?

  d. What would Jesus do?

  e. Will my actions add to the problem or to the solution? If the situation was reversed and I was on the other end, what would I need?

  f. Am I magnifying something which, in a month or two, will make little or no difference but could hurt my future relationship with this person?

Read carefully these words of Jesus: "Don't pick on people, jump on their failures, criticize their faults—unless, of course, you want the same treatment. Don't condemn those who are down; that hardness can boomerang. Be easy on people; you'll find life a lot easier." (Lk 6:37).

Live by these words and you and everyone around you will be happier!

Survival Guide for **June 11**

"BECAUSE OF THE SACRIFICE OF THE MESSIAH, HIS BLOOD POURED OUT ON THE ALTAR OF THE CROSS, WE'RE A FREE PEOPLE. . ." EPHESIANS 1:7

Stop worrying about your condition and start focusing on your position.

Our condition is temporary; circumstances and behavior change all the time. But our position in Jesus is unchanging. Paul says, "anyone united with the Messiah gets a fresh start, is created new . . . " (2 Cor 5:17). That means if we and "united with the Messiah" we are forgiven, and are a free people—present tense.

Redemption depicts a person in prison under a death sentence who is pardoned and released. That is the story of each one of us. Because of our sin we are in prison under a death sentence. But when God, the judge, sees the blood of Jesus on us, all claims against us are thrown out of court, our prison door swings open, and we are set free. Pardoned! Awesome! Even more so because no matter how hard we try or how dedicated we become, we couldn't, in fifty lifetimes, pay off our debt and earn our own freedom. Only Jesus could do that, because only He could offer up the ransom: a life completely free from sin.

But a pardon does no good unless the prisoners know about it. And the last person on earth who wants them to know is the prison keeper. The prison keeper knows that if the prisoners don't know they are free, they will remain in bondage in their minds, and live in bondage as prisoners even though they are free. We are prisoners who have been set free by Christ. The devil is the prison keeper who wants to keep us in bondage.

So when the devil points to your condition, remind him of your position. Tell him, "All right, I did wrong because some areas are still under construction, but I am still loved, accepted, and approved one-hundred-percent by God who has redeemed me through the blood of Jesus and I am free and I am no longer your prisoner!"

Survival Guide for **June 12**

―――

"JESUS SAID, " GET UP, TAKE YOUR BEDROLL, START WALKING." THE MAN WAS HEALED ON THE SPOT . . . "
JOHN 5:8

Picture a wretched street in Calcutta, and you will have an idea of what people witnessed at the Pool of Bethesda.

What did they hear? Endless groans.
What did they see? Faceless need.
What did they do? Walk on by.

But not Jesus; He healed a paralyzed man who had spent 38 miserable years lying on a bed.

But why, when Jesus healed him, did He tell this man to take up his bed and walk? Two reasons occur to me:

(1)   His bed would serve as a constant reminder of what he had been delivered from.

Q: Why did God tell His ancient people to put tassels on the corners of their garments?

A: To help them remember His commandments and obey them.

Q: Why did God tell them to build a monument of stones taken from the Jordan River?

A: To remind them of Who had parted the waters and brought them safely through.

Q: Why did God tell them to keep the Passover?

A: To remind them that their very existence depended on Him.

 (2) His bed would confirm the truth of his healing.

When people asked, "Did that really happen?" there would be evidence; like Jacob's limp.

God knows that although not all of us are fast learners, we are all quick forgetters! So, don't forget your "bedroll."

Survival Guide for **June 13**

". . . IT'S WHAT WE TRUST IN BUT DON'T YET SEE THAT KEEPS US GOING." 2 CORINTHIANS 5:7

A traveler in the Far East was watching a tapestry-maker seemingly shouting instructions at a loom, and threads suddenly appeared in a tapestry. When he asked for an explanation, his guide said, "The man you see is the master weaver. He is shouting to his apprentice behind the loom, telling him what color of thread to use, and where to put it. Only the master knows the design, so the apprentice has to listen carefully and do exactly as he says."

"What happens if the apprentice gets it wrong?" the traveler asked.

"Well," replied the guide, "the master, being the artist that he is, just works it into the design."

Do you feel as if you are standing on the wrong side of the tapestry today, looking at a bunch of knots and threads that seem to have no real purpose? And just when you think you are starting to understand, the Master calls for a thread that changes everything? Don't worry, God is the master Weaver who knows exactly what He is doing.

And don't be so hard on yourself. When you put a blue thread where a red one is supposed to be, or tie a knot in the wrong place, God doesn't fall off His throne.

God takes our mistakes and works them into His overall design.

I, for one, am very glad for that, aren't you?

Survival Guide for **June 14**

"... HE HAD ... DESIGNS ON US FOR GLORIOUS LIVING ..."
EPHESIANS 1:11

Consider this quote from Dean Alfange:

> I do not choose to be a common man. It is my right to be uncommon if I can. I seek opportunity, not security. I do not wish to be a kept citizen, humbled and dulled by having the company look after me. I want to take the calculated risk, to dream and to build, to fail and to succeed. I refuse to barter incentive for a dole. I prefer the challenges of life to the guaranteed existence; the thrill of fulfillment to the stale calm of Utopia. I will not trade freedom for beneficence, nor dignity for a hand-out. It is my heritage to think and act for myself, to enjoy the benefits of my creations, to face the world boldly and say, "This I have done."

That sounds like another man, who wrote,

> This is the only race worth running. I've run hard right to the finish, believed all the way. All that's left now is the shouting—God's applause! Depend on it, he's an honest judge. He'll do right not only by me, but by everyone eager for his coming. (2 Tim 4:7,8).

In the movie *Rain Man* Dustin Hoffman plays a savant: a person who, in a sea of disabilities, has an island of genius. The character he plays In the movie is incredibly gifted with numbers. Other savants have amazing abilities in art and music. The truth is, all of us arrived equipped and empowered to do something special. You have an island of genius inside you. God's given you a gift, no matter how surrounded it may be by a sea of disadvantages. Believe it! Discover it! Develop it! Cherish it! Use it! Glorify God with it!

That is the key to "glorious living."

Survival Guide for **June 15**

**"SMART PEOPLE KNOW HOW TO HOLD THEIR TONGUE;
THEIR GRANDEUR IS TO FORGIVE AND FORGET."
PROVERBS 19:11**

Our emotional intensity level is like the volume level on a sound system; when it Is set too high the risk is run of blowing out the speakers and ruining the system.   To much emotional intensity and we run the risk of blowing everything out of proportion and ruining our relationships.   One disagreement, and we're headed into a new relationship.   Our ride is five minutes late, and it's World War III.   And let's not even talk about how we behave when we're behind the wheel of a car!

Solomon wrote: "Do not be quickly provoked . . . for anger resides in the lap of fools." (Ecc 7:9 NIV).

So, how is your volume level these days?   When it is set too high, your emotions dictate your reactions, you talk without thinking, and you leave a trail of bitterness and pain.   Dad, every time you storm out of the house because you don't get what you want, when you want, the way you want it, has it occurred to you that you are teaching your children to do the same?   Mom, when your daughter hears you say, "All men are alike; they are no good," has it dawned on you that she might grow up never trusting, or allowing herself to be emotionally available to anybody?   How will you feel living with that?

Reduce the volume!   Lower the intensity level!   Destinies are being shaped by your words, your behavior, and your attitudes.   God says, "Refrain from anger and turn from wrath; do not fret—it leads only to evil." (Ps 37:8 NIV).

Today, turn down the volume!

Survival Guide for **June 16**

―――

"... HIS MERCIES BEGIN AFRESH EACH DAY."
LAMENTATIONS 3:23 (NLT)

Recently I came across this story, I liked it and thought I'd pass it along:

> A carpenter I hired had just finished a rough first day
> on the job. A flat tire made him lose an hour of work,
> his electric saw quit on him, and now his ancient pick-
> up truck refused to start. As I drove him home, he sat
> in stony silence. On arriving, he invited me in to meet
> his family. As we walked toward the front door, he
> paused briefly at a small tree and touched the tips of its
> branches with both hands. As he opened the door, he
> suddenly underwent an amazing transformation. His
> tanned face was wreathed in smiles; he hugged his two
> small children and gave his wife a kiss.
>
> Afterward as he walked with me to the car, we passed
> the tree again, and my curiosity got the better of me. So
> I asked him about what I had seen him do earlier. "Oh,
> that's my trouble tree," he replied. "I know I can't
> avoid having troubles on the job, but one thing's for
> sure, they don't belong at home with my wife and
> children. So, I just hang them on the tree every night,
> then in the morning I pick them up again. Funny thing
> is, when I come out in the morning—there aren't as
> many as I remember hanging there the night before."

Isn't that a great story? I think it illustrates perfectly this Biblical truth:
"The unfailing love of the Lord never ends . . . His mercies begin afresh
each day" (Lam 3:22-23 NLT).

I think all of us probably need a trouble tree, don't you?

Survival Guide for **June 17**

". . . IF WE GIVE UP ON HIM, HE DOES NOT GIVE UP . . ."
2 TIMOTHY 2:13

Even people with great faith occasionally flat-line, and God has to resuscitate them: "If we are faithless, He will remain faithful. . . " (2 Tim 2:13 NIV).

Those words relieve us of having to pretend that we never doubt. They liberate us from always having to look like perfect believers who never feel afraid, or alone, or question God when His decisions override our petitions. When our faith crashes and burns, He remains faithful.

Jesus told Thomas he had no faith, and Peter that he had little faith, yet He remained faithful to both of them. The incredible truth is, His faith continues when ours has expired. When we're at our best, it's sometimes hard to tell who has accomplished things. But when we're at our worst it is wonderful to see how much Jesus can achieve in spite of us, rather than because of us.

Paul wrote, "I have been crucified with Christ. My ego is no longer central. It is no longer important that I appear righteous before you or have your good opinion, and I am no longer driven to impress God. Christ lives in me. The life you see me living is not "mine," but it is lived by faith in the Son of God, who loved me and gave himself for me." (Gal 2:20).

When our joy has been crucified by adversity, and our faith falters, what is it that keeps us going? The indwelling "faith in the Son of God!"

Life will occasionally hand us things you don't know how to live with. When that happens, His faith continues, even though ours has collapsed. It's then we realize that Jesus carried us through the funeral, or the divorce, or the sickness, or the moral failure.

Spiritual maturity is us growing up into His faith—not our own!

Survival Guide for **June 18**

"WHAT A WILDLY WONDERFUL WORLD, GOD! YOU MADE IT ALL, WITH WISDOM AT YOUR SIDE. . ." PSALM 104:24

While speaking at the famous free speech arena in Hyde Park, London, author Frank Sheed was talking about the remarkable order and design of the universe, when a heckler shouted, "Even I could make a better universe than your God!" Unruffled, Sheed replied, "I won't ask you to do that today, but would you mind making a rabbit just to establish credibility?"

Nature is a powerful testimony to a creator. Consider this:

—If the Earth was as small as Mercury, its gravitation couldn't sustain the atmosphere we need. On the other hand, if the Earth were as large as Jupiter, its extreme gravitation would squash us like bugs. If Earth were as close to the sun as Venus, the heat would be unbearable; if it were as far away as Mars, every region would experience snow and ice nightly.

—If the oceans were half their size, we would get only 25% of our present rainfall. If they were one-eighth larger, annual precipitation would increase 400% turning the earth into a vast, uninhabitable swamp. Water solidifies at 32 degrees Fahrenheit. But if the oceans were subject to that law, the amount of thawing in the polar regions wouldn't balance out and we'd all end up encased in ice. The salt in the sea to alters its freezing point thus preventing this catastrophe.

David said, "How many are Your works, O Lord! In wisdom You made them all . . . I will sing praise to my God as long as I live." (Psalm 104:24-33 NIV).

If God's workmanship doesn't make you want to stop and praise Him, you need to stop and smell the roses!

Survival Guide for **June 19**

". . . IN ACCORDANCE WITH THE MEASURE OF FAITH GOD HAS GIVEN YOU." ROMANS 12:3 (NIV)

When it comes to building muscle, how much weight you lift is not as important as how many repetitions you do. The more "reps," the stronger you become. So it is with our faith. The weight of our trials is not as important as how many times we lift them. We develop the faith needed to handle the next crisis by surviving the last. We know that since God brought us through that, He can also bring us through this.

It is necessary to experience both success and failure, for built into each is the ability to grow stronger and wiser. David destroyed Goliath, because he had "faith-trained" with a lion and a bear! He also refused to wear King Saul's armor, because he knew he couldn't use somebody else's workout regime to kill Goliath.

Neither can we: "I can't even move with all this stuff on me. I'm not used to this." (1 Sam 17:39).

What you are going through right now is just equipping you to handle what God has for you in the future. It has been allowed so that you can work on your training formula. Have you ever noticed how certain people can lose everything, yet a few years later they're back on top again? That is because they know the formula for success, and that is better than the riches, for the formula will work anywhere. If you can cook, you can cook anywhere. If you can sing, you can sing anywhere. Learn God's training formula for your life and it will work regardless of the circumstances.

Use whatever situation you are in right now as a "faith-training" opportunity!

Survival Guide for **June 20**

"... GO ON YOUR WAY, FROM NOW ON, DON'T SIN."
JOHN 8:11

Can you imagine being caught in the act of adultery? And worse, all the local stalwarts of the faith want to stone you? That was the scene when Jesus stepped in, saved this woman, and said to her, "Go on your way, from now on, don't sin." I imagine Jesus' critics saying, "What do you mean go and don't sin? If she couldn't live that way before, how will she manage it now?" Of course what they were ignoring is that Jesus gives "... the authority (power, privilege, right) to become the children of God..." (John 1:12 AMP).

When we meet Jesus, He gives us the power to become something better. It is as if a light comes on and we discover that now we no longer need what we thought we needed before.

The affair is over. She is now free from what drove her to it. So are we.

If you have met Jesus and heard him say "... go on your way, from now on, don't sin." you now have the power to unhook from that person (or substance, or habit), walk away and say, "I am done with that!" You don't need a long drawn-out discussion or a confrontation or a redefining. Just know, believe and keep telling yourself until it lodges in your soul: "I am not vulnerable to that anymore." Leave it behind! Exercise your spiritual freedom.

Here are four truths about spiritual freedom worth remembering:

1. Those who have used you, for their own advantage, will not take kindly to the fact that you are not available to them anymore.
2. When God looses you from something, it is to join you to something better, otherwise you will go back and seek out your old connections.
3. When Jesus quenches your thirst, you will not have to go back to the old dry wells any more.
4. As you develop a relationship with Jesus, you will begin to attract the right kind of people into your life.

Jesus is saying to you today "... go on your way, from now on, don't sin."

Survival Guide for **June 21**

"... THERE WAS A WAS A SPLIT IN THE CROWD OVER HIM."
JOHN 7:43

Motivational speaker Wayne Dyer tells this story:

> I came home from school one day and asked my mom,
> "What's a scurvy elephant?" She told me she'd never
> heard of one, and asked where I had heard it. I replied,
> "From my teacher." When my mother called the
> teacher, he told her, "As usual, Wayne got it wrong. I
> didn't say he was a scurvy elephant; I said he was a
> disturbing element!"

Do people see you as a disturbing element? They did Jesus. His enemies
said, "He's stirring up unrest among the people. . . " (Lk 23:5). Imagine
that: The Prince of Peace was also the Great Disturber!

Daniel refused to eat the King's meat or bow to his gods, because he had
been sent to bring change, not build a consensus. When we compromise
what is right to gain acceptance with people, we forfeit it with God. We
all have a choice to make! Each of us are where we are today for a reason.
The question each of us need to answer is: Am I willing to become a
disturbing element in order to fulfill God's purpose for putting me where I
am?

Joseph Bayly writes,

> Lord of reality, make me real, not plastic. I don't want
> to keep a prayer list, I want to pray. I don't want to
> agonize to find Your will, I want to obey what I
> already know. I don't want to explain the difference
> between eros, philos, and agape. I just want to love. I
> don't want to tell it like it is, I want to be like You
> want it.

Make that your prayer today too.

Then go be a "scurvy elephant!"

Survival Guide for **June 22**

"WHAT MATTERS IS NOT YOUR HAIR, JEWELERY, CLOTHES...CULTIVATE INNER BEAUTY." 1 PETER 3:3

Fashion designers are concerned with the outward appearance of the models they send down the catwalk. They must have perfect accessories, the right hairstyle and make-up, and the current body shape that is in vogue. Thank goodness it is not that way with God. He created each of us as a whole person with specific features, personality traits and emotional responses. He designed us to be a vibrant, thinking, feeling, fully functioning human being with our own unique attractiveness.

He endowed us with more than just physical appearance (can I hear an amen!). He also gave each of us talents and spiritual gifts—inner qualities He wants developed and displayed for His glory. You see, who you are on the inside should determine how you see yourself on the outside. When your "looks" determines your sense of worth, a few extra pounds or a bad-hair day can wipe you out.

Refuse to live that way! The Bible says, "What matters is not your hair, jewelery, clothes, but your inner disposition. Cultivate inner beauty, the kind that God delights in." (1 Peter 3:3-4).

When your sense of worth comes from God instead of men, you can wear a $5 outfit from a charity shop or a $500 one from an upscale boutique and feel fine either way, because you recognize that your outer appearance doesn't define who you are.

Inner beauty can't be bought, taken off a rack, applied like make-up or put on like a new suit. It's an inside job that always finds a creative and appropriate expression on the outside.

Look at yourself today in God's mirror and try to see what He values most —your inner beauty.

Survival Guide for **June 23**

"I ASK HIM TO STRENGTHEN YOU BY HIS SPIRIT--NOT A BRUTE STRENGTH BUT A GLORIOUS INNER STRENGTH." EPHESIANS 3:16

Dr. Phil, a popular celebrity counselor, recently told his television audience:

> "A lady flew across the nation to tell me how her husband had left her for another woman. The woman who came to see me was young, vibrant and beautiful. But suddenly she pulled out a photograph and said, 'Just look at her! He left me for that!' Sadly I thought, 'Ma'am, what you've been conditioned by society to think of as being all-important, really isn't. Outer appearance isn't the biggest issue at all.'"

Advertisers spend billions to get us to decorate a shell that is in a losing battle with Mother Nature and Father Time; all to create what we think will attract others. What we create may momentarily turn a head or two, but it has little or no ability to capture and hold a heart or mind. We think that by enrolling at the latest health club, using the right toothpaste, being seen in the right places with the right people, we will end up enjoying the right kind of life. And when it doesn't work, we get depressed and wonder what went wrong.

Certainly there is nothing wrong with wanting to look our best, but when we become obsessed with our looks we become shallow and superficial. Others quickly lose interest, because they discover that although the box we came in is beautifully wrapped—it is empty.

The real source of attractiveness is "a glorious inner strength." That is what ultimately wins hearts and attracts the right people, for the right purpose, at the right time.

Today, stop gazing into society's mirror and look deeply into God's mirror instead!

Survival Guide for **June 24**

"MARTHA, DEAR MARTHA, YOU'RE FUSSING FAR TOO MUCH AND GETTING YOURSELF WORKED UP OVER NOTHING." LUKE 10:41

Erma Bombeck writes:

> I'm good at worrying. I worry about making introductions and going blank when I get to my mother, or what the dog thinks when he sees me coming out of the shower, or that one of my kids will marry an Eskimo and set me adrift on an iceberg when I'm no longer able to feed myself!

I think Martha could relate to Erma! Martha was so worried that she even tried to tell Jesus what to do: "My sister has left me to do the work. Tell her to help me!" (Luke 10:40 NIV). Worry makes her forget who is servant and who is Lord. Note three things:

(1) Martha was busy serving, but she wasn't enjoying it. Doubtless, she wanted to please Jesus; it Is just that she allowed the work of the Lord to become more important to her than the Lord of the work. Has that happened to you?

(2) Satan didn't take Martha out of the kitchen, he just stole her purpose for being there. He doesn't turn you against the church, he just makes you focus on yourself. He doesn't take away your ministry, he just disillusions you by saying you are overworked, underpaid and unappreciated.

(3) God values our attitude more than our service. Jesus said, "One thing only is essential. Mary has chosen it. . ."(Luke 10:42) And what was it? Mary worshipped at Jesus' feet.

"Do everything without complaining" (Philippians 2:14 NIV). A bad attitude spoils the gift brought to the altar. Jesus prefers the quiet devotion of a sincere heart to the noisy attitude of a complainer. I have never met a complainer who was not a worrier. The message of Martha is not that serving is wrong but rather that worry can cause us to serve from the wrong motives.

Today, vow to serve God as an act of worship instead of as a means of alleviating worry!

Survival Guide for **June 25**

". . .WHAT DO WE DO THEN TO GET IN ON GOD'S WORKS?" JESUS SAID, "THROW YOUR LOT IN WITH THE ONE THAT GOD HAS SENT. . ." JOHN 6:28-29

An old man took his first flight on an airplane. After he got off the plane, somebody asked him what he thought of it. "Fine," he replied, "but I never did put my whole weight on it."

Ridiculous? Of course it is, but no more ridiculous that when we refuse to put our whole weight on the finished work of Calvary.

Satan is sneaky. Instead of leading us away from God's grace, he makes us question it or try to earn it. When the disciples asked Jesus, "What does God want us to do?" He didn't say work harder, pray longer, give more. Instead, He said, "Believe in the One He has sent."

When the Philippian jailer asked, "What do I have to do to be saved, to really live?" They said, "Put your entire trust in the Master Jesus. Then you'll live as you were meant to live." (Acts 16:30-31). Salvation is about believing—not behaving! Does that mean God doesn't require obedience? Not at all. God requires both. Acts 16:33 tells us that the Philippian jailer and his family were baptized that same night.

The problem is we don't have enough of either to qualify: ". . .be holy and blameless in his sight." (Ephesians 1:4 NIV). "Blameless?" Wow! The only way any of us will pull that off, is if God credits some of His righteousness to our accounts. And He does! Charles Wesley wrote: "Clothed in His righteousness alone, faultless to stand before Thy throne. On Christ the solid rock I stand; all other ground is sinking sand."

So how can we be "holy and blameless?" By abandoning our own efforts and trusting in Christ alone. That means putting our whole weight on Him and trusting Him enough to obey Him as The Father empowers us to do so.

Then and only then can we can stand before God in His righteousness, not our own!.

Survival Guide for June 26

"LET THE WORD OF CHRIST—THE MESSAGE—HAVE THE
RUN OF THE HOUSE. GIVE IT PLENTY OF ROOM IN YOUR
LIVES. . ." COLOSSIANS 3:16

How does the Spirit of God make us like the Son of God? Through the
Word of Christ. That's why Satan fights to keep us from reading our
Bibles: "(God's) gracious Word can make you into what He wants you to
be and give you everything you could possibly need."(Acts 20:32).

Especially pay attention to the word "Everything."

God's Word is seed. It is filled with potential life. Jesus said "The words
that I have spoken to you are life" (John 6:63 NAS). When we hear from
God, things suddenly come to life in us.

The Bible is more than just a doctrinal guidebook; it generates life, creates
faith, produces change, frightens the devil, causes miracles, heals hurts,
builds character, transforms circumstances, imparts joy, overcomes
adversity, defeats temptation, infuses hope, releases power, cleanses our
minds, brings things into being, and guarantees our future forever.

We can't survive spiritually without God's Word. It is as essential to our
life as food. Job said, "I have treasured the words of His mouth more than
my daily bread." (Job 23:12 NIV). God's Word is the spiritual
nourishment we need to fulfill our life's purpose.

The Bible is called our milk, bread, solid food and sweet dessert (see 1
Peter 2:2; Matthew 4:4; 1 Corinthians 3:2; Psalm 119:103). This four-
course meal is the Spirit's menu for daily strength and growth. Peter
writes, "crave pure spiritual milk, so that by it you may grow up." (1 Peter
2:2 NIV).

Today, do whatever it takes: rearrange your priorities, sacrifice lesser
things, discipline yourself, but make a commitment to spend time daily in
God's Word!

Survival Guide for **June 27**

"LET THE WORD OF CHRIST—THE MESSAGE—HAVE THE RUN OF THE HOUSE. GIVE IT PLENTY OF ROOM IN YOUR LIVES. . ." COLOSSIANS 3:16

Are you suffering from spiritual malnutrition?

Spiritual malnutrition can be hidden until a crisis hits. For your soul to prosper, God's Word must become your first priority. Jesus said, "If you abide in My Word, then you are truly disciples of Mine" (John 8:31 NAS).

What does it mean to abide in God's Word?

It means accepting God's Word as our highest authority. It means God's Word becoming the compass we rely on for direction, the counsel we listen to for making wise decisions, the benchmark we use for evaluating every relationship and action. In other words, it must be the first and last Word in our lives.

Most of our troubles occur because we base our choices on such unreliable authorities as:

> culture – "Everybody's doing it"
> tradition – "We have always done it this way"
> reason – "It seems logical"
> emotion –"It just feels right".

All these authorities are flawed because they come from us, not God. What we need is a perfect standard that will never lead us in the wrong direction. Only God's Word rises to that standard. Solomon says, "Every Word of God is flawless" (Proverbs 30:5 NIV).

These words from the Apostle Paul should become your rule-of-life: "I believe everything that is Written." (Acts 24:14 NIV)

When God tells you to do something trust His Word and just do it!

Survival Guide for **June 28**

"LET THE WORD OF CHRIST—THE MESSAGE—HAVE THE RUN OF THE HOUSE. GIVE IT PLENTY OF ROOM IN YOUR LIVES . . ." COLOSSIANS 3:16

Reading, receiving, researching, remembering and reflecting on God's Word are useless—unless you "act on what you hear" (James 1:22). This is the hardest step of all because Satan fights it intensely. We can get so focused on not missing the next Bible Study that we fail to put into practice what we learned at the last one.

Jesus said, "Everyone who hears these words of Mine and puts them into practice is like a wise man who built his house on the rock." (Matthew 7:24 NIV). The safety of the "rock" comes from obeying the truth, not just knowing it: "Now that you know these things, you will be blessed if you do them." (John 13:17 NIV). Want to be blessed? Start doing what God says.

One of the reasons we avoid personal application is because it is difficult, even painful. The truth will set us free, but first it often will make us miserable! God's Word reveals our motives, exposes our flaws, rebukes our sin and demands change. That is why we need to discuss our personal applications with others. We learn from others truths we would never learn on our own. Others help us to see and apply what we miss.

The best way to "act on what you hear" is to write out an action plan. Your plan should be personal (involving you); practical (something you can do); provable (with a deadline to do it). D L Moody said, "The Bible was not given to increase our knowledge, but to change our lives." To which I say, Amen!

If your Bible knowledge is greater than your Biblical practice, don't stop learning—just start putting what you learn into practice.

Make yourself a Bible action plan and then stick to it!

Survival Guide for **June 29**

"... CONDUCT YOUR LIVES IN LOVE..." 2 JOHN 1:6

Before you get up in the morning and rush into your day, pause and pray: "Lord, don't let me waste this day. Whether or not I get anything else done, help me to spend today loving You and loving others because that is what your Word says life is all about."

The more time we give to someone, the more we reveal their importance to us. It is not enough to tell them they are important; we must prove it by investing time in them. The best way to spell "love" is T—I—M—E! The essence of love is not what we think or feel about others rather the essence of love is how much we give of ourselves to them.

Men tend to have a harder time understanding this than women. Lots of husbands say, "I don't understand my wife and kids. I provide everything they need. What more could they want?" They want—you! They want focused attention. Love concentrates so intently on another that it forgets itself. That kind of attention says, "I value you enough to give you my most precious asset—my time." This is true whether you are a working dad or a guy in college. Of course, it is true for women as well as men, but most women I know do a better job of living this out than most men I know.

NOW is the best time to express our love because we don't know how long we will have the opportunity to do so. Circumstances change. People die. Children grow up. Friends move away. We have no guarantee of tomorrow.

There is no better time to express your love than right now.

Who do you need to start spending more time with? What do you need to cut out of your schedule to make that possible? The best use of life is love. The best expression of love is time.

The best time to love is—NOW!

Survival Guide for **June 30**

"I LOOK UP. . ." PSALM 121:1

(1) Wake up. Life is not a dress rehearsal. Live each day as though you will not be around tomorrow—for you might not be.

(2) Dress up. When you get up each morning, put on a good attitude; attitude determines how you view your day. Life is like a piano; everything depends on how we play it. Only 10% is about what happens to us; the other 90% is about how we respond to it.

(3) Shut up. You are not learning while you're talking: "He who guards his lips guards his (soul)."(Proverbs 13:3 NIV). You will save yourself untold heartache and impress others by listening, observing, and speaking only after you have thought things through.

(4) Stand up. Establish your values and your vision according to God's Word—nothing else. Not everybody will agree, nonetheless: ". . . stand firm. Let nothing move you." (1 Corinthians 15:58 NIV).

(5) Reach up. Paul wrote, "I keep trying to reach the goal and get the prize for which God called me." (Philippians 3:14 NCV). Focus on your goals. Refuse to settle for less than God's highest and best

(6) Lift up. Max Lucado writes, "Worship is a 'thank you' that refuses to be silenced; an act of gratitude offered by the saved to the Savior, the healed to the Healer and the blessed to the Blesser." So lift up your voice in praise today.

(7) Look up. Follow David's example, "I look up . . . my strength comes from God . . ." (Psalm 121:1-2)

Survival Guide for **July 1**

"TAKE GOOD COUNSEL AND ACCEPT CORRECTION—THAT'S THE WAY TO LIVE WISELY AND WELL." PROVERBS 19:20

What exactly should a coach do?
(1) Observe
(2) Instruct
(3) Inspire.

At first, the thought of having someone evaluate you may be intimidating. But think about it this way: people are watching you anyway, so why not plant a coach amongst the crowd? The following is a list of areas in which you might consider inviting a coach (or mentor) to evaluate you:
(a) spiritual development
(b) personal discipline
(c) family relationships
(d) decision making
(e) handling finances
(f) conflict resolution
(g) goal setting and strategic planning.

Create an environment where coaching is not only allowed—it is encouraged. Don't wait until you are in trouble, invite a coach into your life to help you avoid trouble. Actually, what you learn early determines how you behave later. What you don't know can hurt you; it can put a lid on your potential. You owe it to yourself and those who depend on you to open the doors of evaluation.

And don't let it stop with you. Pass on to somebody else what you have been given. Jesus said, ". . .You have been treated generously, so live generously." (Matthew 10:8). No, you are not too young (or too old for that matter) to be a coach to someone. You are not responsible for knowing everything. You are just responsible for sharing what you know with others. As you pour into their cup what God and others have poured into yours, they will go further, faster too.

Get a coach and be blessed . . .
THEN . . .
Become a coach and bless others!

Survival Guide for July 2

". . .GOD IS STRONG, AND HE WANTS YOU STRONG."
EPHESIANS 6:10

Generally speaking, God calls us to step out and do things we don't feel qualified to do.

Why? So that we learn to lean more on Him. However just because God calls us to step out in new areas that doesn't mean we won't make mistakes. Being human we most certainly will. But instead of being discouraged, knowing God uses new experiences to teach us to lean on Him helps us accept our mistakes as part of the learning curve and go on to greater things. Often we look at a task and think, "There's no way I can do this." Statements like that show that we are looking through the wrong end of the telescope.

We are looking at the road ahead instead of God.

When God called Joshua to take the place of Moses, He promised him: ". . .In the same way I was with Moses, I'll be with you. . ." (Joshua 1:5). Now if God promises to be with us (and He does), that is all we need. His strength is best shown through our weakness (see 2 Corinthians 12:9).

Whatever ingredients are lacking in the natural realm you can withdraw from your account in the spiritual realm: ". . .be strong in the Lord—be empowered through your union with Him; draw your strength from Him—that strength which His [boundless] might provides" (Ephesians 6:10 Amp). What kind of "might"? "Boundless"! Where do we draw strength from? The ultimate source—God.

Christ empowers and equips you as you fellowship with Him, so stop selling yourself short. Armed with His might you have more capabilities than you think and you are able to do a lot more than you have done in the past.

Today, put your confidence in God and stop doubting yourself!

Survival Guide for **July 3**

"MY HEART WILL DANCE AND SING TO THE TUNEFUL
TRUTH YOU'LL SPEAK." PROVERBS 23:16

Are you being criticized?

I am an expert on handling criticism through long years of practice! Let's start with these three suggestions:

(1) Understand the difference between constructive and destructive criticism. Learn how to interpret criticism by asking:
> (a) In what spirit is it given?
>> If your critic's attitude is kind, rest assured the criticism is meant to be constructive
> (b) When is the criticism given?
>> When somebody criticizes you publicly, usually their intentions aren't the best
> (c) Why is the criticism given?
>> Solomon says, "The purposes of a man's heart are deep waters, but a man of understanding draws them out." (Proverbs 20:5 NIV). Hurting people hurt others, so always ask, "Is the criticism given for my benefit, or just from personal hurt?"

(2) Don't take yourself too seriously. Face it, occasionally we all do stupid things. Blessed are those who can laugh at themselves and learn from their blunders.

(3) Look beyond the criticism and see the critic. Is it someone you respect? Are they constantly critical? If so, don't place too much value on what they say; they are probably just projecting their frustration on to you—like the 12-year-old boy who hadn't spoken since he was born. After being served oatmeal for breakfast several weeks in a row he shouted, "Yuck, I hate this stuff!" His mother jumped up, hugged him and said, "We thought you couldn't talk. Why haven't you ever spoken to us?" Bluntly he exclaimed, "Because up until now everything's been okay." Some folks talk only when they are ticked off.

The important question is does your critic sincerely want to help you?

Survival Guide for **July 4**

_____

**"TAKE GOOD COUNSEL AND ACCEPT CORRECTION—
THAT'S THE WAY TO LIVE WISELY AND WELL."
PROVERBS 19:29**

Here's some more advice for handling criticism.

(1) *Watch your attitude.* A negative attitude can be as destructive as a critical spirit. I ran across this saying online and liked it immediately: "A chip on your shoulder usually indicates wood higher up." Peter writes, "You have been called for this purpose, since Christ also suffered for you, leaving you an example for you to follow in His steps, Who committed no sin, nor was any deceit found in His mouth; and while being reviled, He did not revile in return; while suffering, He uttered no threats, but kept entrusting Himself to Him Who judges righteously." (1Peter 2:21-23 NAS).

(2) *Realize that good people get criticized.* Jesus was called a glutton (see Matthew 11:19); a drunk (see Luke 7:34); a friend of questionable characters (Matthew 11:19). People whose minds are polluted and whose vision isn't clear, won't understand behavior based on obedience to God. So, when your ideas and values conflict with theirs, try to be understanding.

(3) *Stay physically and spiritually in shape.* Exhaustion has a profound effect on the way we act and react. Elijah slipped into depression because of weariness. Jezebel was relentless, her opposition sapped his strength. Listen to him whine, "Enough of this, GOD! Take my life—I am ready to join my ancestors in the grave." (1 Kings 19:4). How is that for a downer? Satan will take advantage of our weariness. When we are tired, we can easily become overly sensitive and miss the opportunity for growth that comes with the criticism. I have health issues which make it difficult for me to sleep and I find that I am much more likely to react negatively to criticism that when I was sleeping better.

Criticism is inevitable. Reacting negatively to it is not.

Survival Guide for **July 5**

**"...THEY MADE ME CARE FOR THE FACE OF THE EARTH,
BUT I HAD NO TIME TO CARE FOR MY OWN FACE."
SONG OF SOLOMON 1:6**

Tony Campolo writes:

> Growing up, I knew a man who loomed larger than life to me. He was Edwin Bailey. He ran the astronomical observatory at the Franklin Institute in Philadelphia. I would go there most Saturdays just to spend time with him. His encyclopedic mind fascinated me. He knew something about everything. I was friends with him until he died several years ago.
>
> Once, after he'd suffered a serious stroke, I went to visit him in the hospital. In an effort to make small talk I told him about all the places where I'd been to speak and how I'd come to his bedside right from the airport. He heard me out. Then looking questioningly at me he asked, "You go all over the world to people who, ten years from now, probably won't remember your name, but are you taking time for those who really matter?" That question changed my life. I've decided not to let my time be used up by people for whom I make no difference, while neglecting those for whom I'm irreplaceable.
>
> A pastor friend of mine was recently invited to the White House to consult the President. Quite an honor. But he said "No," because he'd promised to be at a Little League final where his son was playing baseball. The nation and the President survived just fine without him. His son, however, never felt so loved or valued as he did that day.

Today begin putting first things first!

Survival Guide for **July 6**

"THEN DAVID PRAYED TO GOD, 'SHALL I GO AFTER THESE RAIDERS? CAN I CATCH THEM?' THE ANSWER CAME, 'GO AFTER THEM! YES, YOU'LL CATCH THEM! YES, YOU'LL MAKE THE RESCUE!'" 1 SAMUEL 30:8

While David and his men were on the battlefield, the Amalekites attacked, burned down the town and took their wives and children captive. David's soldiers were devastated—even to the point that some of David's men wanted to stone him. What do you do when your successes are suddenly wiped out by tragedy, when even your best friends turn on you?

David did two things that warrant our careful consideration:

—First, he "strengthened himself with trust in his God" (1Sam 30:6). That's the key. When your life suddenly goes into reverse and the very people you thought would stand by you let you down, remind yourself of these three unchanging facts:

1. God is the Lord your God.
2. They can take everything else from you, but they can't take God.
3. When you've nobody left but God—you've got everything you need to get up and start again.

—Second, He "prayed to the Lord" (1 Sam 30:8). Until you hear from God, the jury's still out and nobody else's verdict matters. Here is what God told David: "Go after them! . . . catch them! . . . make the rescue!" Don't just sit there—get up, go after them and get everyone back!

Have you been hurt by old relationships? You will be healed by new ones. Have you been injured by circumstances? You will be healed by finding purpose. Have you been wounded by memory and resentment? You will be healed by love and forgiveness.

Whatever or whomever is attacking you today: "Go after them! . . . catch them! . . . make the rescue!"

Survival Guide for **July 7**

"SMART PEOPLE KNOW HOW TO HOLD THEIR TONGUE; THEIR GRANDEUR IS TO FORGIVE AND FORGET." PROVERBS 19:11

Here are some more thoughts on handling criticism.

(1) Surround yourself with the right people

When you have the option, spend time with those who build you up, not tear you down. Quality time with the right people will galvanize you against the effects of the worst criticism. It will also keep you from becoming critical yourself. If crows attack a hawk, the hawk doesn't counter-attack, instead it soars higher and higher in ever widening circles until the pests leave it alone. Good strategy! Circle above your adversaries rather than stooping to their level: "It is to a man's honor to avoid strife, but every fool is quick to quarrel." (Proverbs 20:3 NIV). If you want to quell your critics, have a good attitude and avoid defensiveness.

(2) Concentrate on your mission—change your mistakes

Most of us do the opposite; when criticism comes we change our mission and concentrate on our mistakes. If you run every time you make a mistake, you will never accomplish anything; you will live in constant frustration. The only real mistakes are the ones from which we learn nothing. So instead of dwelling on your mistakes, count on making some, growing wiser from them and moving on to finish the job. There is an old Arab proverb that says, "If you stop every time a dog barks, your road will never end." Don't let your mistakes become roadblocks; turn them into building blocks.

Since ". . . iron sharpens iron," ask God to help you grow stronger through criticism. (see Proverbs 27:17NIV).

Survival Guide for July 8

"WE PRAY THAT YOU'LL HAVE THE STRENGTH . . . THAT ENDURES THE UNENDURABLE AND SPILLS OVER INTO JOY." COLOSSIANS 1:11

At 67, Thomas Edison watched as most of his life's work went up in flames. Standing in the ashes, he turned to a friend and said, "Thank goodness! All our mistakes are burned up. Now we can start again fresh!"

Every time we risk and fail, if we re-evaluate and learn from it, we have another opportunity to "start again fresh." But be warned—giving up always looks easier than standing up and giving in always seems more attractive than digging in.

Championship-winning NBA coach, Pat Riley, said, "There comes a moment that distinguishes winning from losing. The true warrior understands and seizes that moment by giving an effort so intuitive that it could only be called one from the heart."

The apostle Paul wrote: "We pray that you'll have the strength . . . that endures the unendurable and spills over into joy." (Col 1:11). That strength comes from God and can be found daily in His Word. Spending time with God in His Word is the path to strength.

John Maxwell writes:

> "After you've been knocked down and had the will
> to get back up, the wisdom to plan your comeback
> and the courage to take action, know this: you'll
> experience one of those defining moments—and it
> will define you as either an achiever or a quitter."

Prepare for your "defining moment," because it's coming. If you do, not only will you survive it, you'll go on to greater things. Why? Because enduring the unendurable "spills over into joy."

Survival Guide for July 9

"BE STRONG AND DO NOT GIVE UP . . ."
2 CHRONICLES 15:7(NIV)

No matter how defeated we may feel we are not defeated until we give up—and giving up isn't an option if we want our lives to matter. Can you think of one quitter—just one—who ever accomplished anything worth remembering?

When John Wesley was forbidden to preach in a certain church, instead of giving up, he went to a nearby cemetery where his father was buried and, using his father's tomb as a pulpit, he preached the gospel of Christ. John Knox often had to be helped up the steps into his pulpit. But once he was there, he preached with such passion that Scotland turned to God.

One night, George Whitefield returned from a preaching tour, extremely tired. As he lit a candle and prepared to climb the stairs to his bedroom, he noticed a group of people gathered in front of his house. So he invited them into his foyer and, candle in hand, preached his last message from the stairway. That night he died in his sleep.

Storms come for a reason. They also come for a season. Discover the reason and become wiser. Outlast the season and become stronger—but never, never give up!

Today, "be strong and do not give up, for your work will be rewarded." (2 Chronicles 15:7 NIV).

Survival Guide for July 10

"CALL ME AND I'LL ANSWER. . ." PSALM 91:15

It is impossible to be a healthy Christian without a good prayer life.

How is yours at the moment? Take inventory with these three questions:

1. How is my consistency? If you can't remember when you last took time to pray, its time to do something about it! Without prayer, we're uncovered and unprotected..

2. How is my sincerity? Are my prayers more liturgy than life? Daily, but dull and dry? If so, that's an indication that you don't know enough about Who you're talking to or how He feels about you. The better we know God, the more time we want to spend with Him.

3. How is my faith? Do you wonder if prayer really changes anything? Or why on earth a God in heaven would want to talk to you or hear anything you had to say? If He already knows it all, what can you tell Him anyway? And if He decides everything, why even bother? Prayer is not for God's benefit—it is for ours! Where else can we go to bare our soul without fear and walk away cleansed, comforted, counseled and corrected? Our prayers work, not because of how well we say them, but because of how well God hears them.

Prayer doesn't have to be understood in order to be enjoyed, anymore than electricity has to be understood in order to turn on a light. Just do it. Pray! Flip the switch and trust One who said "let there be light" to turn on the lights.

Forget about the wrapping and just give the gift! It is better to pray awkwardly than not at all. "He will call upon Me and I will answer him" (Ps 91:15 NIV). There it is in black and white—God's invitation to ask and His promise to answer.

Take inventory and take action.

Survival Guide for **July 11**

"LET'S JUST GO AHEAD AND BE WHAT WE WERE MADE TO BE." ROMANS 12:6

Our calling can often be discovered more in our differences from others—than in our similarities. That is why Paul warns against a wrong basis of comparison: ". . . let's just go ahead and be what we were made to be, without . . .comparing ourselves with each other or trying to be something we aren't." (Rom 12:6 - 7).

Here is the score: those who deserve a place in your life will never be threatened by your strengths or your uniqueness. They'll have the maturity to understand that it takes many different players and many different sounds to make up an orchestra. On the other hand, those who don't belong in your life will always try to pour you into their mold, because that's the only way they can measure or control you.

Not everybody will understand you—they are not supposed to. Don't waste the only life you have by trying to win the acceptance of people who don't appreciate your integrity or discern your worth. Love them, pray for them . . . and move on. Jesus said, "A servant is not greater than his master. If people did wrong to Me, they will do wrong to you too." (Jn 15:20 NCV).

Anytime we have to give up being what God made us to be in order to be accepted, the price of acceptance is too high. God accepts you as you are so just walk away from those who don't.

Always remember that in the final analysis, we all will be compared to one standard only: what God calls us to be, not what others want us to be!

Survival Guide for **July 12**

". . .I WILL PUT TOGETHER MY CHURCH. . ."
MATTHEW 16:18

I love the church. But we have made some serious blunders in our attempt to build it ourselves. Fortunately, it's never too late to learn from our blunders. So in that spirit, here are six blunders I believe we've made and need to correct:

1. We have tolerated division. Who needs the devil when we're so adept at hating one another in the name of denominational loyalty?

2. We have cultivated a religious spirit. We have taught that Christianity is about avoiding things like smoking and drinking. As a result we've lost our joy, because intimacy with God cannot be achieved through rule keeping.

3. We have encouraged "super stars." Consequently, some of our preachers have stopped modelling servant-hood and have forgotten that Jesus washed feet.

4. We have equated money with success. We have found a way to "theologize" greed, instead of using our God-given prosperity to reach the world with the Gospel and meet the needs of those around us.

5. We have stayed in the pews and become irrelevant. We freak out when somebody uses rap or rock music to reach this present generation. Instead of engaging the culture, we're hiding from it.

6. We have taught people to be escape-artists. Instead of "occupying till He comes," we fly away like astronauts. We read rapture novels when we should be praying for those living on the verge of martyrdom. Why can't we have their kind of faith? We can—if we're willing to pay the price and commit ourselves fully to God!

I love the church. May God forgive our blunders and lead us to truly let Jesus build His church

Survival Guide for July 13

"IT'S IN CHRIST THAT WE FIND OUT WHO WE ARE AND WHAT WE ARE LIVING FOR" EPHESIANS 1:9

Until in Christ we find out who we are, we will know neither our real worth nor our true purpose. And almost as bad, others will be able to label and control us. "It's in Christ that we find out who we are and what we are living for. . . "

If you struggle with low self-esteem, here is a prayer to help you:

> Father, sometimes I think I am of no use, that I can't do anything right, that nothing I do is ever good enough. Then I remember that when You look at who I am and who I can be—you see Jesus! And He is good enough!
>
> Jesus is good enough that He shed His precious blood to cover my unworthiness. Jesus is good enough that He paid the price for every sin I'll ever commit. Jesus is good enough that He's perfecting me each day. Jesus is good enough that I am the righteousness of God in Christ. Jesus is good enough that He's interceding for me right now
>
> Thank you Father that everything Jesus does is good enough and that, in Him, and only in Him I'm good enough too!

Survival Guide for **July 14**

"WHAT I WOULDN'T GIVE IF THEY'D ALWAYS FEEL THIS WAY, CONTINUING TO REVERE ME AND ALWAYS KEEP ALL MY COMMANDS; THEY'D HAVE A GOOD LIFE FOREVER . . . " DEUTERONOMY 5:29

When God tells us to do certain things, He is not trying to put us in straight-jackets or rain on our parade. No, He's just setting us up to be blessed! Think about that for a moment. On the other end of anything God asks us to do, we should hear the words "that it might be well with you."

Living in peace, instead of always going to pieces, is easier once we learn to listen to God and respond immediately. Don't hesitate. Don't negotiate. Don't rationalize. And whatever you do, don't run. The only thing that's worse than running from obedience is running smack into the consequences of disobedience. Ask Jonah!

"To obey is better than sacrifice. . ." (1 Sam 15:22 NIV). Sometimes we have to sacrifice certain things in order to obey God. But it is better to sacrifice them than to ignore the promptings of His Spirit, forfeit His blessings and live stressed out.

God will sometimes require things of us that:

> a) He doesn't seem to require of others.
> b) He won't explain and we can't understand.
> c) When we have obeyed, we won't see any immediate benefits.

The secret to obedience is to become convinced that God has a unique purpose for your life and that He loves you unconditionally.

Abandon yourself to God in trust, knowing that in the end you will have "a good life forever."

Survival Guide for **July 15**

"BUT EVEN IF HE DOESN'T. . . " DANIEL 3:18

When you can stand up to threats of harm and suggestions of compromise, you have "furnace faith."

Facing a fiery furnace heated seven times over, three young Hebrew men refused to compromise their beliefs or change their behavior: ". . . we have no need to present a defense our God is able let Him deliver us. But if not we will not serve your gods." (Daniel 3:16-18 NRS).

"But if not"—in three words they took faith to a higher level. They knew that God could prevent it, but accepted whatever His plan called for in this particular instance—they would rather die than deny Him.

God can either take us out or bring us through—but what if He leaves us in the adversity longer than we'd like to stay? That takes "furnace faith!" Furnace faith is dead to doubt, dumb to discouragement and blind to impossibility. It knows nothing but success. It lifts up its hand through the threatening clouds and lays hold of the One Who has all power in heaven and on earth. It makes the circumstances bearable and the future brighter. But "furnace faith" is developed only by standing in the midst of the fire until we find that we're not alone in the fire: "I see four men loose, walking in the fire, and they have no hurt; and the form of the fourth is like the Son of God." (Daniel 3:25).

"Furnace faith"—we know we have it when we are as free in the furnace of adversity and affliction, as we are out of it. Furthermore, when our friends see Jesus in there with us, it will convince them more than all our words.

Is your faith "Furnace faith?"

Survival Guide for **July 16**

"FULL OF HOPE, YOU'LL RELAX, CONFIDENT AGAIN; YOU'LL LOOK AROUND, SIT BACK, AND TAKE IT EASY." JOB 11:18

There is a mental condition that is essential to the life God wants us to live. It is the fuel our hearts runs on. It is the single biggest difference between those who persevere and those who give up. It is called hope. It is a powerful force that arouses the mind to explore every possibility and overcome every obstacle.

Hope is what makes couples say "I do," without any guarantees. Hope is what makes couples pick up the pieces after a disappointment and try again. Hope makes composers agonize over a score and artists over a canvas, believing some glimmer of beauty will emerge from the struggle.

As an old man, the painter Henri Matisse was crippled with agonizing arthritis. When asked why he continued to wrap his swollen fingers around a paintbrush every day, he replied, "The pain goes away; the beauty endures." That's hope!

Laboring to paint the ceiling of the Sistine Chapel, Michelangelo grew so discouraged that he wanted to quit, but every morning hope pushed him up the ladder to fulfill his magnificent vision.

Hope made Abraham leave home without knowing where God was taking him.

Hope made Paul defy the system and carry the Gospel to the Gentiles.

Hope is what fuelled the Old Testament prophets to keep taking on the "powers that be."

David said, "For You have been my hope . . .my confidence since my youth." (Psalm 71:5 NIV). Don't lose hope! You can survive many losses, but lost hope paralyses your spirit. "You will have courage because you will have hope." (Job11:18 NLT).

Regardless of your circumstances, keep your hope alive today by staying focused on God.

Survival Guide for **July 17**

"WE KEPT AT IT, REPAIRING AND REBUILDING THE WALL. THE WHOLE WALL WAS SOON JOINED TOGETHER AND HALFWAY TO ITS INTENDED HEIGHT BECAUSE THE PEOPLE HAD A HEART FOR THE WORK." NEHEMIAH 4:6

On May 29, 1953 Tenzing Norgay, a Sherpa born in Nepal, and Edmund Hilary, a New Zealander, accomplished what no other human beings ever had—they stood at the top of Mount Everest, the world's highest peak. Could they have made it without a great team? No way!

Tenzing tells the story:

> For each level we reached, a higher degree of teamwork was required. One group would exhaust themselves just getting the equipment up the mountain for the next group. Two-men teams would work finding a path, cutting steps, securing ropes, spending themselves to make the next leg of the climb possible for others. You don't climb a mountain like Everest by trying to race ahead on your own or by competing with your comrades. No, you do it slowly and carefully by unselfish teamwork. Certainly I wanted to reach the top myself; it was the thing I'd dreamed of all my life. But if the lot fell to someone else I would take it like a man, not a cry-baby. Where would Hilary and I have been without the others? Without the climbers who made the route? The Sherpas who had carried the loads? Those who had cleared the path ahead? It was only through the work and sacrifice of them all that we had our chance at the top.

How do you build a business, a ministry, a career, a meaningful life? The same way you climb a mountain—through others. The slogan "Teamwork makes the dream work" is true.

A dream without a team is a dream unfulfilled. Go to God both for your dream and your team.

Who is on your team?

Survival Guide for July 18

"FREELY YOU HAVE RECEIVED, FREELY GIVE."
MATTHEW 10:8 (NIV)

Jesus commanded us to give—and receive.   There must be a healthy balance between both.   His command to receive keeps us realistic about our personal limitations, our dependency on God—and on others.   His command to give challenges our innate selfishness.   Assimilation and elimination; our body dies without them—so does our soul.

For some of us, receiving is harder than giving. We have no trouble giving insight, giving hope, giving courage, giving advice, giving support, giving money, even giving ourselves.   For givers the greatest challenge is to become gracious receivers.   By receiving, we acknowledge our need of others and that's hard on our ego.   We also reveal to the giver that they have something worth giving; we add value to their lives.   Often it's only in the eyes of the receiver that the giver discovers his worth.

If somebody gives us a watch but we never wear it, is that watch really received?   If they offer us an idea and we don't at least consider it, is that idea even appreciated?   If they introduce us to a friend, but we ignore them, is that friend truly accepted?

Receiving is an art.   It allows others to become part of our lives; even to become dependent on them in certain areas.   It requires the grace to say, "I need you; without you, I wouldn't be who I am."

Receiving from the heart requires love and humility.   Too many people are wounded and never reach out again, because their gifts weren't valued.

So today, try to be a good giver—and receiver!

Survival Guide for **July 19**

"LET'S SEE HOW INVENTIVE WE CAN BE IN ENCOURAGING LOVE AND HELPING OUT" HEBREWS 10:24

There are few things better than a good marriage, or worse than a bad one. Sadly, most fall into the in-between category—just mediocre. Why? Often simply because they've gone too long without maintenance and repairs. If you are married where does your marriage on that scale? Has it quietly fashioned itself into a smooth well-worn rut? Do you take each other for granted? Or, do you, like the couples that go the distance, find new ways of renewing your love and keeping the relationship fresh?

Sam Levison said,

> "Love at first sight is nothing special. It's when two
> people have been looking at each other for twenty-
> five years that it becomes a miracle."

"Wives, understand and support your husbands. . . Husbands, go all out in your love for your wives." (Eph 5:22-25).

I'll close with this exhortation from Max Lucado:

> Someday is a snake whose tongue has mastered the
> talk of deception. "Someday," it hisses, "I'll take her
> on that cruise . . . we'll have time to sit and chat . . . "
> But you know the truth before I even write it, don't
> you? Someday never comes! Wise up! Invest the
> time. Send the flowers. Write the letter. Make the
> apology. Take the trip. Purchase the gift. Do it!
> The seized opportunity brings joy—the neglected one
> brings only regret!

Survival Guide for **July 20**

"... CRIED TO THE LORD, AND HE ANSWERED BY SETTING ME FREE." PSALM 118:5(NIV)

Roger Palms writes,

> When I go fishing I use a variety of lures, but
> there's one they go for every time. Those fish
> have a weakness and because I know what it is
> I can catch them. Sometimes one will pull
> loose, ripping its skin, and go off to heal, but
> the scars will always be there. Sometimes you
> can pull away from Satan too, but not before a
> painful tearing, causing scars that may remain
> for life.

Satan is clever—he customizes his temptations to our particular weaknesses. Maybe you're not susceptible to lust, but how about pride? Or you can't stand the taste of liquor, but how about your appetite for gossip?

It is Satan's oldest strategy—make sin look good. When Eve "... saw its fruit was good she took some." (Genesis 3:6 NCV). By seducing Eve, Satan planned to get at her off-spring. You see Satan is not just after us but after our future—he is after those God plans to bless through us.

But Eve's weakness didn't thwart God's plan. God had already given Eve "... another child in place of Abel whom Cain killed" (Genesis 4:25). Eve gave birth to a son named Seth, who in turn fathered Enosh. With the birth of Enosh, we read that Eve's descendants "... began praying and worshiping in the name of GOD" (Genesis 4:26). Just so, Satan is defeated when we discover God's help in times of temptation. All we have to do is reach for it: "... I cried unto the Lord, and He answered by setting me free." (Psalm 118:5 NIV).

Today, cry out to God—and be set free!

Survival Guide for **July 21**

"URGE EUODIA AND SYNTYCHE TO IRON OUT THEIR DIFFERENCES." PHILIPPIANS 4:2

You can't pray effectively with bitterness in your heart. Even if the other person is wrong, let God use you as a paramedic of His mercy. Apologize, forgive, then tell them you want to see the relationship healed. It may take more than a U-turn to make up the distance between you, but one step, just one, makes the road shorter and, if you stay on course, you'll get to where you ought to be.

Don't fight over "who hit who first." Come on, be bigger than that! You've been asking God to restore things; well, this is part of it! Go ahead; your pride will rebel and, if you let it, fear of rejection will stop you dead in your tracks. But do it anyway and see what happens. Remember, when you forgive, you position yourself to receive God's forgiveness. Can you afford to live without His forgiveness?

Euodia and Syntyche worked hand-in-hand with Paul to build the church, yet the only mention of them is that they held a grudge against each other. Not good! Jesus said that if you hold a grudge you have to forgive before you worship God: "If you enter your place of worship and you suddenly remember a grudge a friend has against you leave immediately, go to this friend and make things right. Then and only then, come back and work things out with God." (Matthew 5:23-24).

Can you afford to live without God's forgiveness?

Go iron out your differences!

Survival Guide for July 22

"GRAIN MUST BE GROUND TO MAKE BREAD . . ."
ISAIAH 28:28 (NIV)

Brokenness isn't a popular subject, especially in a world that applauds bravado. Yet it's usually the price of success. Check the record: in most of the Bible's great success stories there's a chapter on breaking.

How did Moses, prince of Egypt, become the meekest man who ever lived? (Meekness depicts a wild horse that's broken and responsive to the slightest tug of the rein.) Forty years in the wilderness will do it every time! How did Saul, a proud Pharisee, become Paul, a slave of Christ and a servant to every believer? In his own words: "Our light affliction is working for us" (2 Corinthians 4:17 NKJ).

Now there's a new concept for some of us: ". . . affliction working for us. . . ." It is one thing to be broken like the Prodigal because you have disobeyed your Heavenly Father, it's entirely another to be broken in the process of doing His will.

Gideon's 300 men had to break their pitchers before the light within could shine out, and the enemy be defeated. Elisha had to break his plow, sacrifice his security, and follow Elijah, before he could qualify for a double portion. Mary had to expose herself to ridicule and break her alabaster box over the feet of Jesus, in order to receive one of His highest commendations: ". . . wherever the gospel is preached, what she has done will be told of her." (Matthew 26:13 NIV).

If we want to accomplish anything for God, we must be willing to be broken in all areas of life, including ambitions, reputation, desires, and self-will.

The next time affliction comes remind yourself: "grain must be ground to make bread."

Survival Guide for **July 23**

"THE WORD BECAME FLESH AND BLOOD, AND MOVED INTO THE NEIGHBORHOOD. . ." JOHN 1:14

Henri Nouwen says, "Community is the place where the person you least want to live with, always lives."

Here is one woman's story of what that means:

> As a Sociology student, one of my class assignments was to smile at people and then document their reactions. That weekend my husband and I went out for breakfast and were in line waiting to be served. Suddenly everybody around me began to back away—even my husband! As I turned to investigate, a body odor enveloped me and I encountered a homeless man, his blue eyes searching mine for acceptance. Because he'd come inside to get warm he had to buy something, so he ordered coffee. It was all he could afford. Then I noticed other people watching my reaction. I thought, "What now, Lord?" So I smiled and ordered him a sandwich. As he thanked me and squeezed my hand, I realized I was learning an important lesson. By sharing what I had with this man, I was practicing unconditional love and acceptance.

God says, "Suppose a brother. is without clothes and. food. If one of you says, 'I wish you well; keep warm and well fed,' but does nothing, what good is it? Faith, not accompanied by action, is dead." (James 2:15-17 NIV).

When are we who are the church going to learn that true holiness doesn't isolate us from a hurting world, it insulates us, enabling us to mix freely with them and become a solution to their problem?

Isn't that exactly what Jesus showed us when He ". . . became flesh and blood, and moved into the neighborhood. . . ?"

Survival Guide for July 24

"RUN FROM TEMPTATIONS." 2 TIMOTHY 2 : 22 (CEV)

Here are four lessons I know from experience work:

(1) strength in one area doesn't make you immune to weakness in other areas
(2) temptation always returns to the scene of its previous success
(3) flirting with temptation makes defeat certain
(4) failure won't cut you off from God's grace, but it can limit or destroy your potential.

In *Rebuilding Your Broken World*, Gordon MacDonald tells of getting involved in an affair, and the painful steps required to rebuild his life. He recalls a conversation with a friend before things fell apart.

"Friend: 'If Satan were to blow you out of the water, how do you think he'd do it?'

MacDonald: 'In all sorts of ways, but there's one way he wouldn't get me.'

Friend: 'What's that?'

MacDonald: 'My personal relationships. That's one area where I'm as strong as you can get.'"

MacDonald continues:

> A few years after that conversation a chain of seemingly innocent choices became destructive, and in the very area where I had predicted I was safe, my world had to be rebuilt. Where we consider ourselves strongest, is where we're least likely to prepare for attack!

Kenny Rogers sings, "You gotta know when to hold 'em, know when to fold 'em, know when to walk away and know when to run."

When it comes to temptation, that is a good tune to remember. When Potiphar's wife tried to seduce Joseph—he ran! That was the spiritual thing to do: "Run from temptations always do the right thing."

We have a responsibility to live clean and, when we accept that, the Holy Spirit comes to help us deal with the continual attacks on our old nature. . . and sometimes His advice is "run!"

Survival Guide for **July 25**

"IN A WELL-FURNISHED KITCHEN THERE ARE NOT ONLY CRYSTAL GOBLETS AND SILVER PLATTERS, BUT WASTE CANS AND COMPOST BUCKETS—SOME CONTAINERS USED TO SERVE FINE MEALS, OTHERS TO TAKE OUT THE GARBAGE" 2 TIMOTHY 2:20

Many of us have dishes for everyday use and dishes for special occasions. So does God: "In God's house there are utensils of gold and silver wood and clay, some for special use, some for ordinary. If you stay away from sin you will be like dishes made of purest gold—the very best in the house. Christ can use you for His highest purposes." (2 Timothy 2:20,21 TLB).

These verses aren't about salvation; if you are a Christian you are already in the house. Instead, they are about cleaning up your act; otherwise you get to stay with the pot-scrubbers and dishcloths because God can't use unclean vessels in positions of honor. If you're a recovering clay dish who is ready to move up to a special occasion gold dish in order to be used for God's highest purposes, start doing these things:

(1) Edify yourself. Learn to build yourself up by praying "without ceasing;" that's a basic survival skill.

(2) Practice Godliness. Godliness has to be practiced because it doesn't come naturally. Start by controlling your moods, praising when you want to complain, pursuing the right things, and delighting yourself in God's Word.

(3) Stay Faithful. Job said, ". . . when He has tested me, I shall come out like gold." (Job 23:10 NRS). Stay faithful and you emerge from trials stronger and wiser

(4) Examine your Motives. 1 Corinthians 3:13: ". . . the fire will test each man's work." (NIV). The right works done with the wrong motives will be burned up like wood, hay, and stubble. But the gold of the right works done with the right motives withstands the fire.

Today, make it your goal to be used as a special occasion gold dish in God's House!

Survival Guide for July 26

"THE PEOPLE KEPT THEIR DISTANCE WHILE MOSES APPROACHED THE THICK CLOUD WHERE GOD WAS." EXODUS 20:21

No doubt the Israelites wondered, "What does God's presence feel like? What does His voice sound like? What does His glory look like?" Only Moses knew. And it seems that most folks were happy to let it stay that way: "The people remained at a distance, while Moses approached where God was."

Sound familiar? Sounds like S.M.O. (Sunday morning only) Christians to me! They told Moses: "You tell us what God says but don't let God speak directly to us." Why? Were they afraid God might tell them something they didn't particularly want to hear? I don't know, but I do know that when you haven't carried out God's last set of instructions, it's hard to be enthusiastic about the next set.

John writes: "How can we be sure that we belong to Him? By obeying His commandments . . . those who obey God's Word really do love Him." (1 John 2:3-5 NLT). So, how about it? Are you interested only in being a spiritual "peeping tom;" that is an onlooker who gets a vicarious thrill out of watching God move in the lives of others instead of accepting the discipline required to have a personal relationship with Him yourself? Do you want His gifts and His favor, but not the commitment that goes along with them?

God doesn't want us to be infatuated with the Bible, the church, or even His will. More, much more, He wants us to fall in love with Him! He's looking for a bride, not a girlfriend, somebody who'll stick with Him when the going gets tough.

So, are you ready to stop being a "peeping tom" and instead experience God first hand today? Good!

Survival Guide for July 27

**"NATHANAEL SAID, 'NAZARETH? YOU'VE GOT TO BE KIDDING.' BUT PHILIP SAID, 'COME, SEE FOR YOURSELF.'"
JOHN 1:46**

Jesus got criticized just for being a Nazarene. Since criticism comes from all quarters here are tips for effectively handling criticism.

(1) Don't just see if there's a critic, see if there's a crowd.

An old joke goes that a woman invited a well-known pianist to entertain at her dinner party. When it was over, everyone praised his performance except one lady. "I thought he was lousy", she said. Immediately the hostess intervened: "Pay no attention to her. She doesn't know what she's talking about. She only repeats what she hears everybody else say."

See if your critic has a cheering section; if they do, you may need to make some changes. George Bernard Shaw, the Irish playwright, certainly had his critics, but he knew how to handle them. After one opening night, a critic stood up and shouted, "It's rotten!" To which Shaw replied, "I agree, but what are we against so many?"

(2) Wait for time to prove your critics wrong.

Time is our best ally. It forces deception to the surface and allows the truth to come out. When Nathaniel asked concerning Jesus, "Nazareth? You've got to be kidding." Philip answered, "Come, see for yourself." Often, as events unfold, the cause of the criticism will be eliminated and you'll be vindicated.

It is doubtful that any American President had more critics than Abraham Lincoln. The day after he delivered the Gettysburg Address, The *Chicago Times* called it, "Silly, flat, dish-watery utterances." Today millions flock to The Lincoln Memorial, while almost no one remembers the editor who wrote those scathing words.

Here is the bottom line on handling criticism:
When you are criticized, listen.
If the criticism is valid, learn from it and grow.
If the criticism is invalid, ignore it and challenge your critics to "Come, see for yourself."

Survival Guide for **July 28**

―――

"... MY GRACE IS ENOUGH; IT'S ALL YOU NEED ..."
2 CORINTHIANS 12:9

Courage. Many of us come home every night frustrated because of the lack of it.

We don't lack insight, we just lack the courage to do something about our situation!

But people who really experience live are different; they would rather risk criticism and experience failure than remain silent and die on the sidelines never having gotten into the game. These are the people who inspire others to have the courage to follow them. Most folks have a dream they long to fulfill—they just need somebody to take the first step to show them the way. We call them leaders and you can be that somebody.

Without courage we simply accumulate a collection of good ideas and regrets. Most of our missed opportunities would not have been missed had we only been willing to push through our fear and embrace what could be. All of us feel fear, but here is the difference: eventually a true leader's need for progress overwhelms his reluctance to take a risk. She can live more easily with the prospects of having tried and failed, than not having tried at all. He knows that failure is an inevitable part of success. She also realizes that failure looks and feels completely different in the rearview mirror than it does when it is staring at you through the windshield.

The average person fears stepping out into a new opportunity, the true leader fears missing out on it.

If you are afraid to step out today, where can you get the courage to go ahead and take the risk?

From this promise: "I am with you; that is all you need." (2 Corinthians 12:9 TLB).

Survival Guide for **July 29**

"GREAT IS HIS FAITHFULNESS; HIS MERCIES BEGIN AFRESH EACH DAY." LAMENTATIONS 3:23 (NLT)

Philip Yancey writes:

> On my first visit to Yellowstone National Park, flocks of tourists surrounded the geyser; Old Faithful, cameras trained like weapons while a big digital clock predicted the next eruption. We were in the dining room of the inn overlooking the geyser when the clock showed one minute to go. So along with every other diner, we rushed to the window to see the big event. We "oohed" and "aahed" and clicked our cameras; some even applauded. But glancing back I noticed that not a single waiter bothered even to look up. Old Faithful had become so familiar, it had lost its power to impress them.

The Bible says, "The unfailing love of the Lord never ends! Great is His faithfulness; His mercies begin afresh each day." (Lamentations 3:22-23 NLT). Not only do God's mercies begin afresh each day, our sense of gratitude should too. Our days should be saturated in it. Continual gratitude comes from looking beyond our blessings to their source. What source? A source of unfailing love, great faithfulness and mercy that is already at work when our eyes open each morning. Don't miss God's faithfulness because of it's constant presence!

For years I thought that when I had a bad day and struggled and failed God that God turned His back on me out of disgust. Then I read this great verse: "If we are unfaithful, He remains faithful." (2 Timothy 2:13 NLT). That verse changed my life! Be sure you let it impact you. Paul is saying that even when you are unfaithful to God, still He remains faithful to you. What that promise did for me and I hope will do for you is to move me from serving God out of fear to serving God out of gratitude.

Fear instills fear. Gratitude instills love. God is faithful because it is His nature, not because of our faithfulness. How can you help but worship a God with such awesome faithfulness!

Today show your gratitude through loving acts of obedience.

Survival Guide for **July 30**

"IF YOU'RE CONTENT TO BE YOURSELF, YOUR LIFE WILL COUNT." MATTHEW 23:12

When the moment comes for you to stride confidently into the spotlight and fulfill your God-given role, try to remember that there is no room for self-importance and pretence.

This moment calls for:

> (a) stripping away all the lesser roles you have acted out and settled for
>
> (b) discovering who you are and what you are really all about
>
> (c) depending totally on God to help you give the most authentic performance of your life.

Remember Rosa Parks, the African-American woman who refused to surrender her seat and move to the back of the bus? There was more at stake there than just a ride home from work. By simply being herself, Rosa Parks suddenly moved to center stage. She wasn't playing games. She was the real thing, and God shone a light on her soul that day that made history.

When God shines His light on our efforts, little becomes much.

Since God is the only One who knows when your time will come, you must be prepared to live for Jesus until God promotes you: "Be content with who you are, and don't put on airs. God's. hand is on you; He will promote you at the right time." (1 Peter 5:6). Allow the Holy Spirit to be your agent and advance-man. Don't get ahead of Him.

Just be faithful, then when the time is right, He will shine His spotlight on you and you will be moved to center stage.

"Don't put on airs"—God has just promoted to an even bigger role!

Survival Guide for **July 31**

"IF GOD DOESN'T BUILD THE HOUSE, THE BUILDERS ONLY BUILD SHACKS . . ." PSALM 127:1

In God's kingdom, center stage isn't for people who think they have got it all together and deserve public recognition. Nor is it limited to those in leadership and public ministry. No, being given center stage is a call to action.

Trust God's timing and He will groom you for bigger and better things.

But, in preparing for when God puts you center stage, there are some things you must (and must not) do:

(1) Don't try to make it on your own. Because popular wisdom says, "Fake it till you make it," we are tempted to debut in our own strength. Don't do it! If you do, you will get in the way of a much greater production: "If God doesn't build the house, the builders only build shacks. . ." (Psalm 127:1). Trust God and, when your moment comes, He will give you your cue.

(2) Leave the shadows. Are you ready to transform "acting" into an authentic performance that reveals the real you? Fear of rejection is powerful. It takes courage to be yourself. But we gain strength from the struggle and power from the pain when we are willing to risk moving from the shadows into the light.

(3) Confront your inner critic. We are all subject to that little voice which says, "You will never be smart enough, loving enough, attractive enough, good enough to stand in the spotlight." Confront your inner critic with God's Word.

Always remember, when God raises you up, nobody can put you down!

Most of all never ever forget that we step onto center stage by God's grace and for His glory!

Survival Guide for **August 1**

**"I'LL GIVE YOU GOOD SHEPHERD-RULERS WHO RULE MY
WAY, WHO RULE YOU WITH INTELLIGENCE AND WISDOM."
JEREMIAH 3:15**

Picture this: Joshua's soldiers are down in the valley fighting the
Amalekites. Above him, on a hilltop, sits Moses with his hands raised
towards heaven. So long as he does, the battle goes their way. But if you
have ever tried to hold your hands up for long, you will know that you
quickly grow weary and lower them. The moment Moses lowered his
arms, the battle went against Israel. So Aaron and Hur moved to his side,
held up his arms, and the tide turned again in their favor. Notice, it wasn't
Joshua's ability to fight, it was Moses' ability to hold up his arms that won
the day. Two men kept one man from fainting, so that an entire nation
could be saved.

This may sound self-serving, but I believe it is the truth. If your pastor's
arms drop from exhaustion, God will judge you, not him, because you
weren't there to strengthen him. Take a moment and let that sink in!

If God has given you a pastor who leads you and feeds you—support him!

In the Old Testament tabernacle, the candlesticks had to be kept burning
day and night because their light represented God's presence amongst His
people. If a candle so much as flickered, designated servants moved in
immediately to trim it and restore it to its original glow.

It is our responsibility to make sure that the light doesn't flicker in our
community of faith or the fire go out in our pastor/teachers. So pray for
your pastor every day and be sure to encourage him every chance you get.
Over one half of those who enter the ministry leave it within 10
years—because of discouragement.

What a challenge to the lifters of tired arms and the keepers of the flame!

Survival Guide for **August 2**

"MOSES MY SERVANT IS DEAD. GET GOING . . ." JOSHUA 1:2

Joshua had already tasted the joys of the Promised Land, but now he had to go back and wait. Why? Because his assignment was post-dated.

Certain things had to happen first:

(1) Moses had to die. Moses represented the old system. It was good for then, but not for now. Aligning ourselves with what was, instead of what is, is often a sign that we are still looking for approval and that there are still too many folk we need to impress. It is easy to get so tied up with systems and philosophies that, when God says it is time to move, we have to consult somebody else.

In order to reach your destiny, God will give you new instructions, new insights and a new plan for your life. The interesting thing is that the children of Israel mourned Moses' passing, yet they didn't see him die. They had to "reckon" him dead before they could move forward. Who or What do you need to "reckon" dead in order to get moving forward?

(2) Every doubter had to be buried. There were lots of voices around Joshua telling him it couldn't be done, and he had to wait until every one of them died in the wilderness. And every voice of doubt that holds us back has got to die and be buried too; including the voice of low self-esteem, childhood fears, anxieties, yes, even our critics. Gather them up and put them in a box, bury it, stand on top of the grave and say, "Ashes to ashes and dust to dust."

Only when you've taken those two steps are you ready to enter your Promised Land.

Survival Guide for **August 3**

"... YOUR HEART CAN BE CORRUPTED BY LUST EVEN QUICKER THAN YOUR BODY. THOSE LEERING LOOKS YOU THINK NOBODY NOTICES—THEY ALSO CORRUPT."
MATTHEW 5:28

It happened years ago to a prominent religious figure. His addiction to pornography was exposed—twice. Afraid, ashamed and alone, he wrestled with it, preached against it and prayed over it. When did his problem begin? As a teenager. Every time he picked up another pornographic magazine he filed a mental image for the enemy to pull up in moments of temptation. Ultimately it drove him to forfeit and destroy all he held near and dear.

Jesus said, "... your heart can be corrupted by lust even quicker than your body." Are those words compelling enough to stop you from looking lustfully? Or are you willing to suffer the consequences of continually drinking from the well of sexual impurity?

Sometimes the consequences are difficult to envision, but they are there. They come in the form of lost opportunities for intimacy. Every lustful glance damages your present or future marriage bond. The less you desire your mate, the more you'll look for things in them to justify your turning away. You will become critical of them so that you can feel "entitled" to play mind games with others who cross your path. The saddest part is, you will never know what your marriage could have been, because you chipped away at its foundation—one visual turn-on at a time.

Today, turn to God in repentance.

Ask Him to give you a clean heart (See Psalm 51).

Survival Guide for **August 4**

"BE BRAVE. BE STRONG. DON'T GIVE UP. EXPECT GOD TO GET HERE SOON." PSALM 31:24

When prizefighter James Corbett was asked what it takes to become a champion, he replied, "Fight one more round!" "One more round" like:

(1) Somerset Maugham, who earned only $330 during his first ten years as a writer.

(2) Enrico Caruso, who was a factory worker who studied singing for 12 years before getting his first small break.

(3) Gershwin, who composed 100 melodies before he sold one—for $5.

(4) Zane Grey, who didn't sell a single story during his first five years as a writer.

Study the lives of those you most admire and more than likely you'll discover that they spent years surmounting obstacles, facing their deepest fears, learning from repeated failures, rising above the predictions of those who said, "You'll never make it."

If you're looking for a neat, clean, respectable, no-loose-ends formula for victory, forget it. Victory comes after sweat, perspective and dirt under your fingernails. Victory comes after discipline, commitment, and a long-distance view. Victory comes after the tenacious bulldog quality of a Churchill rising in the darkest hours of World War II to tell Great Britain, "What is our aim? I can answer in one word: victory . . . at all costs; victory, in spite of all terror; victory, however long and hard the road may be; for without victory there is no survival."

Don't be discouraged if your dream hasn't yet come true. Make sure that it is from the Lord then keep pursuing it. Pray for wisdom daily. Study and learn. Grow by experience. Keep working.

Victory goes to the man or woman who is willing to "fight one more round."

Survival Guide for **August 5**

"...THE CHIEF OF THIS GODLESS WORLD IS ABOUT TO ATTACK. BUT DON'T WORRY—HE HAS NOTHING ON ME, NO CLAIM ON ME." JOHN 14:30

Have you ever played with a remote controlled car? Its fun because you can move it anywhere at will, because there's a receiver inside the car that responds to the radio control in your hand. Just push the control and off the car goes. But, if you disconnect the receiver inside the car, he can push the controls all day and nothing will happen. That is how unforgiveness works. As long as we keep it inside us, it can be triggered remotely by a telephone call, a face in the crowd, a certain song, a date on the calendar or even a casual comment. What a miserable way to live.

My point is simple: the solution to being controlled by unforgiveness is to remove the receiver. How? By forgiving. No wonder Paul says, "Forgive one another as quickly and thoroughly as God . . . forgave you."(Eph 4:32).

The word forgive literally means "to get it out." It has nothing to do with the other person's response to being forgiven. It's a decision you make because it is the right thing to do. An added benefit is that it is healthy. Forgiveness is like expelling carbon dioxide out of your body, it allows you take in the fresh air of God's grace.

Go ahead . . . exhale! Let all that bitterness and unforgiveness out, begin to take in God's love.

The hardest test of forgiveness is to forgive the guilty. But that's what God did for us and that's what He commands us to do to those who have hurt us. Can you pass that test?

Don't be controlled by unforgiveness any longer—go ahead remove the receiver.

Survival Guide for August 6

"THE SHADOW OF YOUR SIN WILL OVERTAKE YOU; YOU'LL FIND YOURSELF STUMBLING ALL OVER YOURSELF IN THE DARK." PROVERBS 5:22

In Jerusalem there is a cemetery called The Field of Blood. It was paid for with thirty pieces of silver—the reward Judas got for betraying his best Friend. When he got it, he couldn't stand what he'd become in the process, so he hanged himself and his enemies used the money to buy a pauper's graveyard and bury him in it.

What do you really want out of life? What are you willing to pay in order to get it? Before you answer, stop and consider what your actions say instead of what you should say.

Just because others don't know you are living two lives doesn't mean you're getting away with it. You know—and that knowledge will rob you of your peace of mind, your confidence before God and your self-respect. Try buying those! Or living without them! Most things in life are achievable if we have the brains, the money or the connections. But that's not the real issue, is it? What matters is—can we live with ourselves afterwards?

Judas tried to turn back the clock: "He . . . changed his mind, and . . . brought back the money to the chief priests . . . I have sinned, he declared, for I have betrayed an innocent man . . ." (Matt 27:3-4 TLB).

All sin is forgivable but not all consequences can be undone. Some consequences are final and irrevocable.

Be careful about what you really want out of life—because the goals we pursue in life ultimately determine what we become in the pursuit of them.

Survival Guide for **August 7**

**"THAT ENERGY IS GOD'S ENERGY, AN ENERGY DEEP
WITHIN YOU, GOD HIMSELF WILLING AND WORKING AT
WHAT WILL GIVE HIM THE MOST PLEASURE."
PHILIPPIANS 2:13**

Once upon a time I was a competitive weightlifter. To compete
successfully in a weightlifting meet you don't try to lift the weight, you
train to lift it, otherwise you end up exhausted and defeated. I find there
are parallels between physical training and spiritual training and
accomplishing goals.

Spiritually the kind of training we are talking about isn't a teeth-gritting,
white-knuckle, do-or-die attitude toward things like prayer and Bible
reading. Instead, it's training ourselves to be more sensitive to God. It's
learning to do the right thing, at the right time, in the right way, with the
right spirit. For example, say your goal is to read several chapters of the
Bible each day. But while you're reading you feel that God wants you to
linger at a certain Scripture, because He wants to make that particular truth
a reality in your daily life. You only have time to do one or the other. To
train right you linger. Because your goal isn't really to read X number of
Bible chapters but to do the right thing, at the right time, in the right way,
with the right spirit.

The difference between trying and training is like the difference between a
motorboat and a sail boat. You can turn one on and speed away, but with
the other you have to wait for the wind. Jesus said, "The wind blows
wherever it pleases . . . So it is with everyone born of the Spirit." (John 3:8
NIV).

Trying is a motorboat. Training is a sailboat. Trying is easy to do, just
turn on the flesh and speed away. Training is getting positioned to let the
wind do it's work. We can't turn it on or off. We can't engineer it or take
credit for it. But like good sailors, we can train ourselves to "read" it and
respond to it. That's what training is about.

Once we learn to train instead of try we begin walking in the Spirit instead
of straining in the flesh.

Today, spend more time training and less time trying: you will like the
result.

Survival Guide for **August 8**

"EACH OF YOU MUST TAKE RESPONSIBILITY FOR DOING THE CREATIVE BEST YOU CAN WITH YOUR OWN LIFE." GALATIANS 6:5

John H. Holiday, the founding editor of *The Indianapolis News*, got upset one day because somebody spelled "height" as "hight." When a worker checked the original copy and explained to him that he himself had been the one who did it, Holiday exploded and said, "Well, if that's the way I spelled it, then it must be right!" And the newspaper misspelled the word his way for the next 30 years.

Louis Armstrong once quipped, "There are some people, that if they don't know, you can't tell them."

It is time for each of us to stop blaming others, get honest, look in the mirror and say, "I'm responsible for my life, nobody else. I don't write the rules, but I do have to live by them." Solomon says that our wisdom rewards us and our lack of wisdom causes our suffering (Prov 9:12 NIV).

Don't be like the dying man who said to his wife, "Dear, you have been with me through thick and thin. When I got fired you were there. When I lost the business you were there. When my health failed you were there." Then after a few moments, he looked at her again and said, "You know what? You're bad luck!"

That could be a (hopefully humorous) parable of our age. We like to blame anyone other than ourselves. But the truth is so long as we keep blaming others and refusing to accept responsibility for ourselves, we'll never become what God made us to be.

"EACH OF YOU MUST TAKE RESPONSIBILITY FOR DOING THE CREATIVE BEST YOU CAN WITH YOUR OWN LIFE."

Survival Guide for **August 9**

"FRIENDS LOVE THROUGH ALL KINDS OF WEATHER, AND FAMILIES STICK TOGETHER IN ALL KINDS OF TROUBLE." PROVERBS 17:17

We indulge in bad habits because we don't know how to:
   (a) feel our feelings
   (b) face reality, or
   (c) live life on life's terms.

So we seek escape. And we are only ready to give up our habits when they cost too much: when we "hit the bottom." Most of us don't get off the elevator until it can go no lower. Then, and only then, do we turn to God in earnest and commit ourselves to living His way. At that point, His power to overcome is released within us.

Sometimes being free means finding a friend mature enough to keep our confidence, strong enough to hold us accountable and loyal enough not to give up on us. It also involves a commitment on our part to call that person before we get into trouble. The difference between victory and defeat can be as little as five or ten minutes on the telephone, talking and praying with someone who understands.

But watch out for the voices that whisper false messages in your ear:

Shame whispers, "Don't you feel bad about always having to depend on others?"

Deceit whispers, "You fail too often. They will get tired and give up on you."

Fear whispers, "Don't give anybody that kind of control over you."

Pride whispers, "You don't need to tell them you blew it again. Just get up, dust yourself off, and say nothing."

Don't listen to these voices, instead reach for the help that is available.

"Friends love through all kinds of weather, and families stick together in all kinds of trouble."

Survival Guide for **August 10**

"... WE... HAVE DIVINE POWER TO DEMOLISH STRONGHOLDS." 2 CORINTHIANS 10:4 (NIV)

We all have habits—good ones and bad ones. Today I want to talk about bad habits.

Bad habits keep us from growing, excelling and soaring to the heights God has in mind for us. (Psalm 139:23-24 NIV). Bad habits are ways of thinking and acting that become part of our everyday lives; ways of trying to meet a need or fill a void. Bad habits become crutches we use to get through life. But when a bad habit takes control of us, the Bible calls it a "stronghold" (it has a strong hold on us).

Do you have a habit that has become a stronghold? As long as you think you can break it in your own strength, nothing will change. When we operate in our power, we disconnect from God's power. Jesus said, ". . . In the same way that a branch can't bear grapes by itself but only by being joined to the vine, you can't bear fruit unless you are joined with me.. . . When you're joined with me and I with you, the relation intimate and organic, the harvest is sure to be abundant. Separated, you can't produce a thing." (John 15:4-5).

You must come to the place where you make a conscious decision each day, and sometimes each hour of the day, to turn your life and your will over to God. Pray, "Lord, I don't have the ability to overcome this. I choose not to give in to it. Strengthen me now by Your Spirit."

That's a prayer God will answer, for He always empowers our choices when they line up with His will!

Whatever your struggle today, remember, ". . . we. . . have divine power to demolish strongholds."

Survival Guide for **August 11**

"I DO NOT FIGHT LIKE A MAN BEATING THE AIR."
1 CORINTHIANS 9:26 (NIV)

If you try to fight every battle on every front, you will wear yourself out and be ineffective to boot.

Fighting a battle without a good cause is like pouring water on a burning shack: unless someone's in danger, it's probably not worth saving. Conserve your strength for when there is something really important at stake.

A sure way to loss your fights is to

- (a) fight the wrong battles;
- (b) fight at the wrong time:
- (c) fight other peoples battles for them;
- (d) fight because you constantly need to win in order to feel good about yourself;
- (e) fight a battle that's already been lost, but your pride won't let you accept it.

A strategy for winning your fights is to

- (a) Use discernment;
- (b) Stay focused on your goals. Keep your eyes on the prize God has set before you. (Phil 3:14).

If the enemy can't defeat you, he will either seek to distract with some "side issue" or disqualify you personally by getting you to make bad choices. Either way, he wins and you lose.

 "Therefore I do not run like a man running aimlessly; I do not fight like a man beating the air. No, I act in such a way so as not to be disqualified from receiving the prize." (1Cor 9:26 paraphrase).

Survival Guide for **August 12**

"THE SPIRIT OF GOD WAS MOVING. . ." GENESIS 1:2 (NAS)

Our unchanging God is a God of change. He's always on the move. In Genesis we read, "In the beginning. . . the Spirit of God was moving . . ." (Genesis 1:1-2 NAS). God is still moving today. When He moves, things change and those who move with Him grow.

Scientists conducted an experiment in which they placed an amoeba in a stress-free environment. Conditions were ideal. It had no adjustments whatsoever to make, yet it died. Why? Because change and challenge are as essential to growth as food and water. "Getting comfortable" is good for the short term but staying comfortable inhibits growth.

God moves! If we are going to move with Him we have to:
   (1)   forget about our comfort
   (2)   refuse to settle for where we are
   (3)   abandon our old ideas on how things ought to be done.

The disciples left everything to walk with Somebody they didn't even begin to comprehend. They dreamed of a Messiah Who would establish a kingdom and overthrow Rome, so the crucifixion blew their minds. And the resurrection created problems too, because now they had to preach a controversial Gospel that could cost them their lives.

Following Jesus means yielding:
   (a) the right to know what it will cost us
   (b) the right to know how much it will change us
   (c) the right to know where it will take us.

The disciples didn't know what to make of Jesus. When He walked on the water they said, "He's a spirit." When He ate with them on the shore they said, "He's a Man." For them following Jesus meant accepting the paradox of the incarnation. That hasn't changed. When you decide to follow Jesus, get ready to have your circuits blown and your faith stretched.

Today, get ready to move with God!

Survival Guide for **August 13**

"YOU. . . BECAME MY PARTNERS." PHILIPPIANS 4:15 (TLB)

At midnight November 20, 1988, a 19-year-old woman who had fallen asleep behind the wheel, plunged her car through a crash barrier. It dangled 60 feet in the air. Some motorists stopped, grabbed ropes, tied them to the back of the woman's car and hung on till emergency units arrived. A ladder was extended from below to help stabilize the car while firemen chained the vehicle to two trucks. Every time her car moved she screamed. It took over two hours for passers-by, the California Highway Patrol, tow-truck drivers and firemen—about 25 people in all—to pull her to safety. "'It was kinda funny," Los Angeles Fire Captain, Ross Marshall recalled later. "She kept shouting, 'I'll do it myself!'"

Aren't we all like that (though, hopefully, not to that extreme)? The only problem with trying to do everything on your own is that it doesn't work. Actually, it is quite impossible.

On his office wall, Alex Haley, the author of Roots, had a picture of a turtle sitting on top of a six-foot fence post. The caption read, "You can be sure he had help getting up there!" Haley said, "Anytime I feel too proud to ask for help, I look at that picture."

Somebody within your reach knows something you need to know; something you'll never learn on your own. They're your mentor. Get close to them. Drop your bucket into their well and begin to draw water.

Paul recognized his limitations, so he connected his life to others: ". . . you Philippians became my partners in giving and receiving . . . " (Philippians 4:15 TLB).

Some know how to give but not receive.
Others know how to receive but not give.
Wise men and women know how to do both!

Survival Guide for **August 14**

" . . . HOW GREAT YOUR FAITHFULNESS!"
LAMENTATIONS 3:23

Don't be too hard on Thomas for doubting.

He had already given up his job once, to follow a Man he had seen crucified and buried. So when the disciples said, "Jesus is alive," Thomas wasn't taking any chances. That is what we do when our faith seems to fail, isn't it? Discard it in favor of something we think is absolute: "Unless I see . . . I will not believe it." (Jn 20:25 NIV).

Did Thomas's lack of faith do away with the resurrection? No!

But Thomas almost missed the greatest event of his life because he limited himself to one method of believing—seeing. Yet seeing is not always reliable. Do you think the magician really saws the lady in half, or makes the table float in mid-air? For generations scientists "saw" through telescopes and told us the earth was flat, and that the sun revolved around it! Today's scientific "fact" can become tomorrow's scientific nonsense.

Every time we fly, trusting a pilot you have never even met; or drive a car, trusting the other drivers on the road will stay in their lane, we are operating in faith. We can't function without it.

The real question is, who is worthy of our trust?

The only sure answer is—God!

Indeed, Heavenly Father, "How great Your faithfulness!"

Survival Guide for August 15

" . . . EVEN BETTER BLESSINGS ARE IN STORE FOR THOSE WHO BELIEVE WITHOUT SEEING." JOHN 20:29

There are times when faith seems to make no sense at all.

How can a sea be parted, or one man defeat an army, or the world be created by a Word? Non-Christians think we're simple minded for believing such things. Yet, they often base their entire future on the stock market, or are willing to sell their home and move their family halfway across the country based on a promise—or a ninety-day probationary period. Talk about faith!

What is the difference? Their faith is in man—ours is in God.

Who is wiser? Jesus said, "Embrace this God-life. Really embrace it." (Mark 11:22). That takes our faith from the unreliable, and places it in a God Who is faithful, dependable, and sure. We can't see tomorrow, but we trust the One Who does. We can't trust ourselves, so we depend on His wisdom to know what's best for us. Sounds smart to me!

Even some who call themselves Christians are doubters. When you tell them God's blessed you in a certain way, they say, "Yes, what did you do?" Because they haven't developed their faith, they go around like Delilah, trying to find out the secret of yours.

The simple truth is, when you walk with God, sometimes He just blesses you. He does it because He promised to, because He can, and because it pleases Him.

Today, "Embrace this God-life. Really embrace it!"

Survival Guide for **August 16**

". . . THE ENERGETIC HAVE SOMETHING TO SHOW FOR THEIR LIVES" PROVERBS 13:4

Thomas Starzls became interested in organ transplants when he was a surgery resident in medical school. In 1958, he sewed new livers into dogs whose livers had been removed, but all of them died within two days of the operation. A year later he found a way to stabilize circulation and the dogs lived for a week. In March 1963 he performed the first human liver transplant, but his patient bled to death. That failure, and the hepatitis epidemic that spread through artificial kidney transplant centers worldwide during the 1960's, forced his liver transplant program to be abandoned.

But he refused to quit!

In 1968, Starzls reported the results from new transplant trials. All seven children involved had survived, although four died within six months—an encouraging but not outstanding result. By 1975 only two liver transplant programs were left in the world.

Twenty-three years after he first began, Starzls and his team found success—19 out of 22 patients lived for long periods after transplant. Starzls was criticized, even vilified by the medical establishment for even attempting liver transplantation. But he persevered. And we should all be glad he did!

Today liver transplants are routinely performed in hospitals around the world and people who once had no hope are now living happy and productive lives.

Thomas Starzls was energetic!

By energetic I mean the type of man Jack London was describing when he wrote, "The proper function of man is to live—not just exist. Therefore I shall not waste my days by trying to prolong them. I shall use my time!"

"I shall use my time!"

That just about describes "the energetic," doesn't it?

Survival Guide for August 17

"LET THE PEACE OF CHRIST RULE IN YOUR HEARTS . . ."
COLOSSIANS 3:15 (NIV)

If you don't have peace about a decision you have made, don't proceed: "You will go out with joy, and be led forth with peace . . ." (Isaiah 55:12 NIV).

Jesus said, ". . . my peace I give you: I do not give to you as the world gives . . . " (John 14:27 NIV). The world offers a feeling of peace that operates only when everything's going well. But when all hell is breaking loose around you and yet you're able to remain calm, you're experiencing "the peace of God, which transcends all understanding." (Philippians 4:7 NIV).

How do we get this peace? By trusting Jesus with our entire lives! That transfers our problems from us to Jesus.

> "Let Him have all your worries and cares, for He is always thinking about you and watching everything that concerns you. Be careful—watch out for attacks from Satan. He prowls around like a hungry, roaring lion, looking for some victim to tear apart. Stand firm when he attacks. Trust the Lord. And remember that other Christians are going through these sufferings too.

> "After you have suffered a little while, our God, Who is full of kindness, He personally will come and pick you up, and set you firmly in place, and make you stronger than ever." (1 Peter 5:7-10 TLB).

Survival Guide for **August 18**

_____

**"MY FATHER AND MOTHER WALKED OUT AND LEFT ME,
BUT GOD TOOK ME IN." PSALM 27:10**

Has death or divorce robbed you of a parent? Are you still grieving for
lost hugs and birthdays without your mom or dad? The loss of a parent
can cause you to struggle all your life to find your identity. Or if you grew
up listening to endless arguments and never seeing affection displayed, it's
easy to think that's normal and when you discover that it isn't to wonder,
"How can I ever be a decent spouse or parent when I still feel like a lost
child?"

David said, "My father and mother walked out and left me, but God took
me in." (Ps 27:10).

If you have lost a parent to death or divorce God can hold you and heal
your pain. When you're hurting, God can put you on His couch and be
your "Wonderful Counselor." (Isa 9:6). When you feel like an orphan,
God can be to you an "Everlasting Father" who never abandons His kids,
no matter what. With your Heavenly Father you know you are safe and
protected, because that's what loving fathers do. You're His child, which
means if something's important to you, it's important to Him. What's
more, He can send people into your life who'll be to you, the father, the
mother, the brother, or the sister you never had: "God sets the lonely in
families . . . " (Ps 68:6 NIV).

Today, don't focus so much on your losses that you fail to see God at
work, or recognize those He sends into your life to make it better.

Survival Guide for **August 19**

"IT'S NOT GOOD FOR THE MAN TO BE ALONE . . . "
GENESIS 2:18

While these words were written about Adam and Eve and are usually applied to marriage they are also a general truth for all of us, men and women.   Our culture of self-sufficiency tends to create isolation.   The more we are isolated the more everything becomes magnified.   Paranoia abounds until we may even think that people who don't go out of their way to become our friends, are actually plotting against us.

The answer to isolation is connection. By connecting with others, we're able to see that our monsters are only knee-high, and most of our fears are made of smoke and mirrors. No wonder God said, "It is not good for the man to be alone" (Gen 2:18 NIV).

If you have bought into our societies doctrine of self-sufficiency and its corollary: isolation, consider this thought-provoking poem by Charles H. Towne.

Around the corner I have a friend,
   in this great city that has no end.
   Yet days go by and weeks rush on,
   and before I know it, a year is gone.
   And I never see my old friend's face,
   for life is a swift and terrible race.
He knows I like him just as well
   as in the days when I rang his bell.
   And he rang mine—we were younger then;
   but now we are tired, busy men.
   Tired of playing a foolish game,
   tired of trying to make a name.
"Tomorrow," I say, "I will call on Jim,
   and let him know that I'm thinking of him."
   But tomorrow comes and tomorrow goes,
   and the distance between us grows and grows.
   Around the corner, yet miles away,
   then comes the news. . . Jim died today!

And that's what we get, and deserve in the end, "around the corner—a vanished friend!" Don't wait until it is too late—today reconnect with people in your life who really matter!

Survival Guide for **August 20**

"LIKE A WARRIOR'S FISTFUL OF ARROWS ARE THE CHILDREN OF A VIGOROUS YOUTH" PSALM 127:4

Most college students that I meet are ready for sex. Unfortunately, some of them mistake that as meaning that they are ready for marriage and a family. But are you? No more tantrums; no more staying home from school (or, more than likely work!) because you don't feel like going; no more going out whenever you want to go out and party. Marriage means growing up!

Every team needs a game plan and a good coach; without them, an NFL team can play worse than a college team. That is the job of parents in a family. The most important job a parent has is not making a living or giving the family a nice house to live in. The most important job of a parent is to create a game plan for the family and coach the family to execute the game plan. What values will you live by? What are you going to do with your children's unique personality, gifts, and talents?

"Like a warrior's fistful of arrows are the children of a vigorous youth." (Ps 127:4). Be prepared to shoot those arrows as far as you can, using all the strength God has given you! Be ready to give your children purpose and direction. Prepare to aim them toward a worthy goal, and help them to reach it by having direction in your own life now. What is your purpose? Are you living it out every day?

If you want to create a better future, don't squander your youth. Invest your days wisely. Determine where you want to go, and start taking steps to get there. Before you try to lead anybody else, make sure you know how to follow God yourself.

Are you ready for marriage and a family or just ready for sex? Believe me, it is worth the wait to get the order right and know that you are now ready for the children that sex may bring!

Survival Guide for **August 21**

**"FOR TO ME TO LIVE IS CHRIST, AND TO DIE IS GAIN."
PHILIPPIANS 1:21 (NIV)**

For me, to live is Christ . . . to die is to gain. Those words don't work for any other life purpose. Try it:

a)   For me, to live is money . . . to die is to leave it all behind.
b)   For me, to live is fame . . . to die is to be quickly forgotten.
c)   For me, to live is power . . . to die is to be replaced by others.
d)   For me, to live is possessions . . . to die is to depart empty-handed.

Somehow the words fall flat, don't they?

When money is our obsession we can never get enough, and we live in constant fear of losing it. When fame is our goal we become competitive and manipulative lest others upstage us. That breeds insecurity. When power and influence drive us, we become self-serving and head-strong. That makes us arrogant. When possessions become our gods, we become materialistic. That breeds greed and greed is never satisfied.

Whether you have or don't have, are known or unknown, live or die—only Christ can satisfy. And death? That only sweetens the pie. J.B. Philips paraphrases Paul, "Living to me simply means Christ, and if I should die, I merely gain more of Him."

The bottom line is this: the secret of living is the same as the secret of joy; both revolve around Christ.

Cultivate a Christ-centered, Christ-controlled life, and you can say with Paul—"for to me to live is Christ, and to die is gain!"

Survival Guide for **August 22**

"... UNLESS A GRAIN OF WHEAT IS BURIED IN THE GROUND, DEAD TO THE WORLD, IT IS NEVER ANY MORE THAN A GRAIN OF WHEAT. BUT IF IT IS BURIED, IT SPROUTS AND REPRODUCES ITSELF MANY TIMES OVER." JOHN 12:24

What do you say to those who believe in miracles when they don't get one? Or when your life suddenly hits the wall? Or your home or business burns to the ground and your insurance won't cover it? Or your girlfriend, boyfriend, or spouse gets involved with somebody else? There lie your hopes for a relationship that would last forever. There lie the ashes of what you had to lose, in order to gain what God has in store for you next. It's both a place of death and a place of birth. And it hurts!

To reach the next dimension of anything, something you presently have may be the sacrificial offering required. Jesus taught that some things in our lives must die, in order to be reborn to the next level.

Is that what is happening to you?

When trouble comes, our questions often place God's integrity on the line. Indeed He has to be extremely secure, to stick to His plan in the face of our vacillating and complaining.

It is not until we look back that we realize what we went through was just the bar mitzvah (coming of age) of our ability to trust; the time weak faith evolved into a faith previously beyond our grasp. It is on the other side of pain that our faith gets its diploma, and from then on, refuses to be intimidated by anyone or anything.

Hang in there, especially in times of pain, graduation is worth the effort!

" . . . a grain of wheat. . . dead to the world. . . reproduces itself many times over."

Survival Guide for **August 23**

"EVEN THOUGH YOU'RE NOT MUCH RIGHT NOW, YOU'LL END UP BETTER THAN EVER." JOB 8:7

George's first job as a landscaper was removing a big tree stump for a farmer. It was also his first time to use dynamite. With the farmer watching, George calculated the size of the stump, the right amount of dynamite, and pushed the plunger. Suddenly there was an explosion, the big tree-stump rose gracefully into the air, and came crashing down—right on top of the cab of George's new truck! Filled with admiration, the farmer turned to him and said, "Son, with a little more practice, those stumps will land in the bed of that truck every time!"

No matter what we are doing, few of us ever get it right the first time. When Thomas Edison was developing the light bulb he made a thousand attempts before the lights came on. His answer to his critics is legendary: "I didn't fail 999 times, the electric light bulb was just a one-thousand-step process!" It's all in how you choose to see it, isn't it?

What will you learn or accomplish if you give up? Instead of dwelling on how far short you fell, look at how close you came to success. My experience is that if m life is failure-free I'm not taking enough risks. My experience is also that when I'm not taking enough risks I'm not growing in obedience to God.

Refuse to allow the opinions of others to limit you. The road to success is through multiple failures. The people who tell you today that you couldn't or shouldn't, will be the first to claim credit tomorrow when you succeed. Don't let that make you resentful, instead let it motivate you to keep pressing forward.

Practice wouldn't be necessary if failure didn't precede success.

Most beginnings are rocky at best but without those rocky beginnings there are no spectacular endings!

Today, take that risk you've been putting off because of fear of failure.

Survival Guide for August 24

"THESE HARD TIMES ARE SMALL POTATOES COMPARED TO THE COMING GOOD TIMES, THE LAVISH CELEBRATION PREPARED FOR US." 2 CORINTHIANS 4:17

Jesus said we would have problems (John 16:33). Nobody gets a free pass. Solve one problem and another is waiting to take its place. They are not all big, but they are all necessary to spiritual growth. How do you measure the strength of anything? By testing it: ". . . don't be shocked that you are going through testing. It will prepare you." (1 Peter 4:12-13 CEV).

David wrote: "The Lord is close to the brokenhearted." (Psalm 34:18 NLT). The most life-changing experiences will often come during the darkest days—when your heart is broken, you feel abandoned, you are out of options, your pain levels are through the roof—and you turn to God. That is when we learn to pray heart-felt, honest-to-God prayers. When we are in pain we don't have the energy for superficial ones.

God could have kept Joseph out of jail, Daniel out of the lions' den, Jeremiah out of the slimy pit and Paul from being shipwrecked, but He didn't. And the result? Every one of them was drawn closer to God—and impacted their world!

Our problems force us to look to God and depend on Him, instead of one another. This is especially hard on super-achievers like Paul: "We saw how powerless we were to help ourselves; but that was good, for then we put everything into the hands of God, Who alone could save us." (2 Corinthians 1:9 TLB).

You will never know that God is all you need until God is all you have.

Today place all your needs into His capable, loving hands, and watch what happens.

Survival Guide for **August 25**

"GOD CAN DO ANYTHING, YOU KNOW—FAR MORE THAN YOU COULD EVER IMAGINE OR GUESS OR REQUEST IN YOUR WILDEST DREAMS! HE DOES IT NOT BY PUSHING US AROUND BUT BY WORKING WITHIN US, HIS SPIRIT DEEPLY AND GENTLY WITHIN US." EPHESIANS 3:20

There are words in the Bible that have so much life and power in them that they are stronger than any therapy. God can give us a Word that goes back into our past and heals our yesterday, secures our today, and anchors our tomorrow. That is why Satan clutters our lives with so much junk that we don't have time for God's Word. He knows that the Bible will unmask him and reveal God's power potential that is lying dormant within each Believer.

Before Jeremiah rose to prominence as a prophet God told him:

(a) "before I formed you in the womb I knew you." (Jeremiah 1:5 NIV). Your parents didn't get the first look at you, God did. Nothing about you surprises Him. In spite of what you have been through, He hasn't changed His mind about who you are or what you are destined to become.

(b) "before you were born I set you apart." (Jeremiah 1:5 NIV). Stop looking for acceptance in places where you don't belong. You are on a mission from God. That is why the enemy tries so hard to take you out. Once you understand that, your struggles begin to make sense.

Only as we read God's Word will we begin to sense the awesome, mind-renewing, thirst-quenching, life-changing potential that was deposited within each of us from before the foundation of the world: "Now to Him Who is able to do immeasurably more than all we ask or imagine, according to His power that is at work within us." (Ephesians 3:20 NIV).

Start tapping into God's power potential within you today!

Survival Guide for **August 26**

". . . LET'S NOT ALLOW OURSELVES TO GET FATIGUED DOING GOOD . . ." GALATIANS 6:9

Most of us underestimate the time it takes to achieve anything of lasting value. You have to be willing to pay your dues. James Watt spent 20 years laboring to perfect the steam engine. William Harvey worked day and night for eight years to demonstrate how blood circulated in the human body. Then it took him another 25 years to convince the medical establishment he was right.

Cutting corners is a sign of impatience and poor self-discipline. The way to any breakthrough is follow through.

Albert Grey says, "The common denominator of all success lies in forming the habit of doing things that failures don't like to do." If you find yourself continually giving in to your moods and impulses, you need to change your approach to doing things. The best method is to set standards for yourself that require accountability. Suffering a consequence for not following through will keep you on track like nothing else. Once your new standards are in place, work according to them, not to your moods; that will get you going in the right direction.

Self-discipline is a quality that is developed only through practice. Successful people have learned to do what does not come naturally. They are willing to confront discomfort, distractions, fear, and act in spite of them. R H Macy, founder of Macy's Department Stores, failed at five different professions—whaler, retailer, gold-miner, stockbroker, estate agent—before he finally succeeded. What sustained him through failure after failure? Two things: purpose and persistence.

Purpose and persistence are what separates those who do good, from those who merely dream of doing good!

Survival Guide for **August 27**

"PRACTICE THE SERVANT LIFE" MATTHEW 5:41

Servanthood begins in the mind.

"Let this mind be in you which was also in Christ Jesus, Who made Himself of no reputation, taking the form of a bondservant." (Philippians 2:5-7 NKJ).

Do you serve others to build your reputation or to meet needs? Both can't be your goal at the same time. God is always more interested in our attitude than in our achievements. King Amaziah lost God's favor because "He did what was right in the sight of the Lord, yet not with a true heart." (2 Chronicles 25:2 NRS). True servants have certain attitudes.

True servants focus on others, not themselves.

Real humility is not thinking less of yourself—but thinking of yourself less. A lot of what we do is just self-serving: we serve to be admired or to achieve our own goals. Some of what we do is manipulation, not ministry; we are really thinking about ourselves and how noble and wonderful we are. We even use service as a bargaining tool: "God, I will do this for You, if You will do that for me."

True servants don't use God for their purposes, they let God use them for His.

Self-forgetfulness is a daily struggle, a lesson we must relearn over and over again. We can measure the size of our servant's heart by how we respond when others treat us like servants. How do you react when you feel taken for granted, bossed around or treated as an inferior?

Jesus said, "If someone takes unfair advantage of you, use the occasion to practice the servant life." (Matthew 5:41).

Today, practice the servant life!

Survival Guide for **August 28**

"GOD'S PLAN FOR THE WORLD STANDS UP, ALL HIS DESIGNS ARE MADE TO LAST." PSALM 33:11

What will eternity with God be like?

All I know is that it will be beyond my wildest dreams since Paul wrote "No mere man has ever imagined what wonderful things God has ready for those who love the Lord" (1 Corinthians 2:9 TLB). C S Lewis captured this concept on the last page of the last book in *The Chronicles of Narnia*:

> "For us this is the end of all the stories, but for them
> it was only the beginning of the real story. All their
> life had only been the cover and the title page: now
> at last they were beginning chapter one of the great
> story, which no one on earth has read, which goes
> on forever, and in which every chapter is better
> than the one before."

One of the most damaging aspects of modern living is short-term thinking. Most of us think of eternity only at funerals, and then it's shallow, sentimental thinking. Only a fool goes through life unprepared for what will inevitably happen.

We need to think more about eternity. Just as the nine months we spent in our mother's womb were preparation for life, so this life is preparation for the next.

Want some good news?

If you have a relationship with Jesus you don't need to fear death. It may be the last hour of your time on earth, but it won't be the last of you. Your time on earth is just the blink of an eye, but the consequences of it will last forever.

So make Jesus your priority—get an eternal perspective and start living each day with the end in view!

Survival Guide for **August 29**

"BUT ONE THING I DO." PHILIPPIANS 3:13 (NIV)

Howard Hendricks writes,

> "As a young leader, my biggest mistake was
> allowing my time to be eaten up with things outside
> my core competencies. I wanted to set the pace for
> others, to demonstrate that nothing was beneath me,
> so I devoted an inordinate amount of time to things
> I wasn't good at—things I'd never be good at. At
> the same time I invested little energy into
> developing my strengths. I worked hard but not
> smart. Finally, I realized that my true value lay
> within the context of my giftedness—not the
> number of hours I worked. There were some balls
> I'd no business juggling. When I finally got the
> courage to let them fall to the floor, I began to excel
> in juggling the two or three balls I was created to
> keep in the air in the first place. And the amazing
> thing is, people came long and picked up the other
> balls. What I couldn't relinquish were the
> opportunities they'd been waiting for. What
> drained me fuelled them."

Of the two or three things that take up most of your time, which of them
are in line with your core competencies? That is where you must focus
your energies. That is where you'll excel. Within that narrowed context
you will make the greatest contribution. And best of all, you will enjoy
what you do.

"But I can't afford to focus all my energies on one or two things." Maybe
not yet, but that should be your goal. It is something you should be
working toward if you ever hope to maximize your potential.

Focus!

Survival Guide for **August 30**

"THOSE WHO HAVE BEEN GIVEN A TRUST MUST PROVE FAITHFUL." 1 CORINTHIANS 4:2 (NIV)

God not only deals with us about spiritual and moral issues, He deals with us also about our money:

"He called ten of his servants and gave them ten minas. 'Put this money to work,' he said, 'until I come back.'" (Luke 19:13 NIV). When he returned, "He sent for the servants to whom he had given the money to find out what they had gained with it." (Luke 19:15 NIV).

It is wise to have goals for our life, but God's greatest goal for mankind is: "This gospel of the kingdom will be preached in the whole world then the end will come." (Matthew 24:14 NIV). This can be accomplished through the printed page, media, local churches, campus ministry, missions, humanitarian relief and probably a dozen other ways. They all have one thing in common (beyond the obvious): they aren't cheap!

Our favorite prayer, "Lord, meet all my needs," won't get the job done.

Someone has to believe God for more than just their own needs, step out in faith, and say, "Lord, Your kingdom is my first concern. I will sign the check, You fill in the amount. One day I want to be able to see You face-to-face and declare, 'I have invested every ounce of energy, every talent, every penny You entrusted to me to fulfill Your purposes in the earth.'"

That is a steward's prayer.

If you can't pray that prayer today, drop to your knees, repent and start changing your priorities.

Survival Guide for **August 31**

**"LET US WORSHIP GOD IN A WAY THAT WILL PLEASE HIM."
HEBREWS 12:28 (TEV)**

In John 4, a Samaritan woman with a checkered past tried to debate Jesus as to the best time, place and style for worship. But Jesus told her these issues were irrelevant. Where you worship God isn't as important as why or how much of yourself you offer to Him in the process: ". . . Those who worship him must do it out of their very being, their spirits, their true selves, in adoration" (John 4:24). Worship is your spirit responding to God's Spirit. Worship is not a matter of saying the right words—we must mean what we say. Heartless praise isn't praise at all.

We may worship imperfectly, but we must never worship insincerely.

The best style of worship for you is the one that authentically represents your love for God based on your background and personality. If God intentionally made us all different, why would we all be expected to express our love for Him in the same way? There's no one-size-fits-all style of worship. You don't glorify God by trying to be something He doesn't need one more of. God wants you to be yourself: "That's the kind of people the Father is out looking for: those who are simply and honestly themselves before Him in their worship." (John 4:23).

Mindless worship is meaningless worship. Jesus called thoughtless worship "meaningless repetitions." (Matthew 6:7 NAS). Even biblical terms can become tired clichés from overuse. If someone approached you and repeated, "praise you" 50 times, you would probably think *for what*?

Wouldn't you rather receive two specific compliments than 20 vague generalities?

So would God!

Survival Guide for **September 1**

"(THE SACRIFICE ACCEPTABLE) TO GOD IS A BROKEN AND CONTRITE HEART." PSALM 51:17 (AMP)

There are two types of brokenness in the Bible. One is the result of being hurt and mistreated. The other is when we do something wrong and aren't just sorry we got caught, but genuinely regret grieving God. That kind of brokenness softens our hearts, removes rebellion, and clothes us with humility.

Ever seen a cowboy try to tame a wild horse? The first time he jumps on, the horse has a fit—it bucks and kicks until he's thrown off. But gradually, as the horse is broken, it becomes gentle and a joy to ride. It is the same with us. When we first come to God our flesh is wild and out of control, so He puts His "spiritual reins" on us and harnesses our energies into doing His will and not our own. Now instead of living by our impulses, we follow the leading of His Spirit: "No discipline seems pleasant at the time, but painful. Later on, however, it produces a harvest of righteousness and peace for those who have been trained by it." (Hebrews 12:11 NIV).

If you are struggling with God's correction today, exchange your struggle for a snuggle. Snuggle up into His arms and say,

> "Father, I ask You to break me and make me the person You created me to be. Help me to accept Your discipline and begin making the changes You require, for I long to please You in all that I do."

Survival Guide for **September 2**

"WE WILL NOT COMPARE OURSELVES WITH EACH OTHER." GALATIANS 5:26

True servants concentrate on their God-given assignment—not on what somebody else is doing.   Competition between God's servants is illogical—we are all on the same team: ". . .we will not compare ourselves as if one of us were better and another worse.   We have far more interesting things to do. Each of us is an original." (Galatians 5:26).. Our goal is to make God look good, not ourselves.

This is an area where many of us need to just grow up and get over our petty jealousies.

True servants don't complain of unfairness, don't have pity-parties and don't resent those not serving in the same way. They just trust God and keep serving.   When we are busy serving, we won't have time to be critical.   It is not our job to evaluate others: "Do you have any business crossing people off the guest list or interfering with God's welcome? If there are corrections to be made or manners to be learned, God can handle that without your help." (Romans 14:4).

God is the evaluator, not us.

Nor is it our job to defend ourselves against criticism. Let God handle it! Nehemiah's response to his critics is a classic: "My work is too important to stop now and visit you." (Nehemiah 6:3 CEV).

One of the most beautiful acts of love shown to Jesus was criticized by His own disciples.   When Mary took the most valuable thing she owned, expensive perfume, and poured it over Jesus, they called it ". . .a waste." (Matthew 26:8). But Jesus called it "significant." (Matthew 26:10).

There is only one opinion that matters—God's!

Service for Christ is never wasted, regardless of what others say

Survival Guide for **September 3**

"WHAT YOU SAY ABOUT YOURSELF MEANS NOTHING IN GOD'S WORK. IT'S WHAT GOD SAYS ABOUT YOU THAT MAKES THE DIFFERENCE." 2 CORINTHIANS 10:18

If our sense of self-worth is based on anything other than God's approval, it will be difficult to serve with the right motives. True servants accept jobs that insecure people consider beneath them. Jesus washed the feet of His disciples? Could you do that?

Insecure people always worry about how they appear. They hide their weaknesses beneath layers of protective pride. The more insecure we are, the more we need people to serve us, and the more we work for their acceptance.

Henri Nouwen writes,

> "In order to be of service to others, we have to die to them; that is, we have to give up measuring our meaning and value by the yardstick of others thus we become free to be compassionate."

Our service should not be based on the response of those we are serving, but on obedience to God alone.

True servants don't need to cover their walls with plaques or insist on lofty titles. Paul writes, "You may boast about yourself, but the only approval that counts is the Lord's approval." (2 Corinthians 10:18 CEV).

If anyone had a chance to name-drop it was James, the half-brother of Jesus. What credentials, growing up with Jesus as your brother! Yet he simply referred to himself as ". . . a slave of God and the Master Jesus . . ." (James 1:1).

Our service to Christ shouldn't be an obligation or a job, it should be a joy: "Bring a gift of laughter, sing yourselves into his presence." (Psalm 100:2).

Imagine what would happen if even 10 percent of us got serious about our role as true servants!

Survival Guide for **September 4**

"WHILE I WAIT FOR GOD AS LONG AS HE REMAINS IN HIDING, WHILE I WAIT AND HOPE FOR HIM." ISAIAH 8:17

You wake up one morning and all your "spiritual feelings" are gone. You pray, but nothing happens. You rebuke the devil, but it doesn't change anything. You go through spiritual exercises, have your friends pray for you, confess every sin you can imagine, then you go around asking forgiveness of everyone you know. You fast, still nothing. You begin to wonder how long this spiritual gloom will last. It feels like your prayers bounce off the ceiling. In utter desperation you cry out: "What's the matter with me?"

Nothing! This is a normal part of the maturing of our faith in God. We all go through it! It's painful, but absolutely vital to developing our faith. God is always present, even when we are unaware of Him. His presence is too profound to be measured by intellect or emotion. He's more concerned that we trust Him, than that we feel Him.

Faith, not feelings, is what pleases God.

So what can you do when you're going through a time when God seems distant?

Remind yourself that He is not, regardless of your feelings.

Focus on God's unchanging love for you.

Cling to His promises.

During times of spiritual dryness, rely on God's Word, not your emotions. Realize that God is taking you to a deeper level of maturity. Any friendship based on emotion is shallow indeed. So don't be troubled by trouble. God's grace is still in full force.

Jesus is for you, even when you don't feel Him.

Survival Guide for **September 5**

"THERE'S AN OPPORTUNE TIME TO DO THINGS, A RIGHT TIME FOR EVERYTHING ON THE EARTH."
ECCLESIASTES 3:1

Many of the tomatoes we eat are picked before they are ripe so they won't bruise during shipping. Then before they're sold they're sprayed with carbon dioxide gas to turn them red instantly. Now gas-ripened tomatoes are all right, but they're no match for vine-ripened ones that are allowed to mature slowly. They are filled with flavor.

We worry about how fast we grow; God is more concerned with how flavorful we are!

The moment you open your life to Christ, He establishes a beachhead. You may think you've surrendered all, but there are areas you're not even aware of yet. You can give God only as much of you as you understand at that moment! But that's fine. Once God is given a beachhead, Christ begins a campaign to take over more and more territory until your life is completely His. Satan fights back. We call it spiritual warfare

The battle rages and there are struggles and battles, but the outcome is never in doubt: "He who began a good work in you will carry it on to completion." (Philippians 1:6 NIV).

We are obsessed with speed, but God is more interested in stability. We want the quick fix, the shortcut, the on-the-spot solution. We want a sermon, a seminar or an experience that will instantly resolve our problems, remove our temptations and release us from growing pains. Get real! Maturity is never the result of a single experience, no matter how powerful or moving. Healthy growth is gradual growth.

Paul describes it this way: ". . . our lives gradually becoming brighter and more beautiful as God enters and we become like Him." (2 Corinthians 3:18).

Survival Guide for **September 6**

"THE PHRASE "ONE LAST SHAKING" MEANS A THOROUGH HOUSECLEANING, GETTING RID OF ALL THE HISTORICAL AND RELIGIOUS JUNK SO THAT THE UNSHAKABLE ESSENTIALS STAND CLEAR AND UNCLUTTERED." HEBREWS 12:27

Tests and trials determine where we are spiritually. Under pressure, you get to meet—the real you. Jesus said to Peter, "Satan has asked for you, that he may sift you as wheat." (Lk 22:31 NKJV). The word sift means "to shake as in a sieve, inwardly to try one's faith to the verge of overthrow."

Some of us would have said Satan was attacking Peter, that he needed to pray and rebuke him. But Jesus told Peter, "I have prayed for you that your faith should not fail and, when you have returned to Me, strengthen your brethren." (Lk 2 2:32 NKJV).

Jesus did not pray that Peter would escape his intense shaking. No, He prayed that his faith wouldn't fail in the process. The Master knew that out of this trial would emerge new character, the type Simon Peter needed to fulfill his destiny and strengthen others.

There are five reasons for shaking something:

1) To awaken it.
2) To remove dead fruit or leaves.
3) To mix two things together thoroughly so they can't be separated.
4) To bring it closer to its foundation.
5) To harvest what's ready.

If God's permitting your life to be shaken today, then take a closer look. He may be doing it because He wants to . . .
    awaken you . . .
    remove the dead things of the past that are still clinging to you . . .
    make you and Him inseparable . . .
    place you on a strong foundation . . .
    or make you more fruitful.

Hang in there: God may continue His shaking until only "unshakeable things" are left!

Survival Guide for **September 7**

"WHEN I GET REALLY AFRAID I COME TO YOU IN TRUST"
PSALM 56:3

Meteorologists say that a fog capable of covering half a square mile is made up of only one glass of water, divided into 60 million particles. But when it settles, it can obscure your entire vision.

A little fear can do the same thing.

Why do almost half of us suffer from stress-related disorders? Because instead of walking by faith, we think we're supposed to fly like jets on supercharged adrenaline—and we pay for it in terms of fear and anxiety.

It is so easy for fear to replace faith because they have something in common—both challenge us to believe in what we can't see. Fear tries to persuade us to run from something that's not there. Faith tries to persuade us to run to Someone who is.

Billy Sunday said, "Fear knocked at my door. Faith answered. There was no one there."

Fear is overcome by faith. By faith—and faith comes by hearing the Word of God (Romans 10:17). Feed your faith on the Scriptures, and your fears will starve to death! I find that when I spend the first 15 minutes of my morning filling my mind with God's Word—that day there's no room left for worry .

The antidote to fear is to do what David did: "When I get really afraid, I come to You in trust. . . "

It really comes down to which is in control—fear or faith.

The next time you are afraid, get into God's Word and put faith in control!

Survival Guide for **September 8**

". . .AND SO WE ARE TRANSFIGURED MUCH LIKE THE MESSIAH, OUR LIVES GRADUALLY BECOMING BRIGHTER AND MORE BEAUTIFUL AS GOD ENTERS OUR LIVES AND WE BECOME LIKE HIM." 2 CORINTHIANS 3:18

The church today cannot be stagnant. It needs to be a moving, functioning, vibrant body, with a destination in mind, a map in hand, packed and ready to go to the next level with God. It cannot be satisfied to remain within the framework in which it started, because it's afraid of offending people.

How can we pray for growth, then be afraid of change?

To be growing means to be ever evolving, ever becoming, moving from "faith to faith." (Rom 1:17 NAS) The People of Israel had to move when the cloud moved, otherwise they were left behind. (Ex 13:21).   Think about that!

The word "church" means "the called-out ones." The trouble is that most of us know what we've been called out of—we just haven't discovered yet what we were called into. And until we discover that, we'll keep going in circles and stay in the wilderness.

My experience has been that just about the time I get used to something, God will take me somewhere else; somewhere I've never been before. I think that is characteristic of being "called out." When we have been "called out," we can't stay where we are and have God's blessing.

God blesses those who are willing to change their methods, their motives, their attitudes, their perspectives—and anything else that stands in the way of being "called out."

Today, look up and pray, "Father, whatever it costs, change me so I can help rather than hinder your church."

Survival Guide for **September 9**

"GOD CAN DO . . . FAR MORE THAN YOU COULD EVER IMAGINE OR GUESS OR REQUEST IN YOUR WILDEST DREAMS!" EPHESIANS 3:20

William Carey was called a dreamer for studying foreign languages and the travel-logs of Captain Cook. Many who came to his workshop when he was a cobbler scoffed at the big map he kept on the wall of his workshop so that he could pray every day for the nations.

When he became a minister, he once addressed a conference on, "Is the Great Commission for today?" When he finished speaking, an older clergyman got up and publicly rebuked him, saying, "If God wants to convert the heathen, He'll do it without your help or mine." Carey was silenced for the moment—but not stopped. Soon afterwards, he lived out his dream by carrying the gospel to India and eventually became the father of modern missions!

When your dream is God honoring and you begin to pursue your dream, someone will always emerge to try and steal it. Often, it'll be someone who never had a dream of his own or, if he had, he copped-out and abandoned it. It may be a classmate, churchmate, or workmate who has given up on life and dropped-out. It could even be a family member who has burned out and now constantly reminds you of what God can't do or wouldn't do through someone like you. Never let a cop-out, a dropout, or a burnout cause you to give up the dream God has put in your heart!

What do you dream about?

What has God enabled you to see that does not yet exist?

God can't be out dreamed . . . so keep your dream alive!

"God can do . . . far more than you could ever imagine or guess or request in your wildest dreams." (Eph 3:20).

Survival Guide for **September 10**

"... WHILE HE WAS EATING DINNER, A WOMAN CAME UP
CARRYING A BOTTLE OF VERY EXPENSIVE PERFUME.
OPENING THE BOTTLE, SHE POURED IT ON HIS HEAD."
MARK 14:3

Don't keep the alabaster box of your love sealed up until your friends are gone.

Break it open. Pour it out. Fill their lives with it while you still can. Those words you've thought of saying a thousand times, say them now while their ears can hear them and their hearts can still be touched. Those flowers you've been meaning to send, do it this week and brighten their day while they can enjoy it. Fortunes are spent to engrave words in granite and marble that should've been spoken earlier by human lips.

The crowd in the house saw the woman break open the alabaster box of ointment. They even argued about it. They missed the whole point. If they had only known what was coming. That very night, Judas would set wheels in motion that would lead Jesus to His death. Time and opportunity were running out. She chose this day to demonstrate her love to Jesus. Jesus said, "She pre-anointed My body for burial." (Mk 14:8). How did she know? She didn't. She simply didn't put it off and thereby offered Jesus a kindness before it was too late.

Joseph of Arimathea brought 100 pounds of the same ointment to anoint Jesus after He was dead, yet not a word is mentioned about his post-mortem kindness. She brought one pound and poured it on Jesus while He was still living and Jesus said, "Wherever the gospel is preached . . . what she has done will also be told, in memory of her." (Mk 14:9 NIV).

If you have an alabaster box you've been thinking of breaking open, today would be a good time to do it.

One act of kindness while your loved ones are still here will mean more than 101 when they are gone.

Break it open!

Survival Guide for **September 11**

**"OVERWHELM THEM WITH APPRECIATION AND LOVE!
GET ALONG AMONG YOURSELVES, EACH OF YOU DOING
YOUR PART." 1 THESSALONIANS 5:13**

No matter how much you love someone or how gifted they are, they will get on your nerves from time to time.

An old Irish saying goes, "When you buy a gold mine, you get the dirt too."

Can you imagine being John Mark traveling with the apostle Paul? World changers aren't necessarily good companion material. Movers and shakers generally aren't very patient with those who don't share their vision or respect their schedule. John Mark took all he could take (apparently) and left Paul in the middle of a missionary journey. (Acts 13:13).

To say the least, Paul wasn't very happy about John Mark's behavior. When Barnabas wanted to take John Mark with them on their next journey, Paul exploded—breaking up the team rather than taking John Mark along. (Acts 15:38). I wonder if God recorded this story to remind us that sometimes great people don't act very great?

Clearly, Paul mellowed with age and realized that he hadn't handled the situation very well and was humble enough to change his mind about John Mark. Later he wrote: "Get Mark and bring him with you, because he is helpful to me in my ministry." (2 Tim 4:11 NIV).

Since even the best people in the world will get on our nerves from time to time, it is good to remember that people usually act out of their fears, their unmet needs and their unhealed hurts. So, when others get on your nerves lower your voice, open your heart and be willing to reconsider. Paul gives us the Biblical motive: "Look for the best and always do your best to bring it out."

Never be too proud to change your mind about a person who gets on your nerves.

That is a true sign of growth.

Survival Guide for **September 12**

"GOD WAS WORKING FOR GOOD IN EVERYTHING HE DID."
GENESIS 39:3

Write this down: "My heavenly Father wants good things for me."

What parent wouldn't?

If God wants good things for us why do we keep failing? Often I've found my answer to that question in one or more of these three areas:

1. A negative attitude.   A palm-reader said to her customer, "You will be sad, miserable and poor until you're 30." The customer asked, "What happens when I'm 30?" The palm-reader replied, "Then you'll get used to it!" I hope that brought a smile, but the truth is success requires the right soil, the right seed and the right climate in order to grow. Opportunity is the soil, taking advantage of the opportunity is the seed, and attitude is the climate of life. Attitude, our perspective, can bring either life or death to the seed we sow. Therefore, watch your attitude.

2. A selfish outlook. If others sense that we really don't care about them, they can actually help us to fail or at least stand by and do nothing to keep it from happening. On the other hand, we can survive a lot of mistakes when others help us out because they remember our kindness. Jesus said, "You're blessed when you care. At the moment of being 'careful,' you find yourselves cared for." (Matthew 5:7).

3. A wrong priority. Sometimes failure is just the result of a wrong priority—putting ourselves ahead of God. This leads to mismatched abilities, interests, personalities and values. A wrong priority can lead to us spending our life climbing the ladder of success, only to look back and realize it was leaning against the wrong wall.

"In everything you do, put God first and He will direct you and crown your efforts with success." (Proverbs 3:6 TLB).

God wants good things for you—but on His terms not yours!

Survival Guide for **September 13**

"MOST OF ALL, LOVE EACH OTHER AS IF YOUR LIFE DEPENDED ON IT. LOVE MAKES UP FOR PRACTICALLY ANYTHING." 1 PETER 4:8

When Peter says, "Above all (most important), love each other deeply," (1Pet 4:8 NIV) he is talking about an active love.

"Love each other deeply" surely is the kind of love that:

1. Encourages others. Even the apostle Paul needed that: "Then the God who lifts up the downcast lifted our heads and our hearts with the arrival of Titus." (2 Corinthians 7:6). Imagine being remembered as "the man who encouraged the apostle Paul." If Titus never did anything else, that made him a success. When you encourage someone, you give them the self-esteem and the motivation to reach for their potential.

2. Trusts others. "If you love someone . . . you will always believe in him, always expect the best of him, always stand your ground in defending him." (1 Corinthians 13:7 TLB). Don't judge others by their actions, while you judge yourself by your intentions. That's a double standard! Give others the benefit of the doubt and treat them the way you'd like to be treated.

3. Yields to others. "Agree with each other and live in peace . . . then the God of love and peace will be with you" (2 Corinthians 13:11 NCV). Fighting produces bruised and resistant people, but yielding at the right time can deflate the argument and save the relationship.

In his book *Make a Life, Not a Living*, Ron Johnson writes,

> "Of all the things on earth, what will last for eternity? People! So when you change a life, you're making an investment forever."

Nothing changes people like loving them deeply.

That is, after all, how God changes us!

Survival Guide for **September 14**

"JOSHUA DID WHAT MOSES ORDERED . . ." EXODUS 17:10

Joshua served Moses, but looked only to God for his reward.

No service God gives us to do is beneath us since our reward comes not from the person we serve but from God.

If you pray "God, use me," be prepared for Him to ask you to serve someone else. If you make the mistake of looking to that person for your reward and it doesn't come, you'll feel used and resentful.

We don't live by the world's rules but by God's.

God wants us to honor Him on the job by performing with excellence. He's the one who calls us to the highest standards of behavior. He is the one who says it is not okay to use your roommate's cell phone to call your grandma in Chicago: "Good work will get you good pay from the Master. . . " (Ephesians 6:8).

God balances the scales and rewards us according to our service; not what others think we are worth.

Stop striving and get back to serving: "God is not unjust; He will not forget your work. . . " (Heb 6:10 NIV).

Be encouraged: Serving others brings God rewards—and that is reward enough!

Survival Guide for **September 15**

"MASTER . . . CALL ME TO COME TO YOU ON THE WATER.
HE SAID, COME AHEAD. JUMPING OUT OF THE BOAT,
PETER WALKED ON THE WATER . . . BUT WHEN HE LOOKED
DOWN AT THE WAVES . . . HE LOST HIS NERVE AND
STARTED TO SINK. HE CRIED, 'MASTER, SAVE ME!'
JESUS. . .REACHED DOWN AND GRABBED HIS HAND . . ."
MATTHEW 14:28-31

I find three applications for our walk of faith from Peter's walk on water:

(1) It takes more than one step to get to our goal. This wasn't a little two-person rowing boat where you could just hop over the side. It was a ship. To get to Jesus, Peter had to climb down, keep walking, and keep his eyes on Him. In other words, he had to persevere. To get to our spiritual goal so must we.

(2) There is no faith walk without fluctuation. One moment it feels as if you're walking, the next, as if you're sinking. That sinking feeling is often an attack of the "what-ifs." What if you get too far from the boat and you can't make it to shore? What if the money doesn't come through for your mission trip? What if you haven't prayed hard enough? Faith means standing on what you used to sink in, and declaring, "I'm going from talking about the presence of God, to walking in the provision of God."

(3) God's power is for people who are sinking. Anybody will invest in a company whose stock is going up; but God will invest in you when you are failing: "He energizes those who get tired, gives fresh strength to dropouts." (Isa 40:29).

If you have started walking toward Jesus but feel you are sinking, reach out your hand and He will lift you up!

Survival Guide for **September 16**

"... A TERRIFIC EAST WIND ALL NIGHT LONG, MADE THE SEA GO BACK..." EXODUS 14:21

The miracle of rolling back the Red Sea happened "all night long." The morning simply revealed what God had done the night before, while they were sleeping. That's good news for insomniacs (like me): God works the night shift! Even in the dead of night when you feel lost and alone, God is still on the job, working "everything in conformity with the purpose of his will." (Ephesians 1:11 NIV).

I love this hymn from my youth:

> When darkness seems to hide His face,
> I rest on His unchanging grace.
>
> When all around my soul gives way,
> He then is all my hope and stay.
>
> On Christ the solid rock I stand,
> All other ground is sinking sand.

You may not be able to always feel His presence, but He is no less present. If you're a student at school, or a young couple hard-pressed financially, or a divorcee struggling to get back on your feet, or you're a servant of God laboring in difficult circumstances, or just lonely and in need of companionship, here are some words to help get you through till the morning:

"I was young and now I am old, yet I have never seen the righteous forsaken or their children begging bread." (Psalm 37:25 NIV).

"... The nights of crying your eyes out give way to days of laughter." (Psalm 30:5).

"None of this fazes us because Jesus loves us." (Romans 8:37).

Be encouraged—God works the night shift!

Survival Guide for **September 17**

". . . IF WE ADMIT OUR SINS—MAKE A CLEAN BREAST OF THEM—HE WON'T LET US DOWN; HE'LL BE TRUE TO HIMSELF. HE'LL FORGIVE OUR SINS . . ." 1 JOHN 1:9

An organization in Los Angeles operates an "Apology Sound-Off Line." It gives callers an opportunity to confess their sins anonymously, for just the price of a phone call. At last count, about 500 callers a day were contacting them. Their clients are people who've given up on organized religion; people who believe God's given up on them; people trying to find peace by saying, "I'm sorry for the things I've done."

We all need forgiveness.

If you're feeling guilty today, I have good news for you: "If we admit our sins . . . He won't let us down; He'll be true to Himself. He'll forgive our sins . . . " (1 John 1:9). Guilt is an anchor that keeps us chained to the past and shuts out any possibility for change. God's forgiveness is what breaks that chain, ends the cycle of blame and frees us to be all He wants us to be.

"But you don't know what I've done.." That's true, but God does and His Word says: "God made Him (Jesus) . . . to be sin for us." (2 Corinthians 5:21 NIV).

Whatever kind of sinner you are, Jesus became it. Whatever sin you have committed, Jesus took it. When you accepted that Jesus, the Son of God, died for your sin it was put to death. Your sin was put in the grave with Jesus when you were baptized. You arose from that watery grave a whole new you. No longer does God even look at you; He looks at His crucified Son, charges your sin to His account, and says, "I forgive you."

Don't keep carrying around the dead weight of sin.

Give it to God today, for His Word says,

". . . come back to GOD, who is merciful, come back to our God, who is lavish with forgiveness." (Isaiah 55:7).

Survival Guide for **September 18**

"MASTERS . . . NO ABUSE, PLEASE . . ." EPHESIANS 6:9

Leaders in God's Kingdom—this Survival Guide is for you.

There is no place in God's kingdom for the domineering, the egocentric, or those motivated by anger toward any individual or group, at any time, under any circumstance. Not only is it contrary to Christ's example but it is also dumb! Learn from Pharaoh the lesson he learned the hard way—when a child of God is abused, the Lord will hear their cry, intervene on their behalf, and the offender will pay a high price.

To be a good leader, you must first learn to be a good follower.

Only then will you understand the challenges of serving someone else "as unto the Lord." If you practice servanthood when you're at the bottom, you'll have no trouble doing it when you reach the top. And that's important, for as a leader you must be able to hear, submit to, and obey the leadings of the Holy Spirit.

Joshua was a great leader because he was first a faithful servant of Moses. He remembered the difficulties of submitting to a flawed human being when he himself became a leader. Any time you forget what it's like to walk in the shoes of those who serve under you, you can easily become insensitive to their needs and abuse your power.

For God to trust you with a leadership position, you must first prove to Him that you can control your need for recognition. God-appointed leaders are servant-leaders. They never lead from personal need. They never lead by threat or force. They lead through a compelling combination of love, vision and righteousness.

Leading God's people is an honor and a challenge—one not for the faint of heart!

Survival Guide for **September 19**

"I WILL SING FOR JOY IN GOD, EXPLODE IN PRAISE FROM DEEP IN MY SOUL!..." ISAIAH 61:10

Here is something funny from the internet:

> "Yes, I'm tired. For a couple of years I've been blaming it on iron poor blood, lack of vitamins, air pollution, saccharin, dieting and a dozen other maladies that make you wonder if life is really worth living.
>
> But now I find out, that ain't it. I'm tired because I'm overworked. The population of this country is 237 million. 104 million are retired. That leaves 133 million to do the work. There are 85 million in school, which leaves 48 million to do the work. Of this there are 29 million employed by the government.
>
> This leaves 19 million to do the work. Four million are in the Armed Forces, which leaves 15 million to do the work. Take from that total the 14,800,000 people who work for the state and city government and that leave 200,000 to do the work. There are 188,000 in hospitals, so that leaves 12,000 to do the work. Now, there are 11,998 people in prisons. That leaves just two people to do the work. You and me. And you're slacking off, reading this.
>
> No wonder I'm tired."

Seriously, if you want to relieve from feeling tired all the time, learn to let go. Let go of . . . looking at the negative . . . needing to fix everybody. . . competing and comparing . . . living only for yourself . . . and all the other stuff that keeps you too tired to enjoy life. Refuse to live that way another day! God has put joy in your well, and a pump in your hand.

Start pumping! Start singing for joy! Start exploding in praise! Start living!

Survival Guide for **September 20**

"HE IS IN CHARGE OF IT ALL, HAS THE FINAL WORD ON EVERYTHING. . . " EPHESIANS 1:22

In the Greek mathematical system, when numbers are added, the total is put at the top, not the bottom. Where we might say, "Jesus is the bottom line," the Greeks would say, "Jesus is the top line." I like that better, don't you? No matter how you cut it, when everything's added up—Jesus is the answer.

God has given Jesus as a gift to us. That makes the Church the most privileged people in the history of mankind, because we have as our head the Lord Jesus Christ.

    (1)   In Him, no weapon formed against us can prosper: Isaiah 54:17
    (2)   In Him, we have authority over the enemy: Luke 10:19
    (3)   In Him, we are tapped into the limitless, universe-shaking power of God: Ephesians 1:19

All things are under His control.

That means the problems you are having in your relationships today are under His control; Jesus has a strategy for your relationships. That means the problems you're having at school or work today are under His control; Jesus has a strategy for your life, your talents, and your dreams.

Just as the head commands the body, so Jesus:

    (1)   directs us by His wisdom;
    (2)   empowers us by His Spirit;
    (3)   moves us by His compassion;
    (4)   completes us by His love.

Everything you need today, absolutely everything, can be found in Him.

Jesus doesn't just have the answer—Jesus is the answer!

Survival Guide for **September 21**

". . .SHE SLIPPED IN FROM BEHIND AND TOUCHED HIS ROBE." MARK 5:27

This woman who touched Jesus faced two challenges.

1) Self-doubt: can a person like me touch a God like Him?
2) Getting through the crowd to Jesus.

The enemy will do everything he can to keep you from getting to Jesus.

You will have to press through the flesh realm to get to the spiritual realm. You will have to say to those who doubt what you are doing, "Excuse me, I have to get to Jesus!" To those who want you to stop and stroke their ego, "Sorry, I don't have time, I have to get to Jesus!" To those who offer you their expert but unscriptural opinions, "Please step aside, I'm on my way to Jesus!"

Just take the first step, and God will work with you.

When justice says, "You can't get to Him," mercy will let you through. When the law tries to stop you, grace will open the door. When the world says, "Don't go," God will whisper, "Come. Just press through; I'm waiting for you!"

Don't expect it to be easy.

This woman had to press through the naysayers and the doomsayers, the doctor's report and the pile of unpaid bills, the laws that shut her out and the folks who preached them. But look what happened! Immediately the strength of Jesus poured into every part of her and she was healed.

Jesus' strength will flow into you too, if you will only press through and touch Him today!

Survival Guide for **September 22**

". . . SHE SLIPPED IN FROM BEHIND AND TOUCHED HIS ROBE." MARK 5:27

I have a little more to say about the sick woman I wrote about in my last Survival Guide.

A lot of people we know are just like her, yet it is hard to tell they are suffering because of the atrocious idea that goes: "If you are really a Christian, you wouldn't have that problem." Unfortunately this philosophy pervades the church today. Yet interestingly, if the suffering is from a problem we have, we're fairly tolerant, but when it's a problem we've never struggled with, we're quick to pass judgment. God forgive us!

All God's heroes had problems.

Samson fought lust. Noah got drunk. David stole another man's wife. What a cast! Yet Hebrews 11:13 refers to them as ". . . people of faith . . ." The truth is, you can be a Christian and still struggle. It's not a lack of faith or not being sold out to Jesus, rather it's a matter of living in a fallen world!

The Bible says about this woman that "a long succession of physicians had treated her, and treated her badly, taking all her money and leaving her worse off than before." (Mark 5:26). It is bad enough to have a problem without having a problem with the people who are supposed to be solving your problem!

Be careful who you allow to attempt to solve your problems for you; they may only be after your money or ego-tripping because they are "fixers" or gossiping about you to everybody they know. The trouble with ungodly counselors is that they'll give you plenty of advice, but not lasting help. (See Psalm 1:1). If you want real help, go to somebody who can help you. Go to Jesus! He's the Problem-Solver, the Direction-Giver, the Burden-Bearer, and the Way-Maker.

Press through—one touch from Jesus—and you are on the road to recovery!

Survival Guide for **September 23**

"HE WHO WALKS WITH INTEGRITY WALKS SECURELY. . . "
PROVERBS 10:9 (NKJ)

Samson is the perfect example of one who did NOT walk with integrity and paid the price. Here are four live choices of Samson's to avoid:

(1) He broke the rules. "Don't become partners with those who reject God. . . " (2 Corinthians 6:14). An ox and a donkey are both God's creatures; but they can't sleep in the same stall or work in the same harness. Their natures are too different. When God says "No" to being yoked with unbelievers, He is not being unfair, He is being protective. Walking with integrity means obeying God's rules!

(2) He lived by impulse. Samson thought he was in love when he was only "in lust." When he was confronted about his choices of women he replied, ". . . She's the one I want" (Judges 14:3). Before it was over, he was betrayed by Delilah. Peter writes, ". . . abstain from sinful desires, which war against your soul." (1 Pet 2:11 NIV). Walking with integrity means living by your principles, not your impulses!

(3) He misused his gift. Samson used his supernatural strength for personal gain: ". . . then you'll give ME . . ." (Judges 14:13). God gives us gifts to fulfill His purposes. When we misuse them, we end up in trouble. Walking with integrity means using your gifts for God's glory!

(4) He was blind to his weaknesses. Samson thought his public strength protected him from private indiscretions. Private imperfections will have public consequences, unless they are faced head on. You can't escape who you really are. No wonder David prayed, "Investigate my life, O God, find out everything about me. . ." (Psalm 139:23). Walking with integrity means acknowledging your weakness!

If you look at your life and see Samson—take action to get back on the path of integrity!

Survival Guide for **September 24**

"HOW BLESSED IS GOD! . . . WHAT A BLESSING HE IS! . . . THE FATHER OF OUR MASTER, JESUS CHRIST, AND TAKES US TO THE HIGH PLACES OF BLESSING IN HIM." EPHESIANS 1:3

When we stumble or face a problem, God doesn't jump off His throne and say, "Tim's in trouble, Sheila's in a mess, I'd better act!" No, He's already placed within His children all that is necessary to handle any situation and overcome it. Maturing in Christ is simply the process by which we learn to work out what God has already blessed us with.

Think about a baby in its mother's womb. He or she already has every gene, chromosome, and trait required—there from conception. Likewise, when we are born into God's family, we don't just get one or two spiritual blessings, we get every thing required for us to grow up. As a baby Christian we don't know who we are or what we have, so the Holy Spirit's job is to reveal it to us through God's Word. So when we go through a crisis, we don't need to go on a quest for faith, or grace, or strength, or anything else. We already have them residing within us if we are children of God! We just must learn to draw on them!

Furthermore, we don't need to go looking for a more powerful person to pray for us. I am convinced that God wants to bring each of His children to the place where each of us can. . . lay hands on our own heads. . . minister to our own needs. . . speak peace to our own spirits. . . command calm within our own hearts!

That will happen, when we learn to acknowledge and activate the spiritual blessings God has already placed within us.

"How blessed is God! . . . What a blessing He is!"

Survival Guide for **September 25**

"... JESUS INSISTED HIS DISCIPLES GET IN THE BOAT ..."
MARK 6:45

I drove from the airport tonight amidst the rain and the winds of Hurricane Francis. What about you—are you in a storm today? If so, here are three scriptures I encourage you to read:

(1) "He climbed a mountain to pray . . . the boat was far out at sea" (Mark 6:46,47). Do you feel as if God's off on a mountain-top somewhere, and you're alone in the storm? That may be how you feel but the truth is He has just temporarily stepped out of the storm to leave you alone with the tools He's given you. How you react now, reveals how much you've learned. Some people think if you have enough faith you can stop the storm, or escape it. But I don't believe that. Sometimes you have to go through the storm before you can truly know if you have faith.

(2) ". . . about four o'clock in the morning, Jesus came toward them. . ." (Mark 6:48). There are things you will learn about God at 3 o'clock in the morning that you won't get from a church service or a book or a tape. Every storm introduces you to a new aspect of His character and a new level of His power. When they came through it, the disciples were "amazed," and you will be too.

(3) "He spoke to them and said, 'Take courage! It is I. Don't be afraid. . . ' and the wind died down. . . " (Mark 6:50,51 NIV).

The presence of anyone supportive helps in a storm, but when it is God who comes to you, you have nothing to fear.

Regardless of the deteriorating circumstances, the illness, the betrayal, the credit report, the GPA, or anything else, remember: ". . .With God on our side like this, how can we lose?" (Romans 8:31).

Take courage—no matter how bad the storm God is still God!

Survival Guide for **September 26**

**". . . I'VE DECIDED THAT I REALLY DON'T CARE ABOUT
THEIR MOTIVES, WHETHER MIXED, BAD, OR INDIFFERENT.
EVERY TIME ONE OF THEM OPENS HIS MOUTH, CHRIST IS
PROCLAIMED, SO I JUST CHEER THEM ON!"
PHILIPPIANS 1:18**

Preaching Christ can be done by all kinds of people and in all kinds of ways. In fact, there are bound to be differences among Christians. Not everyone serves God in the same way. If you have trouble accepting that, read these words of the Apostle Paul's: ". . . the important thing is. . . Christ is preached. And because of this I rejoice. . . " (Philippians 1:18 NIV).

Can you rejoice in that too? Or do you need to keep categorizing everybody?

Get rid of your judgementalism and become broad-shouldered enough to let things be. Leave room for differences.

Applaud good results, even if they weren't arrived at by your preferred method. It takes grace to do that. To do otherwise is to clutter your mind with thoughts that rob you of both love and faith. Remember, ". . .What matters is something far more interior: faith expressed in love." (Galatians 5:6). If you are not careful, you'll become a petty, cranky, grim soul, who has to pour everybody into your mold before you can relax.

I know, I was that petty, cranky, grim soul for many years.

And the worst thing is—it can all be done in the name of God. Cut it out!

If God calls somebody His child, we need to start calling them our brother or sister, otherwise our attitude is worse than their action: "Who are you to judge someone else's servant? To his own master he stands or falls. . . " (Romans 14:4 NIV). They are not our servants, they are God's. They are out of our jurisdiction

Today, stop judging, and get your eyes back where they belong—on Jesus!

Survival Guide for **September 27**

**"I WILL CONTINUE TO REJOICE, FOR I KNOW THAT . . .
WHAT HAS HAPPENED TO ME WILL TURN OUT FOR MY
DELIVERANCE." PHILIPPIANS 1:18, 19 (NIV)**

Paul's desire was to go to Rome and testify before Caesar. As a Roman citizen he had that right. Instead, he was illegally arrested in Jerusalem, misrepresented before the court, incorrectly identified as an Egyptian renegade, lost in the red-tape of political machinery, then granted a trip across the Mediterranean only to encounter a storm and be shipwrecked. When he finally arrived in Rome, they imprisoned him and threw away the key for two years. In total, he received countless welts on his back from the Jews and the Roman cat-o'-nine-tails. And for what? He had never broken a single civil law! All he did was preach Christ and love people. Yet he wrote, "What has happened to me will turn out for my deliverance." (Philippians 1:19 NIV).

How can we develop an attitude like that?

The answer is, instead of asking "Why did this have to happen to me?" ask, "How can I grow stronger, see more clearly, and reap the benefits God has for me in this situation?" Paul chose to count his blessings, not his disappointments. Recently while doing a book search on Amazon I came across a book called 14,000 Things To Be Happy About. That's a lot of things to be happy about! The trouble is, not one of the 14,000 will work, unless we give ourselves permission to be happy. The secret lies in the mindset: ". . . Think about all you can praise God for and be glad about." (Philippians 4:8 TLB).

The secret of joy is thinking "about all you can praise God for" instead of playing the "Why me?" game.

Choose Joy today!

Survival Guide for **September 28**

**"I THANK MY GOD EVER TIME I REMEMBER YOU . . ."
PHILIPPIANS 1:3 (NIV)**

Even the great Apostle Paul needed others.

When Paul was ill he needed Dr. Luke. When he was in prison he needed Titus. For his travel he needed Silas. For his future he needed Timothy.

How important are others? Maybe more than you think.

A rooster minus a hen equals no baby chicks. Kellogg, minus a farmer, equals no Cornflakes. Without the nail factory, what good's the hammer factory? Or the cracker-maker without the cheese-maker? Paderewski's genius wouldn't have amounted to a thing if the piano tuner hadn't tuned his piano before the concert. The surgeon needs the ambulance driver. Rogers needed Hammerstein—and you also need people!

The other side of the coin is—somebody needs you too.

The young need your experience and the old your care. The foolish need your wisdom, and the hurting your compassion. Any time you withhold or withdraw what God's given you, others suffer, and you shrivel. Looking back over my life, I see where I've connected with specific people at every crossroad and milestone. Most of them the world will never know, but to me they were absolutely vital. Each helped me to clear a hurdle, accomplish an objective or reach a goal. Without them, I wouldn't be where I am today. How about you?

God is all-powerful, all-knowing, and all-sufficient. That is what makes it all the more significant when He uses people like us.

Almost without exception, His favorite plan is a combined effort; all of us working for Him, and each of us loving one another in the process.

Survival Guide for **September 29**

"WE ARE VERY FAMILIAR WITH HIS EVIL SCHEMES."
2 CORINTHIANS 2:11 (NLT)

Satan is predictable.

His temptations follow this familiar four-step pattern:

(1) Desire. First he identifies a desire within us, like the desire for revenge, or the legitimate desire to be loved and feel pleasure. Then he suggests we fulfill that legitimate desire in a wrong way. The truth is that if we didn't have desires, temptation couldn't attract us. The Bible says there's: ". . . a whole army of evil desires within you." (James 4:1 TLB).

(2) Doubt. Satan tries to get us to doubt what God has said about sin. Is it really wrong? How come others do it? Doesn't God want me to be happy? The Book of Hebrews warns: ". . . watch out! Don't let evil thoughts or doubts make any of you turn away from the living God." (Hebrews 3:12 CEV).

(3) Deception. Satan's incapable of telling the truth. He's "the father of lies." (see John 8:44). Anything he tells us will either be untrue or half-true. He whispers, "Nobody will ever know. It'll solve your problem. It's only a little sin." But a little sin is like being a little pregnant; it'll eventually show itself.

(4) Disobedience. If we conceive and carry a thought long enough, it will birth a behavior. Every addict starts with one fix and every alcoholic with one drink. Shattered relationships begin with seemingly innocent flirtations. James warns, "But people are tempted when they are drawn away and trapped by our own evil desires. Do not be deceived . . . " (James 1:14-16 TEV).

The solution to the devil's temptations is to be familiar with them so you will see them coming.

Even more important is to live closer to God so that your desires are being met by Him.

Survival Guide for **September 30**

". . . WATCH YOUR STEP AND SAVE YOUR LIFE."
PROVERBS 16:17

No matter how spiritual we become we never outgrow temptation.

Temptation is a compliment; it means Satan fears our potential. So, the closer we get to God the more he attacks us.

While you are praying Satan will suggest an evil thought to distract and shame you. Don't be alarmed. Satan fears your prayers and he'll do anything to hinder them. Instead of condemning yourself, just refocus on God.

Here are two things that will help you overcome temptation:

(1) Identify your patterns. Ask yourself, "When am I tempted?" Usually we're most vulnerable when we're tired, alone, bored, depressed or under stress; when we've been hurt, angry, worried or after a big success or spiritual high. Identify your patterns: ". . .watch your step and save your life." (Proverbs 16:17).

(2) Request God's help. ". . .Call for help when you're in trouble—I'll help you. . ." (Psalm 50:15). So why don't we turn to God more often? Because at that moment we just want to do what we want to do. Right? Or we're embarrassed because we keep giving in to the same temptations. But God doesn't get irritated or impatient with us: "Let us approach God's throne, where we will receive grace to help us just when we need it." (Hebrews 4:16 TEV). If we need to cry for God's help 100 times a day, He will be there for us each and every time.

Just as the roots of a tree grow stronger when the wind blows against it, each time we overcome a temptation, we become a little stronger and a little more rooted in Jesus.

Survival Guide for **October 1**

"DIVERT MY EYES FROM TOYS AND TRINKETS, INVIGORATE ME ON THE PILGRIM WAY." PSALM 119:37

Trying to resist a thought is useless.

It only intensifies our focus on the wrong thing and strengthens its appeal. By resisting it we actually reinforce it. Temptation cannot be defeated by simply resisting "thinking about it." Likewise temptation cannot be defeated by fighting the "feeling" of it. The more we deny how we feel, the more that feeling consumes and controls us.

The quickest way to neutralize temptation is to turn our attention to something else. The battle is won or lost in the mind. Whatever gets our attention will eventually get us. Small wonder the Psalmist wrote: "Keep me from paying attention to what is worthless." (Psalm 119:37 TEV).

Ever watch a food advertisement on TV and suddenly feel hungry? That's the power of suggestion. We naturally gravitate toward what we focus on. Repeating, "I must stop eating so much, or I must stop smoking, or I must stop lusting," is a self-defeating strategy. It keeps the focus on the negative "what we don't want." Redirecting your focus temptation is far more effective. Once our mind is on God, the temptation loses its power. Our mind is our most vulnerable organ, so it must be kept focused in the right direction. Bad thoughts are defeated by replacing them with good ones. This is the principle of replacement. Evil is overcome with good (see Romans 12:21). Satan can't get our attention when our mind is preoccupied with something else. That's why the Bible says: ". . . fill your minds with good." (Philippians 4:8 TEV).

If you're serious about defeating temptation, you must start managing your mind and monitoring your mental intake because, ". . . your life is shaped by your thoughts." (Proverbs 4:23 TEV).

It will take lots of discipline and practice, but with God's help you can overcome temptation by reprogramming the way you think..

Get started today; it is worth the effort!

Survival Guide for **October 2**

"AND IF ONE FALLS DOWN, THE OTHER HELPS, BUT IF THERE'S NO ONE TO HELP, TOUGH!" ECCLESIASTES 4:10

If you are stuck in a repeating cycle of good intention, failure and guilt, you won't get better all by yourself.

Certain temptations are overcome only with the help of a committed friend who prays for you and holds you accountable. Becoming transparent is part of the answer to the lonely struggle to "do it on my own."

"Confess your sins to each other and pray for each other so that you may be healed." (James 5:16 NIV).

Problems grow best in the dark, but when you bring them out into the light they shrink. You're only as sick as the secrets you keep, so take off your mask, stop pretending everything's fine and come out into the light.

Satan wants each of us to think our temptations are unique, so we must never share them. But the truth is, we all fight the same temptations. The reason we hide our struggles from each other is pride. We want others to think everything's under control. Another truth is that whatever we can't talk about is already out of control. If it could be handled by our own effort, it would already have been handled. Willpower and personal resolutions aren't enough. Some problems are too engrained, too habitual and too big to solve on our own. So, if you need help today, humble yourself and ask for it.

Answer this tough question: "What am I pretending isn't a problem in my life? What am I afraid to talk about?" Yes, it is humbling to admit our weaknesses, but lack of humility is the very thing that often keeps us from getting better.

Humble yourself, give up on solving everything yourself and get the prayer support you need!

Survival Guide for **October 3**

"THERE'S SOMETHING HERE ALSO FOR SEASONED MEN AND WOMEN." PROVERBS 1:5

Our highest potential will never be reached without a good coach. It's impossible. You may be good, better than most, but without help you'll never be as good as you could have been.

Why would a world class tennis player like Andre Agassi need a coach, especially one who is not as good on the court as he is? Agassi says: "Tennis requires subtle adjustments crucial to winning, and my coach, Gil, is the best at making them. The older I get, the more valuable he becomes." Why? Because age and experience don't necessarily make us better; often they just deepen the rut we are in.

In the world of athletics, nobody performs his or her way out of needing a coach. Yet many of us operate under the misguided assumption that because we are growing spiritually, we don't need to be coached. We make the mistake of measuring ourselves against others, instead of our God-given potential, so in the end we never become what we could have been. Self-evaluation is good, but the evaluation of others is better. A good coach will always measure your performance against your strengths, not somebody else's. That's because he knows what you're capable of and he'll push you to your limit.

By the way, good coaches are on the scene observing, not back at the office waiting for a report. That's because they're personally invested in your success; a win for you is a win for them.

I encourage you to prayerfully consider getting a coach, especially if you're a coach to someone else!

Survival Guide for **October 4**

"WISE PEOPLE TAKE ADVICE." PROVERBS 12:15

Great leaders are great learners.

Learning requires submission, and submission isn't something we are comfortable with. We think submission is just for "those other people who need to be led." This is especially true in our early years when we're sure we already know it all and use every opportunity to prove it.

Engaging a leadership coach requires a willingness to submit to others. If you're not teachable, you're not reachable. The more you think you know, the less likely you are to place yourself under the influence of those who really know and can help you. This is especially true when you view yourself as more capable, passionate or talented than the folks around you.

A wise person always seeks counsel.

A wise person knows his or her limitations, only the foolish believe they have none. Only the naive or arrogant operate under the assumption that they can make all the right calls without input from others. Here are a few of Solomon's thoughts on seeking counsel:

> "The way of a fool seems right to him, but a wise man listens to advice." (Proverbs 12:15 NIV)

> "Plans fail for lack of counsel, but with many advisers they succeed." (Proverbs 15:22 NIV)

> "Listen to advice and accept instruction and in the end you will be wise." (Proverbs 19:20 NIV).

It is not what your coach knows, it is what he or she sees that makes a coach valuable to you.

A coach is an extra pair of eyes—so why be without them?

Survival Guide for **October 5**

"WATCH YOUR STEP, AND THE ROAD WILL STRETCH OUT SMOOTH BEFORE YOU." PROVERBS 4:26

Every great accomplishment began as a dream in somebody's heart.

All things are created twice: first in our minds, then in our lives.

Dreamers allow their minds to wander outside the boundaries of what is, creating a mental picture of what could be. They're not always the most talented or the best educated—just the ones who refuse to put brackets on their thinking or to limit themselves by what others have done, or failed to do. And that requires courage—lots of it!

On the heels of every dream there is a demon of doubt.

No sooner is our dream conceived than our minds are suddenly filled with all the reasons why it won't work. And certain folks around us will be quick to confirm those fears! In spite of that, we must forge ahead and dream; otherwise we'll spend our lives fulfilling the dreams of others.

Andy Stanley writes:

> I keep a little card on my desk that reads: "Dream no small dreams, for they stir not the hearts of men." More than once that simple statement has kept me from retreating from my dreams. I know from experience that it's impossible to lead without a dream. When leaders are no longer willing to dream, it's only a short time before followers are unwilling to follow. So dream! Dream big. Dream often. Somewhere in those random ideas that flood your mind is one that will capture your heart and imagination. And that seemingly random idea may very well evolve into a vision for your life.

To which I simply say "Amen!"

Take some time to dream today.

Survival Guide for **October 6**

"WE DON'T KNOW WHAT TO DO; WE'RE LOOKING TO YOU." 2 CHRONICLES 20:12

By the time Moses passed the reins of leadership to Joshua, everything had changed. For 40 years, Joshua had been taught to navigate and survive in a wilderness, but now it was time to enter the Promised Land. Can't you hear his thoughts: "I know a lot about wandering, but not much about warfare." No wonder God told him, "Be strong and courageous for the Lord your God will be with you wherever you go." (Joshua 1:9 NIV).

God told Joshua not to be afraid for a simple reason: Joshua was afraid!

Everything about his new situation reeked of uncertainty. The only thing Joshua knew for sure was that God said, "Go." "Then Joshua commanded the people, saying, 'Prepare yourselves, for within three days you are to cross this Jordan.(and) possess the land.'" (Joshua 1:10-11 NAS).

Can you imagine what the people must have thought?

Question: "But Joshua, how are we going to get across the river?"

Answer: "I'm not sure, but in three days be ready to go."

Question: "But Joshua, what are we going to do when we get to the other side?"

Answer: "I'll tell you when we arrive. Just be ready to move out in three days."

We will always be uncertain about many things, especially as we move into new territory. But we can never afford to be unclear or in doubt as to our call, our vision and our destination.

What is the source of such confidence?

God's promise, "I am with you."

Survival Guide for **October 7**

". . . YOU'RE NOT EXEMPT. YOU COULD FALL FLAT ON YOUR FACE AS EASILY AS ANYONE ELSE . . ."
1 CORINTHIANS 10:12

Greater success always leads to great temptation.

Our response to that temptation depends entirely upon the condition of our soul at the time. Nobody plans to fail, but failing to plan usually guarantees failure. My point? Don't wait until you're in the midst of the temptation! Begin preparing—now!

It is not too smart but you can wait until the night before your final exam to prepare, but there's no cramming for a test of character. It comes up like a pop quiz, and you're either ready or you're not.

One way to get prepared is to begin letting others in on what you want to be. Vulnerability paradoxically reinforces our perimeter of protection. Becoming accountable is a powerful incentive to check any behavior that might take us out of bounds. And on those inevitable occasions when we do drift across the line, the fact that someone else knows and will call us on it, is a compelling motivator to take responsibility for our actions and correct them quickly.

Another good preparation tool is to constantly ask yourself: "What small thing in my life right now has the potential to become destructive? And who knows about it other than me?" It's better to expose our struggles to a handful of people who really care about us, than run the risk of being publicly exposed before those who couldn't care less. You owe it to yourself to identify and conquer those baby dragons that have the potential to grow up and wound not only you, but also those who put their trust in you.

". . .You're not exempt. You could fall flat on your face as easily as anyone else. . ."

Survival Guide for **October 8**

". . .URGING YOU ON WHENEVER YOU WANDER LEFT OR RIGHT: 'THIS IS THE RIGHT ROAD. WALK DOWN THIS ROAD'" ISAIAH 30:21

True success is an inside job.

It is your verdict on your life, not somebody else's. It is listening to the voice that says "This is the way walk here," and walking there.

When educator, Parker Palmer, was offered a college presidency, it meant more money, status and influence. Career-wise it required no further thought. But when he asked some trusted friends to help him verify that it was God's will, one asked, "What would you like about being president?"

Palmer replied, "Well, I wouldn't like the politics and fund-raising, or giving up studying and teaching."

His friend persisted, "Yes, but what would you enjoy?"

Palmer writes: "I felt compelled to give an honest answer, one that appalled even me. 'I guess what I'd like most is getting my picture in the paper with the word president under it.' There was a long silence and then my friend asked something that cracked us all up—and cracked me wide open; 'Parker,' he said, 'Can't you think of an easier way to get your picture in the paper?'"

Elizabeth Dole said, "Success is doing something that makes you say, 'Nothing I ever did made me feel this good.'"

How about you? Are you doing what you love for its own sake, not just for money and prestige? If you are, you're truly successful.

God said that you will hear a voice "urging you on whenever you wander left or right: 'This is the right road. Walk down this road.'"

Have you listened lately?

Survival Guide for **October 9**

"SURRENDER YOUR WHOLE BEING TO HIM TO BE USED FOR RIGHTEOUS PURPOSES." ROMANS 6:13 (TEV)

Surrender is an unpopular word; it evokes images of admitting defeat or forfeiting the game. In today's world where winning is everything, surrendering is unthinkable. Yet surrender is at the heart of Christian living. The inability or unwillingness to surrender to God indicates two spiritual problems:

(1) We don't trust God enough. Surrender to God is impossible unless we trust Him, and we trusting God is impossible until we are convinced that He loves us. If you want to know how God feels about you, regardless of kind of life you have lived, visualize Jesus with His arms outstretched on the cross saying, "I love you this much."

(2) We can't admit our limitations. A second barrier to total surrender is our inability to admit that we're not in charge. The oldest temptation is: "You shall be as gods." (Genesis 3:5). Our desire to be "in control" is the cause of so much stress in our lives. We accept our humanity intellectually, but not in reality. When faced with our own limitations we react with anger and resentment. We want to be taller or shorter, smarter or stronger, more talented, more beautiful, or wealthier. We want to have it all and do it all, and we become upset when it doesn't happen. When we notice that God gave others characteristics we don't have, we respond with envy, jealousy and self-pity. Surrender to God is impossible until we admit our limitations.

Surrender.

Surrender is not for the faint of heart, but it is demanded of those who would follow Jesus. Jesus himself said, "If people want to follow Me, they must give up the things they want. They must be willing to give up their lives daily to follow Me." (Luke 9:23 NCV).

Surrendering to God is not done only once, but it is something to do each day—and sometimes each hour!

Survival Guide for **October 10**

―――

"A BRUISED REED HE WILL NOT BREAK, AND A SMOULDERING WICK HE WILL NOT SNUFF OUT." MATTHEW 12:20 (NIV)

What do all these people have in common?

1) A woman cowering before an angry mob that is threatening to stone her.
2) A paralyzed man on a stretcher begging his friends not to give up as they stare at a house overflowing with people.
3) A blind man crying out to a rabbi.

They were all "bruised reeds" and "smoldering wicks" that God refused to give up on.

What could be more fragile than a bruised reed?

Kids playing beside the River Jordan made music pipes out of them. As they were hollowed out and holes bored in them, they were often bruised and discarded. The same reed that once stood tall and strong, nourished and rooted in the riverbed is now hidden in the rushes, bruised and fragile. We can become "bruised reeds" by hurtful words, betrayal, failure, or harsh religion.

What could be closer to extinction than a smoldering wick?

When the oil in primitive lamps was gone and the wick burned low, it was extinguished, thrown away as worthless and replaced. That which once glowed with light is now dark and useless. We can glow faith, light the path for others and still the icy winds of criticism, unforgiveness and judgmentalism can leave us one snuff away from darkness.

The world thinks it knows what to do with bruised reeds and smoldering wicks—break it off and snuff it out! But not Jesus: "A bruised reed He will not break, and a smoldering wick He will not snuff out." No matter how far gone you may feel, you are not beyond the reach of God's grace.

Come back to Jesus today, bruised and smoldering, and let Him make you whole again!

Survival Guide for **October 11**

"THIS MARKS THE PLACE WHERE GOD HELPED US."
1 SAMUEL 7:12

It is a good idea to establish some spiritual landmarks, reminding us of the times God intervened on our behalf. Without them we quickly forget, lose our bearings, or claim credit for things we had nothing to do with.

When God miraculously opened the Jordan River for the Israelites to pass over, He knew something they didn't—that soon they'd come up against Jericho, their biggest obstacle. That's when they would need reminders and a reference point. So He told them to collect 12 stones from the Jordan and build a memorial. This would act as a reminder of His past faithfulness. God was saying, "When you can't cope with the future, check with the past. My goodness will stand inventory." Samuel did the same after Israel defeated the Philistines. He took a stone and named it Ebenezer, saying, "Thus far has the Lord helped us." (1 Samuel 7:12 NIV).

Think of some of the spiritual landmarks in your life "thus far."

Like the day you met Jesus; or specific instances when He guided you; or doors He opened that you thought were permanently shut, or scrapes He brought you through.

Landmarks are important, because whenever we are struggling, they remind us of how God's cares for us. Landmarks help us to see God's past goodness, even when we were unaware of it. Landmarks give us a sense of gratitude for yesterday's blessings and the confidence to face whatever tomorrow brings.

Today, establish some spiritual landmarks by making a record of God's blessings!

Survival Guide for **October 12**

"IMMEDIATELY THEY LEFT THEIR FATHER ZEBEDEE, THE BOAT, AND THE HIRED HANDS, AND FOLLOWED." MARK 1:20

We usually are only one step of obedience away from the next truth God wants to teach us. That's why it is a mistake to always cling to the familiar, to find our comfort zone and dig in. When we stop being stretched we begin to shrink, become complacent, think we can handle things on our own, and stop growing.

That is a dangerous place to be.

If you are restless today and feel as if there is more than you have been settling for, it may be time to consider facing down some old fears and walking through them into some new experiences, new relationships and new opportunities.

When Jesus called James and John they were on familiar turf, doing what came naturally—repairing their fishing nets. But they couldn't stay there and still follow Him. Neither can we! The Bible says, "Immediately He called them, and they left .and went after Him." They had to leave the familiar in order to fulfill their destiny. And just in case you think you're too old to try something new, remember that Abraham was 75 when he discovered his life's assignment. Timothy, on the other hand, was just 17.

Age isn't the issue. Availability is.

It takes guts to leave ruts.

Especially when your rut has rewarded you with a comfortable lifestyle. But if you want to experience God in a deeper dimension—one that will stretch you—you must be ready to leave your comfort zone and follow Him.

Are you?

Survival Guide for **October 13**

"GOD, WHO DELIVERED ME FROM THE TEETH OF THE LION AND THE CLAWS OF THE BEAR, WILL DELIVER ME FROM THIS PHILISTINE." 1 SAMUEL 17:37

David didn't show up at the battlefield with the intention of becoming a hero, he was just delivering bread to his brothers. But when he saw Goliath, he seized an opportunity that other warriors only dream about. Today's opportunities will catch us by surprise—if we're not alert and ready, we'll miss them.

"What" was the question David asked, not "how."

"What needs to be done to rid Israel of Goliath?" If you're truly a leader, you already possess the talent necessary to lead. But your courage is what will establish you as a leader before others. The leaders we revere most walk on to the pages of history through timely displays of courage; courage on the battlefield or in the classroom, courage to defend the defenseless or simply to attempt what nobody else thought possible.

"But I don't have what it takes." Don't worry; neither did David, but God provided. Provision follows courage.

"What" should always precede "how." Don't be intimidated by the immensity of the adversary. With God big isn't always better. He responds to faith! Don't let "how" intimidate you and keep you from asking "what." It's because "how" is so challenging that it provides us with great opportunity. If the pathway to meeting needs was well lit, it would already be crowded. If "how" wasn't a problem, somebody else would have already figured it out.

Doing God's will begins with one word: "What."

"What needs to be done?" "What do You want me to do?"

Are those the questions you are asking? If not, why not?

Those who have the courage to ask "what" and the faith to hang on until God shows them "how" are the ones who don't just take opportunities they make them..

Survival Guide for **October 14**

"DON'T PANIC. I'M WITH YOU. THERE'S NO NEED TO FEAR FOR I AM YOUR GOD. I'LL GIVE YOU STRENGTH. I'LL HELP YOU . . ." ISAIAH 41:10

Dr E.V. Hill tells the story of a young man taking a short cut home through a vacant lot late one night. It was dark and tall buildings cast ominous shadows all around him.

Suddenly he became aware of someone following him. The faster he walked, the faster they walked. Frightened and frustrated, he finally turned to see who was there. But when he did, there was no one there. As he turned to continue home, he heard the noise again. That's when he realized that what he was hearing was just his corduroy pants rubbing together!

So often our fear is just like that—false.

Fear often is the result of two things:

1. Our imagination
2. Our failure to understand how God works.

John says that one of the consequences of fear is that: ". . . fear brings with it the thought of punishment. . . " (1Jn 4:18 AMP). That's why when something goes wrong we often wonder, "Is God punishing me?" The answer is probably "no." but our fear makes us see God in terms of punishment. On the other hand faith makes us see God in terms of love. Fear and faith are present with us each day; the one we choose will rule that day.

When you come up against a fear-producing situation, turn fear into faith by doing these three things:

1) Pray for God's wisdom and protection; He guarantees it (Ps 91).
2) Admit your inner struggle. You are not alone, we all battle with fear.
3) Stand on God's Word: "Do not fear, for I am with you; do not anxiously look about you, for I am your God. I will strengthen you, surely I will help you. . . " (Isa 41:10 NAS).

Choose Faith over Fear today!

Survival Guide for **October 15**

"SO LET'S NOT ALLOW OURSELVES TO GET FATIGUED DOING GOOD. AT THE RIGHT TIME WE WILL HARVEST A GOOD CROP IF WE DON'T GIVE UP, OR QUIT." GALATIANS 6:9

A tour guide at the Washington Monument announced, "Ladies and gentlemen, there is currently a two-hour wait to take the lift to the top." Then he paused, smiled and added, "However, there is no wait should you desire to take the stairs."

There are no lifts to the "top." But there are plenty of stairs! How many we're willing to climb, and how long we're willing to keep at it, determines in large part how high we will go.

A music critic once called Sarasate, the great Spanish violinist, a genius. In reply he said, "Genius? Are they joking? For 37 years I've practiced up to 14 hours a day and now they call me a genius!"

Recently, I read the following little ditty which I thought was so true:

He worked by day and toiled by night,
  he gave up play and much delight.
Dry books he read, new things to learn
  and forged ahead, success to earn.
He plodded on, with faith and pluck,
  and when he won—they called it luck.

There is no substitute for obedience . . . consistency . . . discipline . . . and perseverance. Once you understand that, you are ready to achieve whatever God has in store for you at the top of the stairs.

"Be strong and very courageous. Obey all the laws . . . Do not turn away from them and you will be successful in everything you do." (Josh 1:7 NLT).

Survival Guide for October 16

"THAT BROUGHT HIM TO HIS SENSES . . ." LUKE 15:17

Mark Twain quipped "When I was 14, my dad was so ignorant I could hardly stand him. But by the time I was 21, I was amazed at how much the old man had learned in seven years."

Maturity changes perspective.

When God's will and your will conflict remind yourself that God knows better than you. David wrote, ". . . beauty and love chase after me every day of my life." (Psalm 23:6). The more we see lives ruined by wrong choices, the more we will realize that "there but for the grace of God go I."

Look at the Prodigal: A favored son from one of the best families in town, now penniless, friendless, eating pig swill—trying to satisfy a legitimate hunger in an illegitimate way! That's why we get into extra-marital affairs, go on drunken binges, financially swindle other people, or work ourselves to death, sacrificing our families in the process. We are trying to satisfy a legitimate hunger in an illegitimate way. There is a God-shaped hole in each of us—that nothing but God can fill. Finally, the Prodigal was ". . . brought. . .to his senses. . . ."

Maturity changes perspective.

If we will let Him, God will stop us in the nick of time. He will remind us of who we are and where we belong. Then we will start seeing the mud we are wallowing in, the false friends, the empty achievements, the people around us who are no happier than we are.

If that is where you are right now, come home. Your Father is waiting to wipe your slate clean. He still loves you. The table is spread and your seat is reserved. You haven't gone too far!

Tell the devil to take a hike, get up out of the pig pen, and come back where you belong!

Survival Guide for **October 17**

". . . IN THIS GODLESS WORLD YOU WILL CONTINUE TO EXPERIENCE DIFFICULTIES. BUT TAKE HEART! I'VE CONQUERED THE WORLD." JOHN 16:33

Since it's World Series time again let me begin with a baseball story.

A young baseball player was offered a contract with a major league team. In spring training, he performed well and each week he wired his mother back home in Mississippi to tell her about his progress:

> Week 1: "Dear Mom, Leading all batters; these pitchers aren't so tough."
> Week 2: "Dear Mom, Looks like I'll be in the starting line-up; now hitting .500."
> Week 3: "Dear Mom, They started throwing curve balls today—will be home Friday."

If Jesus had been a baseball fan instead of saying, ". . . in this godless world you will continue to experience difficulties. . . ," He might have said, "Expect life to throw you some curve balls, so be ready for them. Furthermore, when they come, don't duck and don't run—start swinging in the Name of the Lord. Believe God's promises and stand on His Word, for it cannot fail. And remember, until the last innings is over, stay in the game; otherwise, how can God make you a winner?"

When life throws you curve balls cling to these promises:

". . . By His mighty power at work within us, He is able to accomplish infinitely more than we would ever dare to ask or hope" (Eph 3:20 NLT).

". . .thank God! In the Messiah, in Christ, God leads us from place to place in one perpetual victory parade. . ." (2 Corinthians 2:14).

"I am still confident of this: I will see the goodness of the LORD in the land of the living."(Ps 27:13 NIV).

Now hit those curve balls out of the park!

Survival Guide for **October 18**

"A SAMARITAN CAME WHERE HE WAS. AND WHEN HE SAW HIM, HE HAD COMPASSION." LUKE 10:33 (NKJ)

Are you too busy to care about the needs of others? It is easy to get so preoccupied with *being* good instead of *doing* good that we miss opportunities to serve that are right in front of us. No one was busier than Jesus, yet He always responded to those in need.

In Luke 10, Jesus tells of a Jewish traveler who was mugged by a gang and left to die on the road. First a priest and then a Levite passed by. They were religious leaders; surely they would have compassion on this wounded man. But no, they both had important appointments to keep and didn't stop. Then a Samaritan came along. Of all people, he had the most reason to look the other way, because the Jews and the Samaritans were long-standing enemies. But the Bible says, ". . . he came where he was. And when he saw him, he had compassion."

True compassion rearranges our priorities.

The Good Samaritan decided that where he was going wasn't as important as where he was at that particular moment.

What would you have done that day? Do you think you would have acted like this Samaritan? How about when God tries to interrupt your inflexible, tightly organized, set-in-concrete schedule and asks you to take time for someone who is hurting? Are you willing to shelve your personal agenda and do what He wants?

When we are too busy to reach out to those who are hurting, we are just too busy.

Today, ask God to give you the compassion of Christ and to help you to take opportunities to serve others.

Survival Guide for **October 19**

"...YOUR STRENGTH LIKE IRON AS LONG AS YOU LIVE." DEUTERONOMY 33:25

Have the daily pressures in life built to where you feel as if someone has a gun pointed at your head, and is saying, "Get this done—or else?" Have you concluded that that's just how life is supposed to be?

I know how you feel, but is that the way life is supposed to be? I don't think so. I believe our best work is done when we're relaxed, not frazzled. Our best decisions are made when we're at peace, not stressed out. It doesn't help when we . . . force ourselves to go faster. . . to be somewhere else . . . or to be something we're not. Actually, it hurts.

What is the answer? Realize that the person holding that gun to your head is you and "put down the gun!" The job will get done, one-step-at-a-time and your stress level will subside as each small step takes you closer to your goal.

"Putting down the gun" causes two wonderful things to happen:

—First, we enjoy whatever we are doing more—even if it is just organizing your desk or cleaning your house—because now we're focused rather than distracted. Any moment of life not experienced is a piece of life thrown away. Life is too precious for that! I find that it helps if I tell myself, "I'm exactly where God needs me to be, doing what I'm supposed to be doing, so the smart thing is to enjoy it and be as creative as I can in the process."

—Second, by being present in what were doing, our productivity increases and we accomplish much more in the same amount of time.

Each day is a new challenge to "put down the gun" because the strength needed for tomorrow's challenge won't be given during today's chores.

It will be given . . . when we "put down the gun."

". . .your strength like iron as long as you live" (Deuteronomy 33:25).

Survival Guide for **October 20**

"BE STRONG. TAKE COURAGE. DON'T BE INTIMIDATED. DON'T GIVE THEM A SECOND THOUGHT BECAUSE GOD, YOUR GOD, IS STRIDING AHEAD OF YOU. HE'S RIGHT THERE WITH YOU. HE WON'T LET YOU DOWN; HE WON'T LEAVE YOU." DEUTERONOMY 31:6

Moses suffered from low self-esteem.

Don't believe me? Then read his answer when God told him he would lead the Children of Israel out of Egypt: "Who am I, that I should go to Pharaoh?. . . " (Exodus 3:11 NAS) Even after God assured him of victory, he still argued, "Lord, I have never been eloquent . . . I am slow of speech . . . " (Exodus 4:10 NAS).

Can you relate? Do you sometimes feel inadequate? If so, that is good, because we are inadequate—in our own strength.

You see Moses was partially right, he had nothing to say on his own—but the moment he trusted God to provide the answers, things changed. The seas parted, pillars of fire rose in the night and water flowed from rocks.

God has designed a work for you to do and all the inadequacies in the world won't limit Him or change His mind. God will be with you every step of the way. Accomplishing your life work may take time (that's why it is called your LIFE work) and involve mistakes, but if you keep focused on God He'll bring you through the your Red Sea and into the land of your destiny. You can count on it.

In God's eyes there are no losers—only lives being changed day by day, for His glory. The cure for inadequacy is found in God's promises. Grasp them and move forward to meet the challenges He places before you. And as you go, remember these words, " . . . The Lord your God will go ahead of you. He will neither fail you nor for sake you." (Deuteronomy 31:6 NLT). God will go ahead of us when we walk in faith. We need fear neither failure nor being forsaken.

Trust God every day—that is the cure for inadequacy!

Survival Guide for **October 21**

"... MAKE THE MOST OF WHATEVER JOB YOU HAVE FOR AS LONG AS GOD GIVES YOU LIFE. AND THAT'S ABOUT IT. THAT'S THE HUMAN LOT." ECCLESIASTES 5:18

Solomon says, " we should make the most of what God gives, both the bounty and the capacity to enjoy it, accepting what's given and delighting in the work. It's God's gift! God deals out joy in the present, the now. It's useless to brood over how long we might live" (Ecclesiastes 5:18-20). Don't wish your life away by constantly thinking:

a. "If only I had
b. a bigger house
c. a more understanding girlfriend/boyfriend/spouse
d. better grades
e. a better-paying job
f.. a beautiful body
g. a higher IQ
h. the acceptance of a particular person
i.. then I'd be happy!"

Happiness doesn't work like that: "This is the very day GOD acted—let's celebrate and be festive!" (Psalm 118:24). The emphasis is on Today.

My mother is a great cook. When I was a boy I loved to watch her bake. As I put my fingers in the bowl and smudged batter across my cheeks, I learned what took me years later to articulate—that all of life is good.

If you want to enjoy life to the fullest, don't wait for what is in the oven, take the bowl now and scrape it out. People who learn to "scrape the bowl" don't hunger for life because things that others ignore nourish them. Too many of us spend our lives waiting for the "cake to come out of the oven" and miss "scraping the bowl"—yet it is in the "bowl" that we often find the best things in life.

Jesus says, "Look at the birds. . . " (Matt 6:26 NIV). "See how the lilies of the field grow" (Matt 6:28 NIV). "Be content . . ." (Lk 3:14 TLB). Jesus is simply saying "Take the time to enjoy where you are, on your way to where you are going!"

Today don't forget to "scrape the bowl!"

Survival Guide for **October 22**

"BUT I'M GOING TO ESTABLISH A COVENANT WITH YOU. . ."
GENESIS 6:18

In Bible times, a covenant was the strongest promise two people could make to each other. Three symbols sealed it:

1) Swords were exchanged signifying they would always defend each other
2) Shoes were exchanged, meaning they would go to any lengths to defend each other
3) Sacrifices were split down the middle and the covenanters walked between the two halves, declaring that without each other they were incomplete.

God entered into a covenant relationship with His people and promised to bless them: ". . .I'M GOING TO ESTABLISH MY COVENANT WITH YOU. . ."

Like every covenant God's covenant with us includes both benefits and conditions. The benefits include salvation, provision, guidance, and victory—the condition is that we love the Lord our God with all our heart, soul, and mind!

God put symbols of His covenant with Israel into a box called "The Ark of the Covenant" and when they went to war, it always went ahead of them. As a result, no enemy could stand before them. Why? Because God's covenant with them made God himself their ally in battle.

How about God's covenant with us? The covenant sword means He will fight for us. The covenant shoe means He will be there when we need Him. The covenant sacrifice means we are Jesus completes us.

God WILL keep His part of the covenant.

Our part of the covenant is truly loving the Lord which is expressed by our obedience to His Word and our care for His people.

The question is—Will you keep your part?

Survival Guide for **October 23**

"... WALK—BETTER YET, RUN!—ON THE ROAD GOD CALLED YOU TO TRAVEL ..." EPHESIANS 4:1

I would hate to try to count the number of books on the market today telling you how to set your own goals and reach them. But for the Christian goal setting is not so helpful as finding God's goals for us. God is not committed to our goals unless they are also His goals for our life.

We can't just come to God and say, "Here is my idea; please stamp your approval on it." That's not the way it works: "He has created us. . . so that we can do the good things He planned for us long ago." (Ephesians 2:10 NLT).

Our prayer should be, "Lord, show me Your good things you have planned for me to do." We can't compartmentalize life and say, "In this category I'll do things my way, but in this other category, I'll be led by God." Instead, every step we take should be synchronized to the beat of the Holy Spirit.

Walking to the beat of the Holy Spirit means letting God set the pace.

His direction is always right, His timing is always perfect and His results are always best. To stay the course it is critical for us to understand that:

1) God works through us as we engage our minds, open our mouths, move our feet and use our hands to do what He puts into our heart
2) God never stops calling us to take one more step, do one more thing and engage in one more act of faith.

One goal that we can be 100% sure that God honors is the goal to walk with Him.

Today ". . .walk—better yet, run!—on the road God called you to travel."

Survival Guide for **October 24**

"STICK IT OUT. . . SO YOU'LL BE THERE FOR THE PROMISED COMPLETION." HEBREWS 10:36

During the first four years of the life of the Chinese bamboo tree, it grows only a few inches. Then in the fifth year, it grows 90 feet in just 5 weeks. Now the real question is—did it grow 90 feet in 5 weeks—or 5 years? The answer is. . . 5 years! Because if at any time during those first 4 years you'd stopped watering and fertilizing it, it would have died.

The Christian life is a lot like the Chinese bamboo tree.

It is lived on long level plains with spurts of growth to the next level. You stay on one level and learn its lessons until you become qualified to move to the next. Then you suddenly grow like crazy.

How can we tell when one level is ending and growth to the next level is ready to begin? One way I've found is that the grace that accompanied the level I'm on will lift and what was once easy, suddenly becomes hard. When that happens, I've found that God is usually preparing me to grow to a new level.

Paul had a life-changing encounter with God on the Damascus Road, but it took the next 3 1/2 years to detox him from "Phariseeism" and equip him for his life's assignment. For Moses, it took 40 years in the wilderness.

Don't be impatient. Whatever it takes—it takes.

Keep focused on God's promises. Don't give in to the temptation to give up. Spurgeon said, "By perseverance the snail reached the ark." Josh Billings put it this way, "Look at the postage stamp; its usefulness consists in its ability to stick to something until it gets there!"

"Stick it out"—what God has in store for you is truly worth the wait!

Survival Guide for **October 25**

"... BUT IF YOU SAY SO, I'LL LET OUT THE NETS." LUKE 5:5

After they had fished all night and caught nothing, Jesus said to His disciples, "Push out into deep water and let your nets out for a catch (Luke 5:4). This is what I call a real test of faith commandment! It is a real test of faith commandment because all they knew and everything they had tried had not work and now the Lord commands them to do something that seemingly made no sense at all.

Peter responds to this test of faith commandment with flying colors: "... but if you say so, I'll let out the nets. . ." (Luke 5:5). Doubt your doubts, but never doubt God; one word from Him can change everything: "It was no sooner said than done—a huge haul of fish, straining the nets past capacity." (Luke 5:6).

Here are four lessons about a real test of faith commandment:

1) God involves us in one thing to teach us another. He commands them to go fishing but soon He is going to involve His disciples in an even bigger miracle—catching multitudes and bringing them into His kingdom.
2) God uses the familiar to do the incredible. In their workplace, where nothing special ever happened, Jesus suddenly showed up and changed everything. Look for God today in the familiar not only in the unexpected moments of   your life.
3) God moves us from the security of the shore to the risks of the deep. Why? Because we've got to risk the deep water if we're going to enjoy great catches. No risks, no rewards!
4) When we obey God nets break, needs are met, minds are blown and God is glorified.

So remember, the right answer to a real test of faith commandment is:

"... But if you say so, I'll let out the nets!" (Luke 5:5).

Survival Guide for **October 26**

"...WHAT MUST I DO TO DESERVE ETERNAL LIFE?" LUKE 18:18

The rich young ruler was educated and respected. He had already achieved the three P's of success: power, prosperity and posterity. He was a bottom-line guy who cut to the chase and asked, "what must I do to deserve eternal life?" Even the way he worded the question suggests that he thought he could get eternal life the way he had gotten everything else in life—by self-effort. So when Jesus replied, "sell all that you possess he became very sad; for he was extremely rich." (Luke 18:22-23 NAS). He had mistakenly assumed that heaven was just a payment away.

He was wrong.

Paul says, "What the law was powerless to do God did by sending His own Son." (Romans 8:3 NIV). Only a cold-hearted God would sell salvation to those who can afford it. That's a hard concept to grasp, since we have always been rewarded for our performance. But just as we wouldn't impress the space-shuttle crew with a paper airplane we had made, or we wouldn't impress a great artist with our crayon sketches, so our character and good works don't impress God. Eternal life costs more than anyone can afford.

Which is why we need a Redeemer.

Money wasn't this man's problem, self-sufficiency was. His problem wasn't his big income, it was his big ego. It is not just the wealthy who have difficulty grasping this truth; so do the educated, the strong, the good-looking, the popular, even the religious.

To receive salvation we must first declare that we are spiritually bankrupt; that our cupboard is bare, our reputation worthless, and our options gone. We can not approach God demanding justice—we can only come pleading for mercy.

Come to Jesus today.

He has a gift that is not for sale at any price waiting for you!

Survival Guide for **October 27**

"HE CUTS OFF EVERY BRANCH OF ME THAT DOESN'T BEAR GRAPES. AND EVERY BRANCH THAT IS GRAPE-BEARING HE PRUNES BACK SO IT WILL BEAR EVEN MORE." JOHN 15:2

God is at work in our lives today taking away things that don't belong and pruning those that do. What are the things He takes away? Things that have served their purpose . . . things that refuse to change . . . things that will give us trouble in the future . . . things that are standing in the way of something better . . . things that are holding us back . . . things He has not chosen for us!

Have you ever seen a newly-pruned tree? It doesn't look too good, does it? When God begins to cut back certain things in our lives in order to redirect our energies, we won't look too good either.

Sometimes pruning means:

1) having fewer things for a while;
2) letting go of what you thought would always be there;
3) being unable to explain to others why you're even going through this.

God knows what needs to be cut back in your life.

God knows what needs to be cut off.

Trust Him today!

Pray: "Lord, if I needed it, You would let me keep it; so I open my hand to You today. Send whomever You will, take away whomever You want. I'll praise You when they come and I'll praise You when they go, because my hope is built on nothing less than Jesus' blood and righteousness."

Survival Guide for **October 28**

"WHENEVER THE POT THE POTTER WAS WORKING ON TURNED OUT BADLY, AS SOMETIMES HAPPENS WHEN YOU ARE WORKING WITH CLAY, THE POTTER WOULD SIMPLY START OVER AND USE THE SAME CLAY TO MAKE ANOTHER POT." JEREMIAH 18:4

Forming a vessel is a life-long process.

If the Potter does not continually wet the clay, it becomes too hard to be worked.

Think about that.

When we start getting callous, God turns the wheel faster, touches us in just the right place and introduces the water. Do you remember the words, "When you pass through the waters, I will be with you?" (Isa 43:2). Could this be what He's talking about or at least an acceptable application? God will never allow our relationship with Him to be reduced to a formula; it must be ever flowing, ever growing and ever changing. He has many ways to bless us, many stages to take us through, so we must remain pliable.

Even though the pot "turned out badly" it was still in the Potter's hand. How wonderful! God never throws us away; nor is His plan for us thwarted because we have a flaw or struggle in a certain area.

He told Paul, ". . . My strength comes into its own in your weakness. . . "(2 Corinthians 12:9).

Whether we're being lifted out of the mud, or placed on the wheel or made over again, at all times and in every situation—we're always in His hand. Even when we are broken and wounded, when others give up on us, when we think we can't take it another day—at our lowest point, we're still in His hand.

Forming a vessel is a life-long process.

You are a vessel in the hands of the Master Potter.

Survival Guide for **October 29**

"... I'VE NAMED YOU FRIENDS ..." JOHN 15:15

"I'm no longer calling you servants because servants don't understand what their master is thinking and planning. No, I've named you friends because I've let you in on everything I've heard from the Father." (John 15:15).

The difference between a Friend and a servant lies in whether they are entrusted with secrets. Jesus was telling His disciples, "I am bringing you from the place of obedience to the place of intimacy; from functioning without insight, to knowing My mind and my purposes."

Jesus had to see if they could

1) take bad news and still keep a good attitude;
2) trust Him and not try to manipulate things;
3) follow His plan, even when they couldn't see the big picture.

Once they could he said "I'm no longer calling you servants. . .No, I've named you friends."

Before God destroyed Sodom He discussed it with Abraham, because Abraham was "a Friend of God." Before He gave Israel His law, He talked it over with Moses. "The Lord would speak to Moses face to face, as a man speaks with his friend." (Exodus 33:11).

Is such a relationship possible? Yes, but it comes at a price.

David said, "The Lord confides in those who fear him . . ." (Psalm 25:14). God shares things with His Friends that He doesn't with His servants!

Being a servant of the Lord is a wonderful thing. But being His friend is so much better. Both obey Him, but only one is let in on God's secrets.

When you see somebody who is clear-headed in the midst of confusion, yet cool when the heat is on, it could be that they know a secret—shared with them by a Friend!

Survival Guide for **October 30**

"... LIVE A LIFE OF LOVE, JUST AS CHRIST LOVED US ..."
EPHESIANS 5:2 (NIV)

Walking in love isn't automatic when we become Christians.

Our actions are still governed by our will. Without the discipline that comes from God's Word and God's Spirit, we will never grow up to be like our Heavenly Father. God is love and the more like Him we are, the more loving we become towards others; it's that simple.

If you think some people are just naturally more loving than others—think again. Love is a choice; one that costs. We can't love others while we are looking in the mirror or give to others while we are still clinging to what we have. Love costs us time, money and preoccupation with self.

If you are waiting for the love of God to envelop you suddenly and turn you into some sort of floating divine being who goes through life doing wonderful loving things for others, you're going to be waiting a long time. . . forever in fact! There are no pre-packaged Christians, no "microwave" formula that makes God's love gush forth instantly and without commitment.

To be consistently loving, we have to nail our world to the cross and make others our second priority under only our relationship to Jesus.

When Jesus found the woman caught in adultery, He sent her home redeemed and restored. If we are going to be like Him, we have to find people who are hurting, abused, even wrong and minister to them until they are healed, restored and right.

Help hurting people.

That is what it means to "walk in love."

Today start walking!

Survival Guide for **October 31**

" . . . GOD KNOWS WHO BELONGS TO HIM . . ."
2 TIMOTHY 2:19

Even if nobody else ever shows love towards you or values you in any way, if Jesus is your Lord, this verse shatters and dispels all rejection by letting you know that God knows you. Imagine—hand-crafted for a specific purpose, chosen to be special part of His body on earth, at precisely this time and in precisely this location. Wow!

You aren't just a piece of wood that fell through some crack that God found and said, "Oh, all right, let's go ahead and add this to the house." No! You came pre-cut to fit a particular place that nobody but you can fit. You've been selected, just like the cedars of Lebanon—one by one—for the building of a temple.

Stop trying to be like everyone else.

If you give up being who you are in order to become like someone else, you will just end up being something God doesn't need one more of. He made you in a precise way for a precise purpose, so only you will do.

Think: regardless of what you like or dislike about yourself, you must be okay, because God knows you. So what if others don't seem to honor or recognize you. ". . . God knows who belongs to Him. . ." (2 Tim 2:19).

So stop doubting yourself and striving with others.

Today be the unique you that God made you to be.

Survival Guide for **November 1**

". . . THAT'S THE KIND OF PEOPLE THE FATHER IS OUT LOOKING FOR . . ." JOHN 4:23

How well do you know God?

Do you know that He is not just strong, He is all-powerful? Or that He doesn't just gather information and arrive at conclusions He's all-knowing? Or that He's omnipresent; which means wherever you go He is there?

If you can talk about God and feel nothing, you probably don't know Him very well. What is He to you anyway? Your Savior? Your Healer? Your Protector? The level on which we know Him will determine the level on which we worship Him. Therefore, if you want to truly worship God the passion of your life should be to know Him better. And you can do that by only spending time with Him.

Seek His presence not only his provision, else you can end up treating God like a genie; rub the bottle and out He comes and gives you whatever you want. That's more like witchcraft than worship!

Giving to God is a great antidote to the "genie" effect.

Make God Lord of your life including your money. Can you seriously call Him Lord and keep Him out of your wallet?

When the Jews worshipped God, they laid a sacrifice on the altar and it went "up in smoke." Do you get the point? Simply this: true worship focuses on what He gets out of it, not what we get.

A man stood in the ashes of his home. Everything he'd accumulated for the past 50 years had been burned up. In tears he looked up and said, "Lord, I'll never again place my focus on anything but You." That's worship.

That is the kind of worshippers the Father's looking for today.

Survival Guide for **November 2**

". . . I COMPLAINED AND MY SPIRIT WAS OVERWHELMED . . ." PSALM 77:3 (KJV)

Words reveal our thoughts.

The moment they are expressed, they are empowered. Words create a climate both for those speaking and hearing them. Words of joy create a "blessing" climate and words of complaint create a "burden" climate. The climate we're around most becomes our natural habitat.

Those raised in a "burden" climate have a difficult time giving themselves permission to enjoy life. They say things like "nobody understands me . . . everybody expects too much of me . . .I get no appreciation." David said, ". . . I complained and my spirit was overwhelmed." That's how it worked then and that's still how it works!

Most of us complain about things we create ourselves—like our busy schedules. It's easy to gain self-worth from "carrying the world on your shoulders." Whenever you hear a voice in your head saying, "If you don't do everything perfectly . . . and do it on time . . . you're a failure . . . others won't need you . . . love you . . . or respect you," look out, that's the voice of pride! However humble and self-sacrificing it may sound, it's pride.

The "blessing" climate is easier to produce if we figure out what is really important to us. What would change in your life if you knew that you had only a year left to live? I believe three things would change right away:

1) We would place more value on what we have than on what we want
2) We wouldn't be in such a hurry
3) Being right or "perfect" would lose its appeal

"Burden" or "Blessing"—which is your natural habitat?

Make it "blessing" today by counting your blessings and figuring out what is really important instead of complaining and getting overwhelmed!

Survival Guide for **November 3**

"CAST ALL YOUR ANXIETY ON HIM BECAUSE HE CARES FOR YOU." 1 PETER 5:7 (NIV)

The Greek word for "cast" means "throw it away."

What are you dragging around from your past? Old pains, old scars or a torch for somebody who's already moved on? God's Word says "Throw it away." It's draining your life. You're sacrificing your future to an idol that's not worth your worship.

Why would God tell you to do something so radical as to throw away your anxiety? "Because He cares for you."

While you are caring for your anxiety, He is caring for you. It is hard to watch somebody you love twisting in pain because of something they shouldn't even be carrying. God has no problem making the thing leave us alone; His struggle is in getting us to loosen our grip on it. So, He speaks to us, not to what's bothering us and says, "Throw it away."

If you know you have things you need to throw away and you are willing to do it today, pray this prayer:

> "Father, so often we contribute to our own storms. We hold on to things You want us to release, and release things You want us to hold on to. Today I repent of my lack of trust in You. I make a commitment to grow stronger because of this season of pain. Thank You for preserving my mind and letting me live to whisper this humble prayer. If You had not kept Your hand on me, I wouldn't be here. Thank You for another chance. Armed with this experience and Your presence, I know I'll be fine. In Jesus' name, Amen."

Survival Guide for **November 4**

"BE MADE NEW IN THE ATTITUDE OF YOUR MINDS."
EPHESIANS 4:23 (NIV)

How we process information and arrive at conclusions must always be subject to the will of God: " . . . be made new in the attitude of your minds. . ." (Eph 4:23-24 NIV).

When we first start thinking God's way, it feels strange. You might even think, "This is just a put-on." But it is not! Just as new shoes don't immediately feel comfortable, so our new way of approaching life doesn't feel comfortable either. But, as we continue to think new thoughts, we become more and more comfortable with them.

Attitude follows behavior. It works like this—we have to:

a) practice being nice, until we automatically become nice
b) practice loving the unlovely, until acting any other way seems strange
c) practice giving to God, until it becomes as natural as buying stuff for ourselves
d) practice speaking the truth, until even the smallest lie tastes bad in our mouths
e) practice kindness, until every cynical, negative word is purged from our vocabulary.

Attitude follows behavior. It is a matter of practice.

Some people think that practicing doing something contrary to our feelings is hypocritical—feeling one way and acting another. But it is not, it is re-training ourselves to walk God's way and restraining ourselves from walking any other way.

Being "made new in the attitude of your minds" is literally declaring, "Lord, it is no longer a matter of anything goes. From now on, I will practice what Your Word says and what You direct me to do—regardless of how I feel about it."

Survival Guide for **November 5**

"BE GRACIOUS IN YOUR SPEECH . . ." COLOSSIANS 4:6

A Native American fable has it that the sun and the wind got into an argument one day over which was the stronger. When a traveler came down the road, they decided to settle it by seeing who could force him to take off his coat.

The sun hid behind a cloud and the wind blasted him, but that just made him wrap his coat around him more tightly. Then the sun came out with its gentle caressing warmth and shone on him—and he was forced to take his coat off.

Angry words only make others withdraw, shrivel or shut down, especially if they're already insecure. Angry words just confirm their worst fears and opinions about themselves. But gracious words can help them to . . . open up . . . discover what's good about themselves . . . and motivate them to reach higher.

The way you speak to those you speak to today will either lift or lower them. Paul writes, "Watch the way you talk . . . say only what helps, each word a gift." (Ephesians 4:29). Solomon says, ". . . there is healing in the words of the wise." (Proverbs 12:18).

People tend to reproduce the seeds we plant in them.

If we keep telling those around us they are incapable or worthless, they will probably fail. But if we keep praising them and pointing to what is good in them, they will make every effort to justify our confidence.

" Be gracious in your speech. . ."

Today, make your words gracious!

Survival Guide for **November 6**

"IT'S NECESSARY TO OBEY GOD RATHER THAN MEN."
ACTS 5:29

You may have the most expensive car on the road, but if you don't know how to get where you need to go, it will do you little good.

God has given each of us the perfect roadmap.

It is our responsibility to follow it. No matter how timid you are, don't allow anybody to dominate you or tell you where to go. Get back into the driver's seat of your life and take the wheel, for only you know the route God has mapped out for you.

Too often our actions are dictated, not by a desire to obey God, but by a need to please others. We care so much about what certain people think, that every step we take, we look over our shoulder to see whether they're smiling or frowning.

Our first responsibility is to please God, not people. In the end, we are accountable to Him alone. (Rom 14:12). When we dedicate our life to impressing people instead of obeying God what is that if not idolatry? "You shall have no other gods before Me." (Ex 20:2 NIV).

If you are a child of God your first responsibility is to please your Father.

We please our Father by following His roadmap. Get behind the wheel and follow His directions. Along the way you will live a life filled with purpose.

Following God's road map is not just about getting to Heaven—it is about the joy of the journey!

Survival Guide for **November 7**

***

**"I'M STAYING ALERT AND IN TOP CONDITION. I'M NOT
GOING TO GET CAUGHT NAPPING, TELLING EVERYONE
ELSE ALL ABOUT IT AND THEN MISSING OUT MYSELF."
1 CORINTHIANS 9:27**

What did Samson, Solomon, and Saul have in common?

They started strong, but they didn't finish strong. Samson finished up
losing his sight, his strength, his freedom, his testimony, his anointing, his
usefulness, and his life. Solomon ended up bogged down with pagan
wives and concubines. Saul ended up fighting God's anointed.

John Maxwell records these words from John Basagno, pastor of First
Baptist Church in Houston:

> "When I was called to preach at 21, my father-in-law told
> me that only one person out of every ten who enters the
> ministry, will still be in it when they reach 65. I've
> written in my Bible the names of 25 friends who went to
> Bible College with me. I'm a long way from 65, but 20
> have already dropped out. I'm fighting hard to be one of
> those who make it. I want to finish well."

A strong start is important, but it doesn't guarantee a strong finish.

The nine who don't make it are the ones who say, "I have done enough
growing, exercised enough discipline, taken enough advice, dreamed
enough dreams, and set enough goals—now I'm taking it easy!"

The Apostle Paul wrote, "I'm running hard for the finish line. . . I'm
staying alert and in top condition. I'm not going to get caught napping,
telling everyone else all about it and then missing out myself." (1 Cor
9:26-27).

Once the race is begun there is no safe time to quit; no time to "take it
easy"—until you cross the finish line. But you don't run alone—Jesus is
right there with you—all the way.

Remember that, and you will finish strong!

Survival Guide for **November 8**

"LEAVE YOUR COUNTRY, YOUR FAMILY, AND YOUR FATHER'S HOME FOR A LAND THAT I WILL SHOW YOU." GENESIS 12:1

God sent Abraham to a place "that I will show you." (Gen 12:1).

Women tend to understand the idea of going after something without knowing what it is better than men. When I ask Sheila what she is shopping for, she will sometimes say, "I am not sure, but I will know it when I see it!"

There are things we know, that we can't explain: "We have an unction (insight) from God and we know things" (1Jn 2:20 paraphrase). Apparently this is what happened to Abraham: "So Abram left just as God said. . ." (Gen 12:1).

At sea, all waters look alike.

That is why a compass is needed. Either you have one or you don't.

When you see somebody who gets excited about things that aren't there, watch them. Either they didn't take their medication that morning, or just maybe they have a compass. Because they can get excited about the invisible, these people usually end up doing the impossible because they have learned to follow their spiritual compass.

David defeated Goliath because he was the only man who had the faith to do it. He knew this was a life-changing moment. If he missed it, he would go back to tending sheep.

When your "Goliath moment" comes, rise up and say, "This giant is mine, no matter how many others are running away from him."

God has given you a spiritual compass—learn to use it!

Survival Guide for **November 9**

". . . HE HAD HIS EYE ON THE ONE NO EYE CAN SEE, AND KEPT RIGHT ON GOING . . ." HEBREWS 11:27

Start using the spiritual compass God has placed within you.

It is risky, but it will open doors that nothing else will.

Consider the widow in 1 Kings 17, of whom the prophet Elijah requested her last meal. When fear whispered, "You only have enough for yourself," her spiritual compass said, "Give what you have, and God will give you back what you need!" She did, and she outlived her famine.

When Saul saw Goliath, he told David, "You'll never defeat him." (1Sam 17:33 NIV). When David saw Goliath, his spiritual compass immediately pointed toward God and he announced, "The Lord. . . will deliver me. . . !" (1 Sam 17:37 NIV).

Noah built a floating zoo in the desert, because he heard a voice that nobody else did. As a result, his family was saved, his children became leaders in the new-world order, and his name was immortalized.

History is full of them; people like Benjamin Franklin, who dared to fly his kite in a thunder storm and discovered electricity; or Annie Sullivan, who saw in Helen Keller greatness that would inspire the world for years to come.

These weren't perfect people, they were just "compass" carriers who saw what others did not, and had the faith to act on it.

What has God shown you that others don't see?

Whatever it is, that is what He will give you power to perform—if you follow your spiritual compass!

Survival Guide for **November 10**

"I SPILL OUT MY COMPLAINTS BEFORE HIM . . ."
PSALM 142:2

In some of the Psalms David expressed his deepest emotions to God: "I am overwhelmed and desperate, and You alone know which way I ought to turn." (Psalm 142:3 TLB). David acknowledges his pain before God. He allows himself to feel it in his gut. That takes courage, especially when you just want to bury the pain and put on a brave face. This kind of true confession is actually therapeutic. Ever been there?

John Ortberg writes:

> "I regret the pain of failure so keenly that I backed
> away from owning it and learning from it. I could not
> heal and move on. I wanted to bury it so deeply that
> no one would ever guess it was there—not even me.
> I have needed to learn to pray the Psalms of lament."

The Bible doesn't condemn the grieving process; it just warns us not to get stuck in it. Jesus said, "Blessed are those who mourn, for they will be comforted." (Matthew 5:4 NIV).

F.B. Meyer writes,

> "There are some who chide tears as unmanly,
> unsubmissive, unchristian. They comfort us with a
> chill, bidding us to put on a rigid and tearless
> countenance. We may well ask whether a man who
> cannot weep can really love? Sorrow is just love
> bereaved; its most natural expression is tears. Jesus
> wept. The Ephesian elders wept on the neck of the
> Apostle whose face they were never to see again.
> Tears are valuable. Pouring out your heart to God is
> a vital step to becoming whole."

Don't hold your pain in—pour it out to God.

Survival Guide for **November 11**

"... BAD COMPANY RUINS GOOD MANNERS."
1 CORINTHIANS 15:33

God told His people, "If you do not drive out the inhabitants of the land, those you allow to remain will become barbs in your eyes and thorns in your sides. They will give you trouble." (Num 33:55 NIV).

Was God being uncharitable? No, He just understood that if His people hung out with the Caananites, they'd pick up their habits, seek their approval, live by their values, and end up worshipping their gods. That's why He laid down His law so clearly.

John Maxwell writes, "You'll acquire the vices and virtues of your closest associates. The fragrance of their lives will pervade yours." Maxwell is right. You can tell yourself that a bad relationship won't hurt you; or that your good will rub off on them. But who are you kidding? If you put on a pair of white gloves, go into your back yard and pick up dirt, the dirt won't get "glovy," but the gloves will definitely get dirty.

I am not advocating abandoning all relationships with non-followers of Jesus—how could we then be "in the world, but not of it" as Jesus commanded? I am advocating abandoning toxic relationships. A toxic relationship is like a malignant cell; if left unchecked, it will rob you of your health, and maybe even your life.

Cervantes, the author of Don Quixote, wrote, "Tell me your company, and I'll tell you who you are." Take another look at the influences in your life today because they are doing two things:

 (1) molding you
 (2) motivating you.

Just as a constant drip can slowly wear away a stone, the wrong influences can undermine us little by little. But unlike a stone: we can move!

Do you need to move away from any drips today?

Survival Guide for **November 12**

"SOMEONE OF INTEGRITY WON'T VIOLATE A CONFIDENCE." PROVERBS 11:13

Three friends were sharing their weaknesses.

The first one said, "My problem's drinking."

The second said, "My problem's lust."

After a long silence the third said, "My problem's gossip, and I can't wait to get out of here and talk about you guys!"

Information is power.

We trade with it to get what we want, and in the process people who trust us get hurt, and never trust anybody again. And that's sad, because we may have robbed them of the one thing they need most—a safe place to open up and be made whole.

The world looks on as we violate confidence under the guise of "I am just sharing this with you so you can pray about it," and loses respect for us, because in their fraternities and sororities and self-help groups, they actually live by the principle, "What's said in this room, stays in this room."

If somebody will reveal to you another's confidence, do you really think they will treat you any differently? Wise up! We're allowing relationships that were meant to bring out the best in us to degenerate into grapevines.

Ask yourself today, "Am I trustworthy, or is my need to impress others so great that I'm willing to betray a confidence to do it?" Before you answer, take a moment and reread these words: "Someone of integrity won't violate a confidence." (Prov 11:13).

They simply won't!

Will you?

Survival Guide for **November 13**

"... SHE WAS STANDING STRAIGHT AND TOLD, GIVING GLORY TO GOD." LUKE 13:13

When God straightens you up, make sure you glorify Him—nobody else, just Him.

Others may be the instruments God uses, but He alone is the source of every blessing. Don't allow anybody to put you on a guilt trip, or hold you hostage to an act of kindness. When whomever God used to bless you asked God to use them, He assigned them to minister to others. That's a privilege. They shouldn't look to others for their reward; they should look to God for it.

Be prepared: when you start glorifying God, some folks won't understand you. That's because they've never had your problem. This woman had been bent over for eighteen years. Once she was made straight, she couldn't help but give glory to God. Usually praise is related to former pain; the greater the pain the greater the praise! Until you've been bound, you'll never know how good it feels to be free! Until you've walked in somebody else's shoes, you won't understand why they're dancing in them. Jesus said, "When you've received much, you'll love much." (Lk 7:47 paraphrase).

If your friends won't let you glorify God openly, don't change your praise, change your friends. Whether you shout, whisper, fall on your face, or run like the wind, God is worthy to be praised. He commands it. He delights in it. He actually dwells in it.

Today, praise God for all He has done for you!

Survival Guide for **November 14**

"... GENUINE FAITH PUT THROUGH THIS SUFFERING COMES OUT PROVED GENUINE ..." 1 PETER 1:7

Faith and photography have a lot in common.

—Photography, you expose film to the light by opening the shutter;
—Faith, you expose your soul to the Light by opening your heart.

—Photography, the exposed film then goes into a dark room where it passes through a series of chemicals developers;
—Faith, the exposed soul then goes into a dark world where it posses through a series of "faith developers."

—The end result of the photographic process is a perfect picture;
—The end result of the faith process is a perfected soul.

Peter calls faith developers "troubles:" "These troubles come to prove that your faith is pure." (1 Pet 1:7 NCV).

Faith is worth whatever "troubles" it takes to develop it! Faith is what enabled David to survive the javelins of Saul. Faith made him sensitive enough to write poetry, but tough enough to cut off the head of Goliath. Faith is what enabled Joan of Arc to pray even while she burned at the stake for her convictions. Colonel Harlan Sanders said faith took him from living off a $105-a-month Social Security check, to running a $285 billion dollar company, working with only a piece of chicken and 11 herbs and spices.

Would these people have preferred a gentler faith development? Probably. But they understood that you have to go through the "faith developers" to reach your destiny: "... The righteous will live by faith." (Rom 1:17).

Faith is what gets us out of bed, carries us through the day, overcomes each obstacle, and keeps us focused on our goal.

Today, don't be afraid of the darkroom for it is the prerequisite to a powerful faith!

Survival Guide for **November 15**

"... FAITH, IS THE FIRM FOUNDATION UNDER EVERYTHING THAT MAKES LIFE WORTH LIVING. IT'S OUR HANDLE ON WHAT WE CAN'T SEE." HEBREWS 11:1

When our passion for something fades, the grace to accomplish it usually goes with it. Does that mean it's time to leave what we have invested so much in? Here are a few thoughts:

1) Get away and rest. Stress-filled minds are not noted for coming up with good answers. Spend time with God. He already knows your future. (Isaiah 46:10).

2) Remind yourself that you are not the only one involved. If you don't know how (or are unwilling) to pass the baton to someone who can take things to the next level, you lose, they lose, and the dream loses. When you have killed your giant, get out of the way and let the next person kill theirs.

3) Do not just focus on what you are leaving behind. Think also about what you are taking with you when you go; like wisdom, faith for the next challenge, and the joy of knowing you have done the will of God: "I have brought You glory on earth by completing the work You gave Me to do." (John 17:4 NIV).

Faith is the "firm foundation."

It will take you anywhere you need to go. It will stand the tests of any climate, thrive in any economy, and move any mountain. Faith is the voice within you that says, "I can't wait to see what God has for me next."

Faith is the greatest evidence that what God calls you to do, by God's help, you can do!

Survival Guide for **November 16**

"ELIJAH, WHAT ARE YOU DOING HERE?" 1 KINGS 19:9

During the high points in life, it is easy to feel God's love, yet He loves us just as much when we are discouraged because we have fallen flat on our faces. God's love is unconditional; it is not based on our success. Elijah knew for sure that God was with him when he defeated 400 false prophets; called down fire from heaven; resurrected a dead boy; outran a chariot; reprimanded an evil king. Yet when Jezebel pursued him he got so discouraged he said, "I have had enough, Lord. Take my life." (1 Kings 19:4 NIV).

Anytime you feel like that you have had enough, remember that it is not from God.

Sometimes God permits pain in order to produce conviction of sin and repentance for wrongdoing. That kind of pain is our friend. But God is not a God of discouragement. His standard greeting is "Fear not" or "Be of good cheer!"

In his discouragement, Elijah camped out in a cave.

Something important happened when God spoke to Elijah in that cave. God didn't ask, "What are you doing there, Elijah?" No, He asked, "What are you doing here?" God was right there with him. Even the cave of discouragement can be a great place to discover that God is with you. It was in such a cave that David wrote, "You are my refuge, my portion in the land of the living." (Psalm 142:5 NIV).

When you know—really know—that God loves you, even at your lowest points, you can handle the cave of discouragement and come out stronger.

Survival Guide for **November 17**

". . . BE ANGRY. YOU DO WELL TO BE ANGRY—BUT DON'T USE YOUR ANGER AS FUEL FOR REVENGE. AND DON'T STAY ANGRY. DON'T GO TO BED ANGRY." EPHESIANS 4:26

Anger is not a sin; mismanaging it is.

The first thing to remember when you get mad at someone is, it means you care. You wouldn't let someone know how you feel if you didn't. You just need to learn how to express your feelings in a way that brings better results. Instead of yelling at your children for not doing their homework, explain to them how an education can fulfill their dreams, then help them where they're struggling.

"Don't give the devil that kind of foothold in your life." (Ephesians 4:27).

The first territory the enemy wants to take is your emotions, because that's the seat of your power. Don't let him! So what if you have good reason to be angry—so did Joseph. Yet he fed those who imprisoned him, and blessed those who betrayed him. In so doing, he was set free from his anger. Later,when he had two sons, he called the first Manasseh, meaning "God has made me forget all my trouble . . . " (Genesis 41:51 NIV). Would Joseph have become great if he had gone back to seek revenge? No! He fulfilled his destiny and enjoyed God's favor, because he controlled his emotions. He called his second son Ephraim, meaning "God has made me fruitful in the land of my suffering." (Genesis 41:52 NIV).

Like Joseph our anger can be controlled when we realize that in spite of our struggles, God continues to bless us.

Survival Guide for **November 18**

"REMEMBER THOSE WHO HAVE THE RULE OVER YOU, WHO HAVE SPOKEN THE WORD OF GOD TO YOU, WHOSE FAITH FOLLOW, CONSIDERING THE OUTCOME OF THEIR CONDUCT." HEBREWS 13:7 (NKJ)

Some people can take less and do more with it, because of their faith.

Speaking of these people, God says, "Follow them." Let's break this verse down:

a) "Remember those who have the rule over you." Are you willing to submit to authority? If not, your future's not very bright.
b) "Who have spoken the Word of God to you." Who feeds you spiritually? Your hunger, not your talent, determines your future.
c) "Whose faith follow, considering the outcome of their conduct." Who should your mentor be? Somebody whose faith produces the results you want.

Follow the example of how Elisha earned the right to wear Elijah's mantle:

1) He recognized and pursued him, regardless of where the journey took him.
2) He honored him, especially when others did not.
3) He drew water from Elijah's well, until he had some in his own.
4) He served him. If you cannot serve, you will never qualify to be served.
5) He obeying him without glorifying him.

Paul told Timothy to follow him—as he followed Christ.

We don't follow our mentor as much as we follow God in our mentor. We catch our mentor's mantle by receiving his (or her) instructions, standing on his shoulders, and making his hindsight our foresight.

Today, ask God to bring such a person into your life.

Survival Guide for **November 19**

"... HAVING BELIEVED, YOU WERE MARKED IN HIM WITH A SEAL..." EPHESIANS 1:13 (NIV)

A seal is a mark of identification.

A child of God stands out in a crowd because we carry our Father's mark of distinction: ". . God's firm foundation is as firm as ever, these sentences engraved on the stones: GOD KNOWS WHO BELONGS TO HIM." (2 Tim 2:19).

God's seal on your life certifies that you belong to Him.

It means He goes before you to smooth out the rough places, line up the right connections, and arrange things in your ultimate favor.

I know what a lot of you are thinking, "Oh yeah? Well, my life is a mess at the moment!" If you are one of those John wrote this for you: ". . .that's exactly who we are: children of God. And that is only the beginning. Who knows how we'll end up!. . . " (1 John 3:2).

Ever been on a building site? It looks like anything but a building, doesn't it?

That is because it is the beginning only and we don't know how what it will be when completed. But bit by bit under the architect's supervision, blocks, beams, wood and piles of sand begin coming together. You may be a mess right now. In fact if the church is doing its job, there should be lots of messy people in it; people being pulled from situations; people in the process of being restored. No baby comes out of the womb clean and dressed up. Spiritual rebirthing is messy too!

The good news is, if you have been spiritually reborn then you are under construction! There is a plan and a purpose behind all that is going on in your life. Things are coming together.

If you belong to Jesus you are a marked man or woman . . . so be encouraged!

Survival Guide for **November 20**

". . . THE LORD IS THE STRONGHOLD OF MY LIFE . . ."
PSALM 27:1

What are you addicted to? What controls you? What is it that you just "can't live" without? What is it that you constantly turn to for relieving your pain, your loneliness or your frustration?

Addictive behavior is often just an attempt to hide from reality or to put off dealing with areas where we are hurt or angry or afraid.

It is no wonder that all of us have addictions.

Except for overeating, most of my addictions did not fall under the heading of "substance abuse." I was addicted to . . . reasoning . . . worry . . . judgment . . . compliments . . . self-pity. . . pouting . . . control . . . and work. When I realized I was addicted to these things, I determined, that in God's strength, I was going to be free and live a disciplined and productive life.

Everything was great, until the pain started.

If I had not had the inner strength to withstand the pain, I would have given in, which would have temporarily relieved the pain, but started the cycle all over again. In my struggle I learned a great truth: God does not just want to give us strength—He wants to be our strength.

God wants to be our stronghold.

Through His indwelling power, God wants us to know that He can break every addiction in our life My goal is to replace my addictions with Jesus—one by one .

Join me in that goal.

Make a decision today to become addicted to Jesus and His precepts then watch your addictions begin to vanish one by one.

Timothy L. Hudson

Survival Guide for **November 21**

"A GIFT OPENS THE WAY FOR THE GIVER."
PROVERBS 18:16 (NIV)

When you are in the midst of a struggle remember this: God is preparing you for something special. The struggle is just part of the preparation.

Another good thing to remember is: what Satan means for evil, God is able to turn for good (Genesis 50:20).

When God brought David to the palace, he was a wild, uncouth shepherd boy with sheep dung on his sandals. God said, in effect, "You are about to be promoted. I saw you kill the lion and the bear. I was watching when you didn't realize it." Solomon says, "A gift opens the way for the giver . . ." (Proverbs 18:16).(NIV)

David's gift was only a rag and a rock, but when he used it, it was enough to kill Goliath.

Take your cue from David and anytime you fight the enemy:

  a) use only what you are gifted in
  b) don't try wearing somebody else's armor; it won't fit
  c) realize that even if what you have doesn't seem like much, if God's behind it, it is more than enough to do the job.

David's gift opened doors for him, and yours will too—no matter how trivial it may seem. God saw you cleaning the Campus House, driving the Sunday school bus, visiting the elderly. He was listening when others said, "They're just using you." But you did it "as unto the Lord" and now the Lord is going to promote you.

All God needs is a teachable spirit, a yielded heart and this prayerful attitude: "Lord, if you will make me able, I am more than willing."

One final thing to remember when in the midst of a struggle: When we give God what we have, He gives us what He has.

I will take that trade anytime!

Survival Guide for **November 22**

"BLESSED WOMAN, WHO BELIEVED WHAT GOD SAID, BELIEVED EVERY WORD WOULD COME TRUE!" LUKE 1:45

When the angel appeared to Mary he asked her to believe the impossible: that even though she was a virgin she was pregnant.

Biologically, virgins can't conceive.

Neither had she any way of knowing how much depended on her obedience, nor that heaven was already preparing for the Messiah she would deliver. What she did know, however, was that when God speaks, our response is to believe Him and say, "I'm ready. . . Let it be with me just as You say." (Lk 1:38).

Even if we believe God can do the impossible, it seldom enters our mind to think "God is going to do the impossible through me." Mary not only believed God, she staked her reputation and her future on it.

Faith precedes fulfillment: "Blessed is she who believed, for there will be a fulfillment of those things which were told her from the Lord." (Lk 1:45 NKJ).

The moment Mary believed, things began to fall into place.

Everything needed to fulfill God's plan for our life is available to us now. He just needs for us to believe and obey him to grasp it. Just as Mary couldn't imagine the results of her obedience, neither can we. God already has a plan to save our loved ones; to meet our financial needs; to deepen our relationships; to energize us, and maybe even to do the impossible through us.

The question is—will you believe and obey God?

Survival Guide for **November 23**

~~~~~~

". . . NOW I OBEY YOUR WORD." PSALM 119:67

In preparation for air travel, before an plane takes off, the attendants tell you that if the plane gets into trouble you should secure your own oxygen mask before attempting to help others with theirs. That is not selfish—it is smart! Unless you get enough oxygen, how can you help anybody else?

Are your needs being met? Really?

If not, it's time to stop taking care of everybody else and start learning to take care of yourself before you burn out. That may mean establishing some boundaries. It may also mean complaints from those who don't want things to change. In fact, just expect it. Moses recorded that "The whole congregation. . . complained against Moses. . ." (Exodus 16:2 NKJ), but he kept on leading them anyway.

Don't complain about what you permit.

People who regularly violate your boundaries need to be held accountable. The Bible teaches that actions have consequences: "A short-tempered man must bear his own penalty; you can't do much to help him. . . " (Proverbs 19:19 TLB). Or, "He who does not work shall not eat" (2 Thessolonians 3:10 TLB). Stop trying to rescue people from their consequences. Pain is a better teacher than comfort. Sometimes we have to feel the heat before we see the light. David said, "Before I was afflicted I went astray, but now I obey Your Word." (Psalm 119:67 NIV).

Just as an empty kettle cracks when the heat is turned up, we will also crack if we allow ourselves to be drained emotionally and spiritually.

It is not selfish to take care of yourself before taking care of others—it is smart—as long as your motive is to be better able to obey God's Word!

Survival Guide for **November 24**

"BE STRONG. TAKE COURAGE . . ."   DEUTERONOMY 31:6

Roger Crawford is a successful author who speaks to Fortune 500 companies, travels worldwide as a consultant and is a professional tennis player. Not impressed? Would you be if you knew he has no hands and only one foot?

When Roger was born, doctors said he would never be able to walk or take care of himself, but Roger's parents disagreed. They sent him to normal schools, involved him in sports, and taught him to think positively.

Roger says "They never allowed me to feel sorry for myself, or take advantage of my handicap."

One day, he got a call from a man who had read about him. When the two met they discovered they had identical handicaps. Roger got excited thinking perhaps he'd found someone older who might act as his mentor. But he was to be disappointed.

Roger says,

> "Instead I found someone bitter, who blamed all his disappointments on his body. He couldn't hold a job. He blamed that on discrimination, and not (as he admitted) on his constantly being late, absent, and failing to take responsibility. His attitude was, 'The world owes me.'   The problem was the world disagreed! He was actually angry with me because I didn't share his despair. We kept in touch until I finally realized that even if some miracle were suddenly to give him a perfect body, his life wouldn't change much, because—he was more the prisoner of his attitude than of his circumstances."

Roger Crawford's philosophy is worth living by: handicaps can only disable us if we let them.

The real limitations are in our minds, not our bodies.

Survival Guide for **November 25**

"COURAGE! WE'LL FIGHT WITH MIGHT AND MAIN. . .AND GOD WILL DO WHATEVER HE SEES NEEDS DOING." 2 SAMUEL 10:12

In 1902, a 28-year-old aspiring poet received a rejection slip from the editor of the prestigious Atlantic Monthly. Returned with a batch of poems he'd submitted was this curt note: "Not one worthy of publishing."

The name of that poet was Robert Frost.

In 1905, the University of Bern turned down a dissertation by a young Ph.D., calling it "fanciful and irrelevant."

The name of that physics student was Albert Einstein.

In 1894, a 16-year-old boy found this note from his speech teacher in Harrow, England, attached to his report: "Hopeless—seems incapable of progress."

The name of that boy was Winston Churchill.

Even when others offer no hope or encouragement, refuse to quit!

Joab, leader of King David's army, wrote: "Be strong and let us fight bravely. The Lord will do what is good in His sight." (2 Sam 10:12 NIV). Joab knew that as long as we stay on the battlefield, God can give us victory. But if we quit, we remove the opportunity for God to act in that situation.

Never give up when you know you are right.

Believe that all things work together for good if you just persevere. Don't let the odds discourage you—God skews the odds in your favor. Refuse to let anybody intimidate you, or deter you from your goals. Fight and overcome every limitation.

Every winner—every one of them—faced defeat and adversity; they just would not quit!

Survival Guide for **November 26**

"HE LAID HANDS ON HER AND SUDDENLY SHE WAS STANDING STRAIGHT AND TALL, GIVING GLORY TO GOD" LUKE 13:13

As long as she needed their help, the people around this sick woman in Luke 13 had no problem with her. But when Jesus set her free and she started praising Him, they couldn't handle it. Actually, they wanted to throw her out of their "church."

How would you act if you, like the woman in Luke's account, you had been chronically ill for 18 years, and suddenly Jesus made you whole? People fall all over themselves about getting a prize on a TV show. Football fans scream and hug total strangers when their team wins, and the world says it's okay. But show a little emotion because of what God has done for you, and you will likely be called a fanatic. Don't worry about it—it is easier to cool down a fanatic, than heat up a corpse.

When God blesses you, what are you going to do?

Do what this woman did: carry on, and let Jesus deal with your critics.

While she was glorifying Him, He was dealing with them. That is how it works. We just praise God and let Him deal with our critics.

If people are upset because you praise the Lord, that is their problem.

There will always be critics. There may even be one in your house, criticizing you for praising Him in the shower; or at work, mocking you for just giving thanks before you eat lunch. Pay them no mind.

Just keep praising God, regardless of the background noise!

Survival Guide for **November 27**

"... THEY HAD SOUGHT GOD—AND HE SHOWED UP, READY TO BE FOUND ..." 2 CHRONICLES 15:15

We only voluntarily return to places that we find pleasurable.

Which is why it is important to stay in God's presence until we create pleasurable memories strong enough to keep bringing us back. If we do not, we will be lured away by lesser things.

How long should we seek God?

Seek Him until:

(1) You have truly repented. "Godly sorrow brings repentance that leads to salvation and leaves no regret." (2 Corinthians 7:10 NIV)

(2) Your mistakes have been dealt with. "People who cover over their sins will not prosper. But if they confess and forsake them, they will receive mercy." (Proverbs 28:13 NLT)

(3) Your anger subsides. "My [own] peace I now give to you. Stop allowing yourselves to be agitated and disturbed." (John 14:27 AMP)

(4) Your fear leaves. "Do not fear, for I am with you; do not be dismayed, for I am your God. I will strengthen you and help you." (Isaiah 41:10 NIV).

(5) Your strength is renewed. "But those who wait upon GOD get fresh strength. They spread their wings and soar like eagles, They run and don't get tired, they walk and don't lag behind." (Isaiah 40:31).

All these things can be found in God's presence.

Today seek God until your needs are met in Him alone!

Survival Guide for **November 28**

"... THEY HAD SOUGHT GOD—AND HE SHOWED UP, READY TO BE FOUND ..." 2 CHRONICLES 15:15

Memories of the good times he had spent with his father were what eventually brought the Prodigal Son back home (Luke 15:17). Having the right memories of our times with God will draw us back into God's presence, time and time again.

How long should we seek God?

Let me add these answers to yesterday's "Survival Guide." Seek until:

(1) Change begins. "But we all, beholding the Lord, are changed from glory to glory by the Spirit of the Lord." (2 Corinthians 3:18).

(2) You trust that God has a plan for your life. "For I know the plans I have for you," says the Lord. "They are plans for good and not for disaster, to give you a future and a hope." (Jeremiah 29:11 NLT).

(3) You recapture your motivation. "I am still confident of this: I will see the goodness of the Lord in the land of the living. Be strong and take heart and wait for the Lord." (Psalm 27:13-14 NIV).

(4) You receive God's wisdom. "I will instruct you and teach you in the way you should go; I will counsel you and watch over you." (Psalm 32:8 NIV).

(5) Christ becomes the desire of your heart. "Delight yourself in the Lord and He will give you the desires of your heart." (Ps 37:4 NIV).

Have you been spending enough time in God's presence lately?

Today seek God until your needs are met in Him alone!

Survival Guide for **November 29**

"... WHY ISN'T IT ALL RIGHT FOR ME TO UNTIE THIS DAUGHTER OF ABRAHAM AND LEAD HER FROM THE STALL WHERE SATAN HAS HAD HER TIED THESE EIGHTEEN YEARS?" LUKE 13:16

In this passage from Luke, Jesus healed a woman after 18 years of chronic illness. Because He healed her on the Sabbath, some religious leaders made a big deal out of it, and Jesus responded by saying: "You hypocrites! Doesn't each of you on the Sabbath untie his ox or donkey from the stall and give it water? Then should not this woman, whom Satan has kept bound for 18 long years, be set free?" (Lk 13:15-16 NIV).

Notice two things about this encounter:

1) Both their valuable ox and their lowly donkey were given water when needed. It is exciting when somebody famous comes to Christ, but it should be no less exciting when someone unknown comes to Christ. Our "place" in life makes no difference to God! The woman in Luke 13 is never mentioned again in Scripture, yet Jesus thought meeting her needs was important enough to buck the religious establishment.

2) These religious leaders kept their expensive ox and their cheap donkey each in their "place." That is OK for oxen and asses but not for men and women. These religious leaders wanted to keep this woman "in her place." But she refused to stay in their religious stall designed to keep her from wandering into areas where she could find for herself what she needed without their help.

In the words of an old political slogan, "Just say No" to those who want to contain or control you by putting you in your "place." Tell them, "I have decided to live close to the living water. While I appreciate your help, I won't be put into a position where I have to rely solely on you to lead me to what you think I need, or don't need."

Today, refuse to stay in your "place" regardless of who is wanting to keep you there.

Survival Guide for **November 30**

"PERSEVERENCE MUST FINISH ITS WORK SO THAT YOU MAY BE MATURE AND COMPLETE, NOT LACKING ANYTHING." JAMES 1:4 (NIV)

Theodor Seuss Giesel drew cartoons in a "creature-of-the-month" ad campaign for a popular insecticide called "Flit." He wanted to expand into commercial illustrating, but his advertising contract wouldn't allow it. So he tried his hand at writing children's books—and flopped.

After 27 rejections of his first attempt, "A Story No One Can Beat," he was ready to quit. One night, on the way home to burn his manuscript, he ran into an old schoolmate who had just been hired as a children's book editor with Vanguard Press. With a little help, and such as changing the title to "And to think that I saw it on Mulberry Street," Theodor's first book finally made it to press.

Thus began the career of the best-selling children's author of all time, Doctor Seuss. In addition to winning the Pulitzer Prize in 1984, he was awarded eight honorary degrees. By the time he died, his books had sold over 200 million copies. All because he didn't give up.

When should you give up?

When you are absolutely certain that God wants you to head in a new direction—not a minute sooner. Until then: Hold on! Hold fast! Hold out! Who knows what unexpected results the second, the tenth, or even the twenty-seventh try will bring you.

Before you give up, ask yourself these questions:

1) am I convinced it is God's will?
2) am I prepared to put in the time and effort required?
3) am I willing to take the risks involved?
4) am I committed to giving God all the glory?

If your answer is "yes," don't give up!

Survival Guide for **December 1**

"ABSOLUTELY NOTHING CAN GET BETWEEN US AND GOD'S LOVE." ROMANS 8:39

Ever look at your shortcomings and doubt that God loves you? Or wonder how He can care for you, given the things you do?

If so, congratulations, you are a member of the human race.

When I have those thoughts I love to read these words of Paul's: "Do you think anyone is going to be able to drive a wedge between us and Christ's love for us? There is no way! Not trouble, not hard times, not hatred, not hunger, not homelessness, not bullying threats, not backstabbing, not even the worst sins listed in Scripture." (Rom 8:35).

No matter how unworthy you may feel, you cannot shut off, stop, or in any way diminish the flow of God's love towards you. Nothing can change the way He feels about you. Nothing can alter the fact that He's going to continue to love you no matter what you do or say.

Never lose sight of that, because God's love will:
1) heal your emotions
2) cause your self-esteem to grow
3) put a foundation of worth and dignity under you
4) give you a foundation upon which to build character

Knowing you are beloved of God motivates you to discipline yourself.

When you know you are loved it makes you want to meet the lover's expectations.

Experiencing God's love not only causes us to love God, but actually gives us the capacity to love yourself, and then love others. When you can do that, the circle is complete. As Jesus taught loving God and loving others is the essence of the New Covenant..

We are eternally, passionately, tenderly, and unconditionally, loved by God. There's no greater blessing and no greater assurance than that. Knowing that, really knowing it, changes our motivation to obey God from fear to love, from grudging to gratitude, from grief to grace!

Survival Guide for **December 2**

"... PURSUE A RIGHTEOUS LIFE ..." 1 TIMOTHY 6:11

1 Timothy 6 is full of guidance to help us "... pursue a righteous life ..."

—Verse 6 "Godliness with contentment is great gain." (NIV) Be content with what you have, not green-with-envy over what others have. There will always be something that looks bigger and better. Always! Contentment comes from understanding that God knows the "whens" the "wheres," and the "hows" of what we need.

—Verse 7. "We brought nothing into the world, and we can take nothing out of it."(NIV) Enjoy what you have, but never forget: nothing tangible is eternal. No matter what we have acquired, we can't take it with us.

—Verse 8. "But if we have food and clothing, we will be content with that."(NIV) Start thanking God for where you are and what you have regularly. Ingratitude clogs the pipeline of communication.

—Verses 9 -10. "People who want to get rich fall into temptation. . .For the love of money is a root of all kinds of evil. Some people, eager for money, have wandered from the faith. . . "(NIV) God is not opposed to you having money; He is, however, opposed to money having you. Money is neither good nor evil; it simply takes on our personality, and makes us more of what we already are. If we are generous before we have money, we will be more generous when we get it. If not, we will spend our lives clinging to whatever we acquire.

—Verse 11. "Man of God, flee from all this, and pursue righteousness. . ." (NIV)

Pursue righteousness = pursue God.

Follow the guidance of 1 Timothy 6 and you will have a deeper relationship with God!

Survival Guide for **December 3**

"... IT IS HE WHO IS GIVING YOU POWER TO MAKE
WEALTH, THAT HE MAY CONFIRM HIS COVENANT ..."
DEUTERONOMY 8:18

Never laugh at somebody with an idea.

Creative ideas come from God, our Creator. Some of the world's most
successful people got where they are because they had a better idea for
cooking chicken, or writing a computer program. Have you got any ideas?

When God gives us the ability to accomplish something, it usually begins
as a thought. But that thought only becomes a reality when we make a
plan and carry it out. Otherwise, our seed rots in the ground of excuses.
The gifts God gives us are the keys to accomplishing great things for Him.
God does not give out spiritual gifts to be put on display, or wasted on
worthless things, or denied out of a false sense of humility. No, He gives
them to each of us to be invested.

Jesus told of three people who were each given money to invest. The first
two doubled theirs. The third hid his out of fear and was called "You
wicked, lazy servant!" (Matt 25:26 NIV). Risk is praised and "playing it
safe" is condemned. True faith is always going to be risky. That is why
fear is one of our greatest enemies. Fear numbs our spirit and incarcerates
our creativity.

Start using what God has given you.

Stop praying for oak trees while acorns are lying all around. Ideas are the
tiny acorns from which great oaks grow.

Spiritually money is "currency" because it is meant to flow through us to
others. We are meant to be a conduit through which God's blessing is
passed on to others, and by which His kingdom is established in their
hearts.

Wealth is not evil—selfishness is.

Survival Guide for **December 4**

"... ANGER BOOMERANGS ..." ECCLESIASTES 7:9

One day an eagle swooped down and caught up a weasel. As the big bird flew away, its wings suddenly went limp, and it dropped to the ground like a brick. With just one blow, the tiny weasel instinctively had struck the eagle's heart and killed it.

Bitterness has the same instinct.

We all get angry at times, but Solomon says only a fool allows anger to move in and take up residence.

Max Lucado writes:

> "Hatred begins like the crack in my windscreen. Thanks to a speeding truck on a gravel road, my window was chipped. With time, the nick became a crack, and the crack a winding tributary. Now I can't drive my car without thinking about the idiot who drove too fast. Though I've never seen him, I could describe him. He's a dead-beat who probably cheats on his wife, drives with a 6-pack of beer on his seat, and keeps his television volume so loud that the neighbours can't sleep."

Bitterness will sour your outlook. It will break your back, not to mention your spirit. You will buckle under the weight of it. The mountain before us is steep enough without carrying that load. Drop it! Remember, we are never called upon to give more grace than God has already given us.

Want to set yourself free from bitterness today?

Pray: ". . .Father, forgive them; they don't know what they're doing. . ." (Lk 23:34).

Survival Guide for **December 5**

"CATCH . . . THE LITTLE FOXES THAT RUIN THE VINEYARDS." SONG OF SOLOMON 2:15

On Colorado's Long Peak lie the remains of a giant 400-year-old tree. Age, storms, and avalanches couldn't bring it down. What did? A tiny beetle you could crush under your foot. It ate right through the bark and devoured its heart.

Beware of boring beetles or as Solomon said "little foxes."

It is the "little foxes" that ruin the vineyards. Little attitudes that seem harmless; but if you practice them often enough, they become fixed attitudes. Little indulgences that seem harmless; but if you give place to them long enough, they desensitize you to sin. Remember when certain things bothered you? Now you don't give them a second thought.

Every alcoholic started by telling himself, "I can handle it." Every victim of Internet pornography (and they are getting younger every day) started with a look, got hooked on a fantasy, and ended up uncaging a tiger that can devour them and will never willingly go back into its cage.

Before a moral problem got out of hand in the Corinthian church, Paul hit it head on with these strong words: "I also received a report. One of your men is sleeping with his stepmother. And you're so above it all that it doesn't even worry you. You pass it off as a small thing, but it's anything but that. Yeast, too, is a 'small thing,' but it works its way through a whole batch.get rid of this 'yeast.'" (1 Cor 5:1-7).

Why does God make such a big deal out of this?

Because sin hurts us, and anything that hurts one of His children, makes God angry. God is mad at sin, not us.

Our sin doesn't only hurt us, it hurts God and it hurts the family of God!

Survival Guide for **December 6**

"FAITH BY ITSELF, IF IT IS NOT ACCOMPANIED BY ACTION, IS DEAD." JAMES 2:17 (NIV)

Faith must be balanced with works. Some things God will do for us; other things He expects us to do for ourselves. In the wilderness God fed His people manna from heaven, but when they reached the Promised Land they had to go out and work for their sustenance.

Two things determine our future: our purpose and our maturity.

Like any good father, God gives his children only what He knows they can handle at the present time. For example, if we pray for financial security, but do not have the discipline to balance our checkbooks or live within our means, it is unlikely that God is going to answer that prayer. God does not pour new wine into old wineskins.

It is poor stewardship to sport a Rolex watch, but not be able to pay your bills, or have any savings. Contrary to what "name it and claim it" preachers imply, what we wear is not a measure of our faith, and what we drive does not represent our status before God.

Good stewardship is more than just giving financial offerings to God; it is having a plan for our future and the wisdom to live by it. Because Joseph had a God-given plan for the future he and his family prospered, in spite of a worldwide depression.

Bigger is not necessarily better, unless it is because of a bigger purpose.

The question is not how much do we want, but how much do we need to fulfill God's will.

God prospers us for two principal reasons:

1) So that we can help to bring others into His kingdom
2) To show the world what happens when one lives by His principles.

Faith must be balanced with works. Stewardship is one means of having a faith that works.

How is your faith working today?

Survival Guide for **December 7**

"I APPEAL TO YOU, IN THE NAME OF OUR LORD JESUS CHRIST, THAT ALL OF YOU AGREE WITH ONE ANOTHER."
1 CORINTHIANS 1:10 (NIV)

God's team needs to huddle regularly.

The "huddle" is where a team:

1) sets its goals
2) determines the division of responsibilities
3) calls the plays that determine whether it wins or loses.

God calls the plays from overhead, but His team must huddle in order to accomplish them on the field. That means working through things, talking through disagreements, motivating and appreciating each member.

For a team huddle to be effective we must each listen with an open heart.

Don't just hear what your neighbor says, try to understand how they feel. God is the boss, so none of us have the right to act like the Gestapo and enforce our will on others. If you act like the spiritual Gestapo sooner or later you will have trouble, for resentment grows when people feel left out. Every member of the team has got to be part of the decision-making process. Engage each other! Ask God to help you look beyond what you want to what is best for His team.

Do not fall under the spell of instant gratification. What looks good to you today could be taking you off the path to a better tomorrow.

Invite "outsiders" into your huddle. Pretty soon they will no longer be "outsiders."

Respect the privacy of your team. Build loyalty. Huddle regularly in prayer.

When God's team does that, everybody wins!

Survival Guide for **December 8**

"... HE ... SET ASIDE HIS ROBE, AND PUT ON AN APRON."
JOHN 13:4

The secret of great ministry lies in what we are willing to lay aside in order to respond to God's call; like laying aside the comforts of home to go where His name has never been heard or giving sacrificially to support those who go in our place.

Or how about taking the "flak" that comes from being the only light shining in your family or in your classroom or in a workplace where spiritual darkness abounds?

Not once did Jesus say following Him would be easy or cheap.

But Paul did say ". . . all the things I once thought were so important are gone from my life. Compared to the high privilege of knowing Christ Jesus as my Master, firsthand, everything I once thought I had going for me is insignificant. . . I've dumped it all in the dustbin . . . I gave up all that inferior stuff so that I could know (be intimate with) Christ. . . " (Philippians 3:9-11).

In this world where "bigger is better" it is good to remember that for every prominent Christian leader there are a thousand who have never written a book, never sold a single CD or tape, never drew a crowd of thousands or gained national fame by building a 'mega church," but who have laid aside their own desires to do what God is calling them to do. Like Noah, whose membership never exceeded eight souls, they minister faithfully. They want to do more. They hope they will be more "successful." But they lay all their ambitions aside to serve the few. They say, "If I'm not called to help everybody, then, God, please let me help somebody."

If we want to be used by God we must answer this question, "What am I willing to lay aside in order to serve?"

What are you willing to lay aside today to serve God more effectively?

Survival Guide for **December 9**

"I WILL NOT TOLERATE ANYONE WHO . . . SLANDERS" PSALM 101:5 (TLB)

It bothers God when our tongue praises Him on Sunday and tears somebody apart on Monday. James says, ". . . this can't go on." (James 3:10).

Slander stems from pride, from an attitude that says in effect, "I am right and everybody else is wrong." Remember, "All a man's ways seem innocent to him, but motives are weighed by the Lord." (Proverbs 16:2 NIV). I see too many people who come to me hurting from the wounds inflicted on them by Christians. Gossip breaks the spirit.

I went through a period of trying to overcome my tendency to gossip. But I would still tell it to my wife. Although I knew she wouldn't repeat it, I soon realized that, by exposing her to it, I was poisoning her spirit. That's when I decided to change what was coming out of my mouth.

What we say about somebody in a careless moment can color how others see them for a lifetime. Think how different your church or campus ministry would be if whenever you heard another person slandering somebody, you stopped them right away and said, "Excuse me—who hurt you, ignored you or slighted you? Let's pray together so that God can restore your peace, but here we don't talk about people who aren't around to defend themselves." Ninety-nine times out of a hundred the issue would die right there—or the offender would leave—either way the body wins!

Paul writes, "Be completely humble and gentle; be patient, bearing with one another in love." (Ephesians 4:2 NIV).

Today, refuse to let the enemy use your words to hurt others!

Survival Guide for **December 10**

"GET RID OF ALL BITTERNESS, RAGE AND ANGER, BRAWLING AND SLANDER, ALONG WITH EVERY FORM OF MALICE." EPHESIANS 4:31

Criticism is one of the ultimate manifestations of pride, because it assumes superiority. The Bible says that God is at work in each of us (Philippians 2:13). That means when we criticize someone, we're saying, "God, Your workmanship doesn't meet with my approval."

What arrogance!

We all struggle and fall far short, so on what basis do we point out the faults of another? Paul writes, ". . . criticism of others is a well-known way of escaping detection in your own crimes. . . " (Romans 2:1).

Is that why you criticize others?

When we criticize somebody's child, who gets upset? The parents! Why wouldn't it be the same with our Heavenly Parent—God? When we judge His people, we're judging Him. When we tear down His leaders, we're saying, "God, you don't know what You're doing by using such people!"

Look out—criticism kept millions of people out of the Promised Land. Imagine, many died just 11 miles from their goal! They spent their lives wandering in dry places. Maybe that is why you've been going through a dry spell lately. They went around the same mountain (problem) over and over again. (Deuteronomy 2:3). Is that why you've been going in circles lately?

Jesus said, "I've told you these things for a purpose: that my joy might be your joy, and your joy wholly mature." (John 15:11).

There is a direct relationship between the joy we have and the words we speak.

Today—"Get rid of all bitterness, rage and anger, brawling and slander, along with every form of malice."

Survival Guide for **December 11**

"WHOEVER ACCEPTS AND TRUSTS THE SON GETS IN ON EVERYTHING, LIFE COMPLETE AND FOREVER!"
JOHN 3:36

The wealthy English Baron Fitzgerald had only one child, a son. Early in his teens, the boy's mother died. Tragically, in his late teens, the boy died also. In the meantime, Fitzgerald's financial holdings greatly increased due to acquiring artwork of the Masters.

Before his death, Fitzgerald left explicit instructions that an auction be held at which his entire art collection would be sold. A big crowd of prospective buyers gathered. Among them were many well-known museum curators and private collectors eager to bid.

The artwork was displayed for viewing before the auction began. Among the paintings was one that received little attention. It was of poor quality, and by an unknown local artist. It happened to be a portrait of Fitzgerald's only son.

As the auction began the auctioneer read from Fitzgerald's will, which clearly instructed that the first painting to be sold was of "my beloved son." Because of its poor quality, the painting didn't receive any bids—except one. That bidder was the old servant who had helped raise the boy and had dearly loved him. For less than a pound he bought the painting.

At that point the auctioneer stopped the bidding and asked the attorney to read again from the will. The crowd was hushed as he read, "Whoever buys this painting of my son, gets all my art collection. The auction is over!"

Without Christ we have nothing—with Him we have everything!

Survival Guide for **December 12**

"... I'D LIKE TO DO SOMETHING SPECIAL FOR YOU IN MEMORY OF YOUR FATHER JONATHAN ..." 2 SAMUEL 9:7

Mephibosheth, the son of Jonathan and the grandson of King Saul, was lame in both feet because a palace nursemaid had dropped him soon after he was born. When David finally took the throne after Saul's death, he asked, "Is there no-one still left of the house of Saul to whom I can show God's kindness?" (2 Samuel 9:3 NIV). That's when they discovered Mephibosheth, living on a rubbish dump, hiding in fear.

Because of a covenant of love between David and Mephibosheth's father, Jonathan, the death sentence Mephibosheth was living under was lifted and he was brought to the palace to be part of the Royal Family. What a testimony! Lifted from the fall, saved because of another and accepted as a child of the King.

Sound familiar?

But there is one problem—Mephibosheth still sees himself as worthless: "Shuffling and stammering, not looking him in the eye, Mephibosheth said, 'Who am I that you pay attention to a stray dog like me?'" (2 Samuel 9:8). He thought of himself as a dog, so he lay on the floor like one. Not only were his feet lame, his thinking was too.

If you are a Christian then no matter how you feel, you need to know and believe that God sees you

1) in Christ
2) through the blood
3) not as you are, but as you will be when grace completes its work in you.

It is time for a makeover and it must begin in your thinking. Just because life has been treating you like a dog doesn't make you one.

Get up off the floor and take your place at the King's table, for He has made you worthy!

Survival Guide for **December 13**

"ABIDE IN ME, AND I IN YOU" JOHN 15:4 (NKJ)

In our busy world "abiding" is a difficult discipline to learn, but the results are worth the effort: "He who abides in Me, and I in him, bears much fruit; for without Me you can do nothing" (John 15:5 NKJ). Want greater results in your spiritual life? Spend more time with God! Want to abound more? Abide more! It's the branch with the strongest, least-obstructed connection to the vine, that has the greatest potential for fruitfulness.

Easy to say, but hard to do! A hundred-and-one things arise daily to keep us from spending quality time with God. And as for an extended period set aside to wait in His presence—that might take an Act of Congress (at least it feels that way)!

Ten times in six verses Jesus says, "Abide." Why so much emphasis? Because "abiding" is not natural! Jesus knew that in the coming years His disciples would be called upon to produce enough fruit to turn the world upside-down. But you can't even begin to have that kind of impact, without first achieving the one thing you're most likely to forget—more of Him!

Jesus has given us just two options:

1) "If anyone does not abide in Me, he is cast out as a branch and is withered." (John 15:6 NKJ). The word "withered" means the branch has become worthless. Don't spend your life on worthless things! God's will is that we should bear fruit, "and that your fruit should remain." (John 15:16 NKJ). Bearing "fruit" gives you Influence beyond your life span—a legacy that's eternal. That is what I want, how about you?

2) "He who abides in Me, and I in him, bears much fruit; for without Me you can do nothing." (John 15:5 NKJ). If we stay closely connected to Him, if we draw spiritual nourishment from Him, if we allow the power that flows through Him to flow through us we will live fruitful, meaningful lives.

Choose to abide in Jesus and nothing will keep you from living the most abundant life possible!

Survival Guide for **December 14**

"DO NOT AVENGE YOURSELVES." ROMANS 12:19 (NKJ)

Chuck Swindoll tells the story of a lady whose doctor said to her, "You've got rabies." Immediately she pulled out a pad and pencil and began writing. Thinking she was making out her will, the doctor said, "No, no, this doesn't mean you're going to die. There's a cure." "I know that," she said, "I'm making a list of the people I'm gonna bite!"

Revenge is like rabies; sometimes it devastates the one who gets hurt, but it always destroys the one who does the hurting. Revenge is insidious because:

1) it convinces you that it is justified
2) it forces you to get bogged down in bitterness and self-pity
3) it makes you spit in a well you may someday have to drink from
4) it sidetracks you
5) it causes you to take the low road.

"Don't insist on getting even; that's not for you to do. 'I'll do the judging,' says God. 'I'll take care of it'" (Rom 12:19).

We are not to "do the judging" because:

a) we don't really know what is in somebody else's heart
b) we are setting the standard by which we ourselves will be judged.

"Whatever measure you use in judging others, it will be used to measure how you are judged." (Matt 7:2 NLT).

If you have been hurt, forgive!

For your own good, put it into God's hands. He is the only One Who is qualified to handle it.

And He will, if you will let Him!

Survival Guide for **December 15**

"GOD WILL SHOW YOU A WAY OUT SO THAT YOU WILL NOT GIVE IN" 1 CORINTHIANS 10:13 (NLT)

Max Lucado writes:

> "I'm at a desk in a hotel room far from home. The voices that encourage are distant, the voices that entice are near. A placard on my nightstand invites to me to the lounge 'to make new friends in a relaxing atmosphere.' Another on top of the TV promises late-night movies that will 'make all my fantasies come true.' In the phone book several columns of escort services offer 'love away from home.' Voices! Some for pleasure, some for power. The world rams at your door, Jesus taps. The world promises flashy pleasure, Jesus promises a quiet dinner with Him: 'I will come in and eat with him.' (see Revelation 3:20). Which voice will you obey?"

How can tempting situations be handled?

a) By filling your mind with God's Word.
b) By avoiding anything that causes you to desire anyone other than your mate.
c) By realizing that real happiness comes from committing yourself to finding pleasure in the relationship God has already given you.
d) By not being too proud to ask for help.

I used to put a bit of hotdog on the floor near my dog and say, "No!" She never touched it. But she never looked at it either, because if she did the temptation to disobey would have been too great. She just kept looking at my face waiting for my voice command: "OK!"

Psalm 34:5 says, "Those who look to Him are radiant; their faces are never covered with shame." (NIV).

It is hard to give in to temptation while looking at our Master's face and waiting for his voice!

Survival Guide for **December 16**

"... WORD GOT AROUND THAT HE WAS BACK HOME."
MARK 2:1

If you are looking for a nice quiet God who won't disrupt your life, forget about Jesus!

When He comes, He will stir up your academic career, your business, your relationships, your marriage, your finances, because He's a functioning, moving, teaching, touching, powerful God, who won't sit in the corner like an ornament.

In Mark 2 some people opened their homes for Jesus to come and teach.

Maybe they thought, "We will put out a few extra chairs . . . it will be nice to hear a good lesson. . . we could use some prayer." Boy were they in for a surprise! When word got out, people came from everywhere. Jesus filled the house without a TV ministry, a CD or DVD, a brochure, or a donor list.

It got so crazy that four men carrying a sick friend on a stretcher couldn't get in, so they broke open the roof and lowered him down to Jesus. That's what we need in the church today—people who know how to "raise the roof" with their prayers, their praises, and their preaching, and who aren't afraid to do whatever it takes to get to Jesus.

When you let Jesus into any area of your life, He will ask you to give what you think you can't give, do what you think you can't do, and be what you think you can't be. He will rearrange everything. That is because He knows that we tend to stay . . . in the same place, the same rut, give the same testimony . . . for too long.

Today, God wants to take us out of our comfort zones. He wants to stretch us by calling us to do more than we have ever done before.

Are you ready to say "Yes?"

Survival Guide for **December 17**

"THE LORD WHOM YOU SEEK WILL SUDDENLY COME"
MALACHI 3:1 (AMP)

Have you ever awakened with a sense of dread because of something you had to face that day? Yet by bedtime you have come to realize that everything was alright because God suddenly showed up?

God comes "suddenly" because what is sudden to us isn't sudden to God.

God works according to His schedule, not ours.

It was history's greatest prison break: "After they had been severely flogged, about midnight, Paul and Silas were praying and singing hymns; the other prisoners were listening. Suddenly, all the prison doors flew open, and everybody's chains came loose." (Acts 16:23-26 NIV). Notice two things:

1) Paul and Silas did their part—they kept praying and praising
2) God did His part—He suddenly showed up

The result? The prison warden asked, "What must I do to be saved?"

When Moses wanted to see God's glory, God said: "I will make all My goodness pass before you, but you can not see My face. I will put you in a cleft of the rock, and cover you with My hand. Then I will take away My hand, and you shall see My back." (Exodus 33:19-23 AMP). Notice what happens when we are hidden in the cleft of the rock: God comes, and even though we can't see His face we can experience His presence.

Experience God's presence and suddenly everything seems alright.

When faced with a sense of dread what we should do is:

a) Keep praying and praising
b) Know that though we may not be able to see God in the situation, we can experience His presence

The how and when of our deliverance is up to God—just be ready, for God comes suddenly!

Survival Guide for **December 18**

"BRING THE BOOKS, ESPECIALLY THE PARCHMENTS."
2 TIMOTHY 4:13 (NKJ)

Sitting in prison, with virtually no hope of a reprieve, Paul writes to Timothy and says: "Bring my books" (He wants to keep taking in); and "Bring my writing paper." (He wants to keep giving out).

What an attitude!

He doesn't ask for an attorney, because real purpose needs no defense. Time will tell the world whether he was guilty or innocent.

He doesn't ask for better accommodation, for he has "learned to be content." (Philippians 4:11 NIV).

Paul sends for a book, because he knows that as long as you are alive you should continue to grow, otherwise you are just taking up space. Reading allows you to transcend our situation and explore new worlds. Knowledge keeps our minds sharp and our souls free. Peter says, "Grow in grace and knowledge of our Lord . . ." (2 Peter 3:18 NIV).

Paul also sends for writing paper, because he wants to keep making a difference. He ignores his circumstances, grabs his pen and continues to be productive. No tears. No gut-wrenching displays of self-pity. "I've still got something else to say, and I want to say it! I'm not done yet!"

So Paul, who loved athletic allusions, teaches us the most important lesson of all: never get out of the game, for even in the last few seconds, a goal is still possible.

The art of living is to keep giving to the end.

Even on the cross, with nails piercing His hands and His feet, Jesus continued to minister—and He is our example!

Survival Guide for **December 19**

"EACH ONE IS TEMPTED WHEN HE IS DRAWN AWAY BY HIS OWN DESIRES AND ENTICED." JAMES 1:14 (NKJ)

Every day it seems like we hear of a new CEO being led off in handcuffs or of a spiritual shepherd molesting his sheep or a politician in the pockets of special interests. How do good people go bad? In most cases, it happened because:

1) they lost their moral compasses
2) at some point they vacillated, saying "Everybody else does it, why not me?"
3) as their appetites increased, their consciences eroded
4) they surrounded themselves with others who shared the same values, or were willing to look the other way.

"I would never do those things."

Maybe, but what things would you do? Have you reached your hour of testing yet? James writes: "Each one (no exceptions) is tempted when he is drawn away by his own (particular) desires and enticed." What James is telling us is that we are all susceptible to thoughts and impulses, which if not disciplined by strong character, have the potential to destroy us.

"What can I do?"

When Jehosaphat came up against an enemy too big to handle alone, he prayed, ". . . We're helpless before this vandal horde ready to attack us. We don.t know what to do; we're looking to you." (2 Chronicles 20:12).

Jehosaphat understood that:

a) in our own strength we are no match for the enemy
b) no matter how bright we are, we still sometimes don't have the right answers
c) some things are just a job for God

Turning to God in our weakness, releases His power to work in us and through us.

That is the key to handling temptation.

Survival Guide for **December 20**

―――

"GO MAKE (THEM MY) DISCIPLES" MATTHEW 28:19 (NIV)

We each have different gifts, but God has given us all the same mission: "Go make (them My) disciples."

We call this the Great Commission, not the Great Suggestion!

It is not just a commission for pastors and missionaries, it is for each and every one of us. It is mandatory, binding and urgent: "...you must warn them so they may live. If you don't.they will die in their sin. But I will hold you responsible." (Ezekiel 3:18 NCV).

"But I'm not good with words." So what?

If you can interview for a job, make a report in class, or shoot the bull with your friends, surely you can say something on behalf of Christ. Can you imagine having a cure for cancer and keeping it to yourself? Sharing the greatest news is the greatest kindness we can show to anyone.

One problem long-term Christians have is that we forget how hopeless it felt to be without Christ. Another problem is that we mix so much with the churched that we forget how to communicate with the unchurched. No matter how contented or successful the people around you appear to be, without Christ they are empty and lost—eternally lost.

You are the only Christian somebody knows; there are people that only you can reach because of where you are and what God has made you to be.

If just one person is in heaven because of you, your life will have made a difference.

Today, start looking around at your personal mission field and begin to pray, "God, who have You put in my life today who needs to know about Jesus?"

Survival Guide for **December 21**

"MAKING THE MOST OF EVERY OPPORTUNITY."
EPHESIANS 5:16 (NIV)

There is no "magic age" at which excellence emerges, or quality suddenly appears. With God, we are never too young, and never too old.

—Thomas Jefferson was 33 when he drafted the Declaration of Independence.
—Charles Dickens was 24 when he began the Pickwick Papers, and 25 when he wrote Oliver Twist.
—Sir Isaac Newton was 24 when he formulated the Law of Gravity.

But if you think "movers and shakers" can be found only amongst the young, think again:
—Verdi was 80 when he produced Falstaff.
—Goethe was 80 when he completed Faust.
—Tennyson was 80 when he wrote Crossing the Bar.
—Michaelangelo was doing his best work at 87.

And for an extreme example—how about Noah? Noah was 500 when he preached his first sermon, and over 600 when he came out of the ark and helped start the world all over again.

Carpe Diem is Latin for "Seize the day" Seize the "now" moments of your life! The "right" time or the "right" age you're waiting on may never arrive.

James writes,

> "The word for you who brashly announce, 'Today—at the latest, tomorrow—we're off to such and such a city for a year. We're going to start a business and make a lot of money.' You don't know the first thing about tomorrow. You're nothing but a wisp of fog, catching a brief bit of sun before disappearing. Instead, make it a habit to say, 'If the Master wills it and we're still alive, we'll do this or that.'" (Jas 4:13 -15).

The moment, once past, will never return. *Carpe Diem!*

Survival Guide for **December 22**

"JESUS SAID, "RIGHT—AND YOU CAN READ IT FOR YOURSELVES IN YOUR BIBLES: THE STONE THE MASONS THREW OUT IS NOW THE CORNERSTONE. THIS IS GOD'S WORK; WE RUB OUR EYES, WE CAN HARDLY BELIEVE IT." MATTHEW 21:42

Sometimes rejection turns out to be "God's work."

After Joseph had been betrayed by this brothers and slandered by Potiphar's wife, he said, "you meant evil against me; but God meant it for good." (Genesis 50:20 NKJ).

How often has something happened in your life that you later realized was necessary? Upon reflection you realize that If you had not sustained this, or walked through that, you would not be ready for the blessings you are enjoying right now. It is when we see the hand of God in rejection that we begin to understand that what the enemy meant for our destruction, God used for our development.

To be more than a conqueror means to stand up and say:

> "Here is how I see it. It took all I have been through to make me who I am today and to teach me what I know. I choose to be better, not bitter. I trust the faithfulness of God more than ever. If faith doesn't move the mountain, it will give me strength to endure until tomorrow. And if it is not gone by tomorrow, I will still believe that God is able, and trust Him until He acts."

Hang in there!

Your steps (and your stops) are being arranged by God. They are also being observed by Him. When you get over the rejection, you will realize that "the worst thing that could have happened" is, in reality, "God's work" and it will become marvelous in your eyes.

Survival Guide for **December 23**

"HE CAME TO HIS OWN PEOPLE , BUT THEY DIDN'T WANT HIM." JOHN 1:11

Would you spend your last night on earth with someone if you knew they were going to betray you the next day? Jesus did.

He is faithful, even when we are not.

There is no greater opportunity to grow in love than when you have been mistreated. Look at Jesus on the cross: He asked His Father to forgive those who ripped the flesh from His back and drove the nails into His hands.

How we handle rejection reveals whether or not we have truly died to self—for it is impossible to hurt a corpse. On the other hand, being rejected without being offended is one of the greatest demonstrations of spiritual maturity. It is being Christ-like.

In the Old Testament a priest was disqualified from ministry if he had "scabs" (unhealed wounds) (Leviticus 21:20). Perhaps one reason for this prohibition is that "scabs" make us "touchy." So the priest with "scabs" couldn't allow you to get close to him, in case you brushed up against his sore spot. It would show up in the things he said and keep him from functioning the way God wanted him to.

Nothing creates "scabs" quicker than unforgiven rejection.

But God has a solution: "I will restore you to health, and heal your wounds, declares the Lord." (Jeremiah 30:17 NIV).

God wants to heal you, so that through you, He can reach out and make others whole.

Let Him restore you today!

Survival Guide for **December 24**

"MAY GOD GIVE PEACE TO YOU . . . AND LOVE, WITH FAITH
. . . MAY GOD'S GRACE . . . BE UPON ALL WHO SINCERELY
LOVE OUR LORD JESUS CHRIST." PHILIPPIANS 6:23 (TLB)

It is easy to get caught up in the craziness of shopping, parties, gift giving
and family obligations during the Christmas season.   In fact, it's
exhausting just thinking about it all.   Imagine however, that when you
awakened on Christmas morning you found four gifts you had overlooked
tucked away under the tree.

You open the first one, and you are filled with an awesome sense of peace
you have never known before.   You unwrap the second, and experience an
overpowering love for others—even those who have wronged you.   You
open the third, and you are infused with a faith that enables you to trust
God for anything—even things you previously considered impossible.
Finally, you unwrap the fourth gift, and receive such grace, that you can
handle criticism and hurt without retaliating.

Sound far-fetched? Well, it is not at all!

These are the gifts Paul says God wants to give us: "May God give peace
to you . . . and love, with faith . . . May God's grace . . . be upon all who
sincerely love our Lord Jesus Christ." (Eph 6:23 TLB).

What gifts!   And not one of them has to be returned the day after
Christmas: they're guaranteed to last a lifetime.

Peace, love, faith, grace are gifts that God has already given to us—all we
have to do is unwrap them and start using them.

Tomorrow is Christmas Day, the day that changed everything.

Why don't you take a moment and thank God for all His wonderful
gifts—especially for the gift of His Son.

Survival Guide for **December 25**

"HE APPEARED IN A HUMAN BODY." 1 TIMOTHY 3:16

Now that the rush of the modern Christmas season is coming to an end I thought it might be a good time for us to reflect once again on the One whose birth we are celebrating. These words by an unknown author contrast His life with His influence:

> "He was born in abject poverty, yet a choir of angels filled the heavens with songs of His greatness. A star that astronomers still can't explain to this day became the compass that brought world leaders to worship at His crib.
>
> His birth defied the laws of biology and His death defied the laws of mortality. No miracle is greater than His life and teaching. He owned no cornfields or fisheries, yet He spread a table for 5,000 and had bread and fish left over. He never walked on expensive carpeting, yet when He walked on water it supported Him; when He spoke the wind and the seas obeyed Him.
>
> His crucifixion was the crime of all crimes, yet in God's eyes no less a price could have made your redemption possible. When He died, few mourned, yet God hung black crepe over the sun. Those who crucified Him never once trembled at what they'd done, yet the earth shook beneath them. Sin couldn't touch Him. Decay couldn't claim His body. The soil that was reddened with His blood couldn't claim His dust.
>
> For over three years He preached the gospel, yet He wrote no books, built no cathedrals, and seemingly had no great financial resources. Yet 2,000 years later, He's still the central character of human history, the perpetual theme of Christian preaching, the pivot around which the ages revolve—and the only Redeemer of the human race!"

For every other job, God sent a man.
But in order to rescue and renew us, God became a man.
That is the mystery of Christmas.
That is reason to rejoice 365 days a year!

Survival Guide for **December 26**

"LET'S TAKE A BREAK . . . " MARK 6:31

People's needs are endless!

With the best of intentions you try "being there" for them, and before you know it, you Are drained. If that is where you are today, obey these words of Jesus: "Let's take a break." (Mk 6:31).

Jesus understood that solitude is necessary for intimacy with God, and intimacy with God is necessary for long term meaningful ministry to others.

We have to get away from the demands of people, in order to distinguish the voice of God. Job said, "the breath of God Almighty gave me life!" (Job 33:4).

Until God breathes His breath into us, we are just ministering in our own might..

Have you learned yet how to replenish your flagging emotions and drained energies? David said, "You have bedded me down in lush meadows, You find me quiet pools to drink from. True to Your word, You let me catch my breath." (Ps 23:2,3).

In our "busyness is next to godliness" world we need to get into God's presence and let Him restore our souls.

Ponder these three scriptures:

1) "Three times a day he got down on his knees and prayed, giving thanks to his God." (Dan 6:10 NIV)
2) "Every morning you'll hear me at it again. I lay out the pieces of my life on your altar." (Ps 5:3)
3) "Jesus got up, left the house and went off to a solitary place, where He prayed." (Mk 1:35 NIV).

The message is crystal clear to me: I need more time alone with God!

How about you?

Survival Guide for **December 27**

"SKILLED WORKERS ARE ALWAYS IN DEMAND AND ADMIRED." PROVERBS 22:29

Both his wife and his mother were deaf. Maybe that's why Alexander Graham Bell's passion was to change the way people communicated with each other. For five frustrating, impoverished years he experimented with a variety of materials in an effort to make a metal disk that, vibrating in response to sound, could reproduce those sounds and send them over an electrified wire.

During a visit to Washington, DC, he called on Joseph Henry, a pioneer in electrical research, and asked for his advice. Should he let somebody else perfect the telephone, or do it himself? "Do it yourself," the old pioneer told him. When Bell complained about his lack of electrical knowledge, Henry said, "If you don't have it, get it!"

So Bell studied electricity day and night. A year later, while obtaining a patent for the telephone, the officials at the patent office credited him with knowing more about electricity than all the other inventors of his day combined.

Graham is a great model of what it takes to succeed:

(1) vision
(2) hard work
(3) study
(4) hope
(5) persistence

What is it that burns within you? That unlocks your creativity? That energizes you? That could be the key to your future? Don't neglect it! Don't fear it! Don't put if off!

Nehemiah started out as a waiter, yet he ended up rebuilding the whole city of Jerusalem. Why? Because he heard a cry nobody else heard, saw a need nobody else was meeting, and said "Yes!"

That is all God requires of any of us!

Survival Guide for **December 28**

". . . THE GIFT THAT CAME BY THE GRACE OF THE ONE MAN, JESUS CHIRST . . ." ROMANS 5:15 (NIV)

During a conference in Britain on comparative religions, experts from around the world gathered to debate what belief, if any, was unique to the Christian faith. Resurrection? Other religions had accounts of people returning from the dead. Healing? Other religions had reports of miraculous healing too. The debate continued until C.S. Lewis stood up and simply said, "Grace!"

The unmerited favor of God toward us—Grace—is uniquely Christian.

If you were raised to believe that God forgives you reluctantly and only after you have squirmed a while, then grace probably sounds too good to be true. The idea that God's love is unconditional is hard to grasp, because acceptance for most of us has always been based on our performance. But not with God: ". . . it is the gift of God—not by works. . . " (Ephesians 2:8-9 NIV). If you believe you are saved by grace but kept by your own good works, every time you fail you will have to prove to God all over again that you are worthy of His love.

That is not salvation. That is probation!

Relax, God's grace won't run out before you get your act together.

James says, "He gives us more grace" (James 4:6 NIV). Peter says "God is keeping careful watch over us. . . " (1Peter 1:5).

Faith is actively trusting in Jesus. It requires that you let go of your life—die to yourself—and let Jesus live in you. No more is required, no less will do. When Jesus said, "It is finished," He satisfied all God's claims against you.

"But what about doing good works?" Good works are what we are saved for—not what we are saved by.

Good works are like a "P.S." to say, "Thank You Father, for Your amazing grace!"

Survival Guide for **December 29**

"... I'M THE ONLY ONE LEFT ..." 1 KINGS 19:10

Apparently Elijah was convinced that nobody else was as badly off as him.
He felt "terminally unique."

But his feeling was false.

Behind your neighbor's smile, or the nameplate on your professor's door,
there are struggles just like yours that they don't talk about. So they live in
quiet despair. Martin Luther King Jr. was right on many levels when he
said, "We may have arrived on different ships, but we're all in the same
boat now." Paul wrote, "No test or temptation. . . is beyond the course of
what others have had to face. All you need to remember is that God will
never let you down; He'll never let you be pushed past your limit; He'll
always be there to help you come through it."
(1 Cor 10:13).

Before every crown there Is a cross:

- Bunyan wrote *Pilgrim's Progress* in prison.
- Florence Nightingale, too ill to move from bed, reorganized the
  hospitals of England.
- Pasteur, semi-paralyzed by apoplexy, was tireless in his attack
  on disease.
- Francis Parkman couldn't work for more than five minutes at a
  time. His eyesight was so bad that he could only scrawl gigantic
  words on a manuscript. Yet he wrote twenty magnificent
  volumes of history.

You are not "terminally unique!" And you have not been deserted: ". . .
nothing living or dead, angelic or demonic, today or tomorrow, high or
low, thinkable or unthinkable—absolutely nothing can get between us and
God's love. . . " (Rom 8:38-39).

Next time you have an attack of ". . . I'm the only one left. . . " remember
that!

Survival Guide for **December 30**

―――――――――――――――――――――――――――――――――――――

". . . EVERY DETAIL IN OUR LIVES . . . IS WORKED INTO SOMETHING GOOD." ROMANS 8:28

A little boy complained to his grandmother that things were bad.

He was in trouble at school, his dad forgot to give him his allowance, his best friend went fishing without him.

His grandmother, who was baking a cake at the time, listened patiently, then asked him if he'd like a snack.

"Sure," he replied.

So she said, "Here, have some cooking oil."

"No way"' he said.

"Well, how about a couple of raw eggs"'

"Gross!" he exclaimed.

"What about some baking powder?" she asked.

"Grandma, those are all yucky!" he said.

"Yes," she replied. "On their own, all of them seem pretty bad, but when you put them together, they make a great cake!"

Sometimes we ask God for one thing and He gives us another, because, while we think we know what we want, He knows what we really need. The truth is, God knows more about what we need than we do: "He knows us far better than we know ourselves. . . That's why we can be so sure that every detail in our lives. . . is worked into something good." (Rom 8:26-28).

Everything that comes your way today may be "yucky" but together they make a pretty good cake!

Survival Guide for **December 31**

"... YOU WEREN'T BATHED AND CLEANED UP, YOU WEREN'T RUBBED WITH SALT, YOU WEREN'T WRAPPED IN A BABY BLANKET..." EZEKIEL 16:4

Ezekiel gives us some answers on how to last in our walk with God:

(1) We must be "bathed and cleaned up."   Our spiritual protection against spiritual dirt, disease, and death begins in the waters of baptism but continues in "... the washing with water through the Word." (Ephesians 5:26 NIV). Just as we step into the shower every day—we also need to step into the Scriptures daily. Jesus said, "You are already clean because of the Word I have spoken to you." (John 15:3 NIV). Sin will keep us from the Bible, but the Bible will keep us from sin.

(2) We must be "rubbed with salt." In Hebrew culture, they rubbed salt on newborn babies to toughen their skins, so they could be handled without bruising. Too many of us need to be stamped "Fragile—Handle With Care!" We are touchy. If we are corrected, we get defensive. Only when we have been "rubbed with salt" by mature love and non-legalistic correction can you be really open and honest.

(3) We must be "wrapped in a baby blanket." When we are first born into God's family we are vulnerable. We need to be covered and protected. That is the value of Christian fellowship; it wraps us up in the arms of love and says, "You don't ever have to go back to the old life again! You can begin afresh. You can be healed of your painful past. You can have good times and good relationships instead of bad ones."

Have you been bathed, salted, and wrapped up?

Acknowledgement

We all stand on the shoulders of giants. This book is the result of the inspiration of numerous daily devotionals that I have read over the course of my life. I am particularly indebted to "The Word for Today," which was the first internet-delivered devotional I ever read. These "e-devotionals" are what inspired me to reach out to our students through the Survival Guide. As I read over Survival Guides from the last ten years in preparing this book I realized how much the style and content of these devotionals have been influenced by them. I gratefully acknowledge that Bob Gass has had a profound impact on both my life and this book.

Author's Note Regarding Translations

The Bible, the greatest literary work in the history of mankind, has been subjected to a number of translations through the years. Since being translated into English for King James in 1611, many scholars have, particularly in recent years, tried to update the translation to today's more common usage of the language.

In assembling the devotionals in this book, several different translations and paraphrases were used. These translated and paraphrased versions are denoted in parentheses after the verse. When no translation is credited, it is taken from The Message (TM).

Others used in this book, as indicated by the abbreviations below, include:

NKJ, or New King James Version
NIV, or New International Version
NRSV, or New Revised Standard Version
AMP, or The Amplified Bible
NLT, or New Living Translation
TEV, or Today's English Version
PHPS, or Phillips Translation
NCV, or New Contemporary Version
NAS, or New American Standard
KJV, or King James Version

www.ingramcontent.com/pod-product-compliance
Lightning Source LLC
Chambersburg PA
CBHW031041110426

42740CB00046B/217